IN SEARCH OF S(
THE LIFE AND TIMES OF LU(

Frontispiece 'Lucy Etheldred Broadwood' 9 August 1858–22 August 1929
Source: Copyright of Surrey History Centre.

In Search of Song:
The Life and Times of
Lucy Broadwood

DOROTHY DE VAL
York University, Canada

Routledge
Taylor & Francis Group

LONDON AND NEW YORK

First published 2011 by Ashgate Publishing

2 Park Square, Milton Park, Abingdon, Oxon OX14 4RN
711 Third Avenue, New York, NY 10017, USA

Routledge is an imprint of the Taylor & Francis Group, an informa business

First issued in paperback 2016

British Library Cataloguing in Publication Data
De Val, Dorothy.
  In search of song : the life and times of Lucy Broadwood.
  -- (Music in nineteenth-century Britain)
  1. Broadwood, Lucy, 1858-1029. 2. Broadwood, Lucy,
  1858-1929--Ethnomusicological collections. 3. Folk Song
  Society--History. 4. Ethnomusicologists--Great Britain--
  Biography. 5. Women folk musicians--Great Britain--
  Biography. 6. Folk musicians--Great Britain--Biography.
  7. Folk songs, English--Great Britain--19th century.
  8. Folk songs, English--Great Britain--20th century.
  I. Title II. Series
  782.4'216221'0092-dc22

Library of Congress Cataloging-in-Publication Data
De Val, Dorothy, 1955-
  In search of song : the life and times of Lucy Broadwood / Dorothy de Val.
    p. cm. -- (Music in nineteenth-century Britain)
  Includes bibliographical references and index.
  ISBN 978-0-7546-5408-7 (hardcover) 1. Broadwood, Lucy Etheldred, 1858-1929. 2. Folk
musicians--Great Britain--Biography. I. Title.
  ML420.B7782D4 2011
  782.42162'210092--dc22
  [B]
                                                                           2011002916
ISBN 978-0-7546-5408-7 (hbk)
ISBN 978-1-138-26489-2 (pbk)

Contents

List of Illustrations

Acknowledgements

My journey to discover more about Lucy Broadwood and her circle has not been made alone. I am grateful to the late Cyril Ehrlich for first making me aware of her diaries some years ago, and for the many fruitful discussions we had about her, her times and on music generally. I have missed his incisive input, wry humour and gentle guidance as I assembled the narrative of this book, but its spirit still owes much to his wit, personality and style.

I have long had a connection with the Surrey History Centre, (www.surreycc. gov.uk/surreyhistorycentre) first in its incarnation as the Surrey Record Office, Kingston, where I first became aware of the Broadwood archives through my work on the piano firm for my PhD dissertation, in which Professor Ehrlich also played a vital role. The archive also houses the Broadwood family history, including the diaries of and letters to Lucy Broadwood. I am grateful to all the archivists at the Centre under the leadership of, first, David Robinson and then Maggie Vaughan-Lewis, who were without fail always helpful and insightful. I owe a huge debt to Jenni Waugh, no longer with the Centre, but whose encyclopaedic knowledge of Lucy, her times and, above all, the huge quantity of material in the archive, was invaluable to me. Jenni's enthusiasm and passion for this period and its many personalities inspired me to continue when the sheer weight of research material threatened to undermine the whole project. I am also grateful to Robert Simonson for his patience and diligence in helping me choose illustrations for this book. All illustrations are reproduced by permission of the Surrey History Centre.

Sincere thanks are also due to Malcolm Taylor and his staff at the Vaughan Williams Memorial Library at Cecil Sharp House, which holds a vast amount of material related mostly to Lucy's song collecting, as well as the records of the Folk Song Society, of which she was a founder member. There is still much to explore there in the correspondence of Lucy's contemporaries, such as Cecil Sharp and Anne Geddes Gilchrist among others, but I fear this book would have never reached completion had I attempted to go exhaustively through their material as well. Malcolm's intimate knowledge of the collection, plus his involvement in the folk music world generally, made him a valuable source of information in the production of this book.

Working at the British Library, both in the Music Room and in the general collections, has always been a joy owing to the quiet helpfulness of their staff. Likewise the staff at the Bodleian Library (in particular the Music Room) and the Faculty of Music, University of Oxford, under their former librarian John Wagstaff, were particularly helpful at crucial times of my research: I am indebted to John for constant access to the sprawling Frank Howes collection. In London,

I have always enjoyed access to the collections at the Royal College of Music, whose archives have been particularly useful, as was their collection of instruments on which I played my first Broadwood piano, dated 1799. Christopher Bornet, Elizabeth Wells, Oliver Davies, Celia Clarke and Peter Horton have always been helpful and knowledgeable guides. More recently I have enjoyed the use of the well-stocked library of the Faculty of Music, University of Toronto, as well as my home library at York University, which yielded some interesting finds.

Colleagues have been helpful throughout my time researching this book: Chris Bearman shared his notes and encyclopaedic knowledge with me in the early stages, Rachel Cowgill provided useful material on Anne Geddes Gilchrist, and I have learned much from other writers in this field, such as the late Roy Judge, David Gregory, Vic Gammon, Georgina Boyes and numerous others. I have also been fortunate to meet a host of folksong enthusiasts more recently through my membership of the Country Dance and Song Society and the Toronto English Country Dancers. My students at York University, particularly those in my graduate classes, have always provided insight and a freshness of approach. An award from the Research Development Fund of York University made the final stages of writing this book possible.

Above all, I am grateful to my family for their patience and perseverance. My daughter Susanna McCleary has performed many of the songs Lucy collected, even making the effort to learn Scots Gaelic in order to sing the highland songs at two academic conferences. Our joint ventures in this relatively arcane area owe much to the expert guidance of the Toronto Gaelic Learners Association under the leadership of Janice Chan, Kerrie Kennedy and Sharon Brown. Mary Enid Haines brought some of the English songs to a wider public at the first conference of the North American British Music Studies Association in June 2004. There has been little time in my son Mark's life that has not been dominated by Lucy, so I thank him for tolerating my long sessions at the computer as well as my mutterings in Gaelic; likewise, I cannot begin to repay my husband John McCleary, who now knows Lucy all too well and has brought enthusiasm, patience and well-honed editing skills to this project. Like many others he, too, no doubt will be relieved to see its final coming to fruition, though I will make the usual disclaimer that any errors and faults in the following text are completely and utterly my own.

General Editor's Series Preface

Music in nineteenth-century Britain has been studied as a topic of musicology for over two hundred years. It was explored widely in the nineteenth century itself, and in the twentieth century grew into research with strong methodological and theoretical import. Today, the topic has burgeoned into a broad, yet incisive, cultural study with critical potential for scholars in a wide range of disciplines. Indeed, it is largely because of its interdisciplinary qualities that music in nineteenth-century Britain has become such a prominent part of the modern musicological landscape.

This series aims to explore the wealth of music and musical culture of Britain in the nineteenth century and surrounding years. It does this by covering an extensive array of music-related topics and situating them within the most up-to-date interpretative frameworks. All books provide relevant contextual background and detailed source investigations, as well as considerable bibliographical material of use for further study. Areas included in the series reflect its widely interdisciplinary aims and, although principally designed for musicologists, the series is also intended to be accessible to scholars working outside of music, in areas such as history, literature, science, philosophy, poetry and performing arts. Topics include criticism and aesthetics; musical genres; music and the church; music education; composers and performers; analysis; concert venues, promoters and organisations; the reception of foreign music in Britain; instrumental repertoire, manufacture and pedagogy; music hall and dance; gender studies; and music in literature, poetry and letters.

Although the nineteenth century has often been viewed as a fallow period in British musical culture, it is clear from the vast extent of current scholarship that this view is entirely erroneous. Far from being a 'land without music', nineteenth-century Britain abounded with musical activity. All society was affected by it, and everyone in that society recognised its importance in some way or other. It remains for us today to trace the significance of music and musical culture in that period, and to bring it alive for scholars to study and interpret. This is the principal aim of the Music in Nineteenth-Century Britain series – to advance scholarship in the area and expand our understanding of its importance in the wider cultural context of the time.

Bennett Zon
Durham University, UK

Introduction

A biography of Lucy Broadwood is long overdue. Some years ago, when I first encountered her diaries, which she kept meticulously almost daily until her death, I was excited and overwhelmed by the detail and how much they revealed about her life. But the diaries were a mixed blessing. Written primarily as an *aide mémoire* of daily life and not as a document for posterity, their very detail threatened to stifle the overall narrative of a fascinating life. Their bulk also threatened the completion of this project, as I struggled to sift wheat from chaff and to correlate the information in the diaries with the mountains of other documents. I also struggled to identify and keep track of the cast of thousands that populate their pages. The diaries chronicle 47 years of a very full life: though not a literary diarist like her younger contemporary Virginia Woolf, Broadwood connected with a large number of people, many of whom were already famous, or would become so.

Most of the documentation of Broadwood's life is held in the Surrey History Centre (SHC), Woking, and in the Vaughan Williams Memorial Library (VWML), London; her compositions can be found in the British and Bodleian Libraries. In addition to the diaries, the SHC holds a huge archive of family information in the form of letters, other family diaries, miscellanies, photographs and much else, while the VWML collection focuses on her folksong research, with particular attention to her fieldwork. Her publications range from original compositions and arrangements to volumes of folksong and exhaustively researched articles for the *Journal of the Folk-Song Society*. While vast, this material has crucial gaps: where the diaries record many letters received from certain people, virtually none of those letters survive. For example, there is nothing at all from James Campbell McInnes, who played a significant role in her professional and personal life and who certainly kept an ongoing correspondence with her in the early 1900s; did Lucy herself destroy those letters, or were they culled after her death? Important entries about the family business are invariably brief, or written in German script. Always circumspect about her private life in her diaries (no doubt to protect against the prying eyes of various maids), the entries only hint at the truth.

Though Lucy Broadwood was known mainly as a collector of folksong, her life embraced a larger world, and her folksong work has to be seen in the context of mainstream musical London and a huge network of friends and relations. Like some of her contemporaries, such as Vaughan Williams and Fuller Maitland, Broadwood was as at ease with the musical establishment as she was with her folksong contemporaries, though she tended to keep the two worlds separate. She could hold her own with scholars as much as with the farm labourers from whom she collected folksong, though until the end she remained conscious of her class and status as a lady. She was also conscious of her family background and made frequent trips to Switzerland to investigate her Tschudi origins. Equally proud of her English and Scottish family ties, she extended her collecting into highland Scotland while continuing to proselytize for English folksong.

The bourgeois origins and inclinations of Broadwood and her contemporaries have brought down a hail of criticism and opprobrium upon their work. Though it is easy with hindsight to criticize the sometimes patronizing attitude associated with earlier collecting, it is also important to realize that the Victorian collectors were simply products of their time. The move from the library-driven armchair methods of earlier generations to a new, living field approach inevitably brought challenges. In fact, the early collectors were extraordinary individuals in their own right: men such as Frank Kidson and Sabine Baring-Gould could well join Strachey's list of 'eminent Victorians'. The obsession with collecting resulted in a certain objectification of their fieldwork and differing approaches to their presentation and dissemination: Kidson's and Baring-Gould's approaches could not have been more different. Broadwood herself vacillated between presenting her tunes, Kidson-fashion, in melodic form for a specialized audience and publishing polite, edited versions with accompaniments for middle-class delectation, in the style of Baring-Gould. As a singer herself, she could sing her tunes almost anywhere and was probably more adept at getting tunes from informants than many of her contemporaries. It is interesting to see her methods change as she adapted to the evolving technology of the phonograph and its use by iconoclastic collectors such as Percy Grainger. Unlike Sharp, who disapproved of Grainger's methods, Broadwood embraced them, ultimately adopting them herself. It is an easy and unfair game to focus only on the shortcomings of the early collectors; a more nuanced approach is needed.

Quite apart from folksong or other musical concerns, Broadwood's life offers some insight into Victorian and Edwardian womanhood. As the youngest of a large Victorian family, dominated by women, she was particularly well placed to benefit from the experience of her older siblings and to observe the foibles of the family as a whole. During the writing of this book I was constantly reminded of the Bennets in *Pride and Prejudice*. Though the period covered by this book is later than Austen's era, the Broadwoods, like the Bennets, were part of a rural community, looked after their tenant farmers, knew the neighbours and went to all the local balls. They were equally happy in a town environment, where they spent 'the season'. While none of Lucy's sisters appeared to be as silly as the younger Bennet girls, their mother, Juliana, is often somewhat reminiscent of Mrs Bennet as she tried to manage her growing household and make suitable matches for her daughters. Religious, devoted to husband and family, and concerned with the minutiae of daily life, Juliana was for some years the archetypal Victorian wife, staunchly bearing children and burying two, eventually becoming an invalid, though perhaps not one as tiresome as Mrs Bennet. It seems clear that towards the end she was indeed weary of life itself. Her two sons, having been dispatched to private schools and then Cambridge, were not often present, though they returned to the estate from time to time for some hunting and shooting with their father. A typical Victorian gentleman of his class, Henry Fowler Broadwood was as fond of sport as his middle name suggests and, while clearly a loving husband and father, had to devote time to his ailing business which was struggling as the market and technology changed. This was a female family writ large: both sons proved to be ineffectual in business and in life, and there was a tacit family acknowledgement that the women of the family would have managed the business better.

In *Destined to Be Wives* Barbara Caine has written of the Potter sisters, having originally set out to write a biography of the most famous sister, Beatrice Webb. Late nineteenth-century London society was closely knit enough for the Broadwoods to have known the Potters, and indeed Lucy refers to Beatrice and her sister Mary Playne occasionally in the diaries. The Broadwood sisters were certainly not all destined to be wives, though four of them (Katherine, Edith, Mary and Evelyn) chose this course of life and had families of their own. Katherine's tragically premature death in faraway India and the arrival of her three traumatized children on the Broadwood doorstep must have made the younger sisters reflect on the merits of married life: as the oldest and favourite sister 'Katty' had had responsibility for raising them and had amused them in their early years with her clever poems and wit. Later, the chronic illness of their sister Mary – admired for her efficiency and capability – and the death of her infant daughter must have given them pause. Whatever the reason, Lucy joined her sister Amy in remaining single; one suspects that Bertha never intended to marry. Nevertheless, to reject marriage in the 1880s was a defiant gesture, and both Amy and Lucy suffered ill-health and depression throughout their lives, perhaps due to the insecurity and inevitable loneliness of being single. At the same time, it is difficult to assess whether their married sisters were any happier than they were: none had particularly easy lives, and indeed they might have resented the relative freedom that Amy and Lucy enjoyed.

Broadwood achieved adulthood as the suffragist movement began to take hold but, though sympathetic, she did not join its ranks. She became a Primrose Leaguer instead, though later she befriended Mary Neal and went to hear Millicent Fawcett. Though she took part in charity concerts for the less privileged in London, she was never a crusading social reformer; she left such work to Bertha. A Conservative in ordinary life, she was also a conservative suffragist. Like Elizabeth Bennet, she had no formal education beyond that provided by private governesses at home, but nonetheless emerged well-read, critical and articulate. Lucy's erudition flowed from her own diligence and interest, for few Victorian women of her generation could have boasted her vast literary knowledge and ease with languages. The Broadwood library must have helped, and we know from the early diaries that she used her leisure time, which must have weighed heavily on many a young woman of that period, for extensive reading and music practice when she wasn't indulging her other passions of painting and writing clever poetry. She became a competent pianist and, with instruction into her adulthood, a capable singer. She developed a taste for travel early and joined the family on an ill-fated grand tour of Europe in 1887, just short of her thirtieth birthday. A bit of a closet bluestocking, she chose various female models and even began to enjoy the novels of about the emerging 'New Woman' of the 1880s, commenting favourably on Sarah Grand's *Ideala*. The 1880s and 1890s saw her take up bicycling – the hallmark of newfound female independence and a passport into the villages which would yield her songs. She also used her musical training in tentative forays into public performance – again on the model of the 'New Woman' – but at the last minute she retreated from the public gaze and into the comfort of her study: *English County Songs* was the result. Broadwood would have made an ideal university professor: it is tantalizing to speculate what effect the Cambridge education her brothers received as a matter of course would have had on her.

Broadwood found her *raison d'être* in editing the *Journal of the Folk-Song Society*, which in effect became her life's work. In 1899 she achieved a measure of independence as she moved into her own flat after the death of her mother and became a founder member of the Society. Paradoxically, this also became a time when she began to savour the full pleasures of living an adult life in London, finding an unexpected distraction in the company of a strapping young baritone from Lancashire. Always torn between her 'folk' and art music lives, the allure of this conflicted young man pulled her yet again into the art music world, away from her collecting and perhaps also away from her determination to remain single. It also pulled her away from her class. She became his mentor if not a lover, setting the tone for many of her future relationships with younger musicians. It was only when an unknown schoolmaster and principal of a minor music school in north-west London came to shake up the ailing Folk-Song Society that she was jolted back into the world of folksong. Cecil Sharp – sometime principal of the Hampstead Conservatoire but never remotely a member of the musical establishment – proved to be her nemesis in many ways, and his reputation eventually totally eclipsed hers. The studious Broadwood was no match for the publicity-churning whirlwind that was Cecil Sharp, and the battle lines were soon drawn.

The inevitable comparison between Broadwood and Sharp brings into the focus the divide between the Folk-Song Society and its later counterpart, the English Folk Dance Society. Broadwood's scholarly disposition led her beyond music into folklore, a movement that was attracting another group of enthusiastic amateurs. Established some 20 years before the Folk-Song Society, the Folklore Society already had a journal and a committed group of researchers, including outstanding women role models such as Alice Gomme and Charlotte Burne. Broadwood's inclination towards mysticism led her away from the dusty Anglicanism of her youth to the liberal sermons of progressive London clergymen and then on to comparative religion and into the mysticism of George Mead and the Quest Society. She indulged in the typical Victorian parlour games of mind-reading and visualizing, and was even known to consult a fortune-teller. She also became preoccupied with exploring the question of Shakespeare and his authorship of the plays and sonnets, an activity, along with her researches into freemasonry and Rosicrucianism, which I have not dwelt on here. Living in the shadow of Westminster Cathedral, she was also not far from the ethereal music of Elizabethan composers, brought to life by Richard Terry, in whom she found a kindred spirit. Meanwhile, Sharp, the pragmatist, was focusing on music and dance, bringing both into the classroom and cementing his reputation as the avatar of folk music. Broadwood had no real interest in taking folksong into schools; she tended to agree with Kidson that they would be devalued by doing so. The approaches of the contemplative, reticent Broadwood and the self-publicizing, driven Sharp could not have been more different.

In the end, Broadwood's generosity to others – usually perceived as a feminine trait – proved to be her undoing. Too often she sacrificed her own work in order to publish the work of others in the *Journal*. Her valuable work in Scotland was delayed so that she could publish the collection of Frances Tolmie, a gesture of female allegiance, but one that meant that she never saw her own Gaelic songs in print. For the most part comfortably off herself, she was acutely aware of the less fortunate among her friends and made sure that the neediest among them received Civil List support. The plaque in memory of her mentor Alfred J. Hipkins was the result of her petitioning many friends.

Broadwood always maintained close female friendships, and these became her mainstay in later life. Abandoned first by her dashing but troubled baritone and then by her niece with whom she had shared her flat for many years, she turned to her old friends for comfort and support, eventually admitting a favoured few into her inner circle. The friendships with Mary Venables and Fanny Davies stand as testament to the power of female networking in the war years and beyond: careers changed, money was short and hardship abounded. Broadwood's last decade was not an easy one as she confronted a changed society and her own declining health. Her final reliance on her maid, May Scrivener, is a poignant reminder of how interdependent we all are.

The following biography attempts to trace the main threads of Broadwood's life, as well as to situate it in the context of the society in which she lived. Her friends have become my own ghostly friends, as I move between my own busy twenty-first-century life and the shadows of a century ago. I have concentrated on the narrative of her life rather than dwelling on or analysing the tunes she collected: there is enough material in that area for another book and opportunities for bringing it to life through performance. I have found it difficult to refer to her throughout the text only as 'Broadwood'; in her own time she was usually addressed as 'Miss Broadwood', but in a biographical text this seems rather cumbersome and formal, so the reader will find her referred to as 'Lucy' most of the time. There is something to be learned from a woman who survived the transition from the gentility of a mid-Victorian life to the harsh modernity of the twentieth century and its attendant social changes. In addition to adapting her lifestyle to shifting times and customs, she also adjusted her scholarly practices without dropping her standards. By the time of her death, the musicology of folksong and cultural anthropology (which would in turn influence ethnomusicology) were still in their infancy, but her work set high standards for future scholars. And perhaps we also have Jane Austen to thank for influencing Broadwood's keen mind, eye and ear, which in the end made her work stand out from all the others.

Chapter 1

Lyne

The country house of Lyne stands on the borders of Surrey and Sussex, near the villages of Capel and Rusper, 'on the *line* of two parishes, the greater position in Newdigate, the lesser in Capel'.[1] Even at the beginning of the twenty-first century there is a pleasant rural air about this part of England, with its quiet country pub and Norman church and churchyard. Lyne itself, a gracious country house standing in fields at the end of a sweep of driveway, is now home to several owners of luxury flats, but it has not lost its nineteenth-century character and dignity.

Illustration 1.1   Lyne, photographed by Henry Fowler Broadwood, c. 1865
Source: Copyright of Surrey History Centre.

---

[1]   John Shearme, *Lively Recollections* (London: John Lane Bodley Head, 1917), p. 155.

For it is at Lyne that this story really begins. Though no longer in their ownership, Lyne will always be associated with the Broadwood family. It was purchased in 1799 by James Shudi Broadwood, who substantially rebuilt the original seventeenth-century farmhouse (which dated back to the thirteenth century) to accommodate his family. He also purchased surrounding properties, establishing a large estate which took in the villages of Capel, Rusper and Newdigate, and its extensive grounds became the family seat for over a century and a half. By 1855 the estate had taken in holdings with pleasant rural-sounding names such as Osbrooks, Gages, Caffells, Temple and Clowes, among others.[2] James's father, John Broadwood, founder of the important piano firm, had moved from humble origins as a cabinet maker in Scotland to join harpsichord maker Burkhardt Tschudi in London, later turning to piano manufacture as the new instrument began to enchant London in the late eighteenth century. Subsequently he married Tschudi's daughter, Barbara, and their oldest son, James Shudi, became a partner in the firm in 1795.

With the acquisition of Lyne, James Shudi became a country squire and from about 1820 kept detailed records of the estate yields.[3] He was no longer a mere piano manufacturer, but part of the landed gentry. The house was extended with the addition of a library in 1830 and tower in 1838, and throughout the 1830s he was much concerned with local politics. His brother Thomas was appointed as sheriff in 1833, and James himself was sworn in at Lyne as High Sheriff of Surrey in 1835 and Justice of the Peace in 1837.[4] By 1838 he was writing confidently: 'I am become quite a working justice & verily believe I am nearly as competent as the majority of my fellow magistrates.' A pillar of the local church, James also financed an extension to the Capel church to provide seating for some 70 children as an inducement for them to attend services. In 1837 he was appointed to the Capel parish committee to consider commutation of tithes.

Although the family always maintained a town home in London, Lyne remained their spiritual home. James Shudi's first wife, Sophia Colville, gave birth to a second son, James Preston, at Lyne in 1800; John, an older son, had been born in 1798 and became Lyne's second owner on his father's death in 1851. However, tragedy struck when Sophia died at Lyne in the summer of 1801. James Shudi remarried in 1804, re-establishing a Scottish connection in his choice of wife, Margaret Schaw Stewart (1778–1849), daughter of an army surgeon and born in Dominica. This second marriage produced three sons, Henry Fowler (b.1811), Thomas Capel (b.1817) and Walter Stewart (b.1819).

James Shudi's community involvement extended to an interest in local music-making. The Lyne estate included a number of tenanted farms, and in such a rural community folksong was still to be heard. Old customs such as wassailing were still observed, where country folk would visit the local gentry. James Shudi and

---

[2]   Surrey History Centre (hereafter SHC), Broadwood records, SHC 3529/1.
[3]   SHC 6975/1/2.
[4]   SHC 6975/1/2.

his successors seemed to maintain a paternalistic relationship with their servants, who joined in with family music-making at holiday times, notably Christmas. One old retainer, William Boxall, had served the family for years and wrote fulsomely about these occasions. Papers from this period include a number of folksong texts and notes about traditional customs, such as wassailing:

> About thirty years ago the boys used to come into the orchards,
> & after striking an apple tree with a stick, repeat the following:
> 'Stand fast root
> Bear well top,
> Pray God send
> A good howling sap,
> On every twig, apples big,
> On every bough, apples now,
> Hats full, caps full,
> Half quartern sacks full,
> Holla, boys, holla.'
> Upon which they blew a horn & hallooed.[5]

John Broadwood and 'Old English Songs', 1843

All of this had an effect on James Shudi's oldest son, John, who became a 'gentleman clergyman' or 'squarson'– meaning he did not have to preach much – living in Worthing from 1841 to 1847 and at Wiggonhold, before moving to Lyne. While in Worthing, he joined forces with G.A. Dusart, who had been the organist at the chapel of ease there from 1825, and privately published a collection of local folksongs in 1843.[6] The title page, with its confusing jumble of fonts, gives evidence as to the inspiration:

> John Broadwood, OLD ENGLISH SONGS *as now sung by the Peasantry of the* WEALD OF SURREY AND SUSSEX. *and collected by one who has learnt them* by hearing them sung every Christmas from Early Childhood *by* The Country People *who go about to the Neighbouring Houses, Singing.* 'WASSAILING' AS IT IS CALLED AT THAT SEASON.

> The Airs are set to Music exactly as they are now Sung *to rescue them from oblivion and to afford a specimen of genuine Old English Melody.* THE WORDS ARE GIVEN IN THEIR ORIGINAL ROUGH STATE. *With an occasional slight*

---

[5]   Vaughan Williams Memorial Library (hereafter VWML), Cecil Sharp House, Lucy Etheldred Broadwood (hereafter LEB), File 1, item 6.

[6]   Further information and background in Stanley Godman, 'John Broadwood: The Earliest Folk Song Collector', *West Sussex Gazette*, 30 January 1964, SHC 2297/12.

alteration to render the sense intelligible. Harmonized *for the Collector in 1843* *by* G.A. DUSART, ORGANIST TO THE CHAPEL OF EASE AT WORTHING.

Dusart provided leaden accompaniments in church-hymn style, initially ironing out any archaic-sounding modalities in the tunes and harmonies. Broadwood, who played the flute, was keenly aware of the modal nature of some of the tunes and insisted on their being presented in their original state. Dusart's accompaniments are less than inspired, but the collection affords some insight into what John Broadwood might have heard locally. The wassailing tune is none other than 'God rest ye merry Gentlemen' with different words; in all there are 16 songs, including the usual seasonal songs to celebrate the harvest and the plough, rosebuds in June and the pleasures of 'A sweet country life'. The volume opens with 'The Moon Shines Bright', a Christmas song on a religious text, and ranges through a variety of ballads ('The Noble Lord') to sea songs such as 'The Privateer'. The book was privately published by Balls & Co. of 408 Oxford Street London, 'for private circulation'. It was a pioneering effort of its time, though it owed something to editions published earlier in the century by John Bell, John Clare, Chappell, William Sandys and others.[7]

Henry Fowler Broadwood and the Family Firm

The year 1851, the year of John Broadwood's removal to Lyne, was also the year of the Great Exhibition, in which the Broadwood family exhibited its internationally renowned pianos in Joseph Paxton's Crystal Palace. Though a triumphant display of British industry, the Exhibition also featured the inventions from the Continent, where both French and German makers showed a competitive edge, particularly where pianos were concerned. The Broadwoods could no longer count on the family name and their appointment to the royal family to keep their business flourishing in the light of advancing competition from Germany, a situation that would plague Henry Fowler's tenure as director of the firm.

It is significant that 1851 should have been the year that Henry Fowler took over the firm upon his father's death. Somewhat of a *bon vivant* like his uncle Henry, who was a high-living MP and, true to his middle name, fond of hunting and sport, he had had a wide-ranging education, first at public school (Harrow) and then in France and Heidelberg, which gave him some linguistic facility in both French and German, not uncommon among his class at this time: it was good for business. Returning to England, he attended first St John's College Oxford, but moved to Trinity College Cambridge after just two months, possibly at his father's

---

[7]   For more on these early collectors, see the excellent survey by E. David Gregory, *Victorian Songhunters: The Recovery and Editing of English Vernacular Ballads and Folk Lyrics, 1820–1833* (Lanham, MD: Scarecrow Press, 2006).

behest because he had got in with 'the wrong set' in Oxford.[8] No intellectual, like many of his wealthy gentleman friends, he did not take a degree.

In appearance he was very like his great-grandfather, Burkhardt Tschudi, with his 'heavy eyebrows, southern eyes, restless nature and courtly manner'.[9] On coming down from Cambridge, he had been quickly put to work in the factory, learning the trade from the bench upwards and learning the basics of tuning from his father. He became a partner on 10 May 1836, with a one-fifth stake in the business, the older men (James Shudi and Thomas) taking two-fifths each.[10] By 1851 he had had the benefit of nearly two decades' experience, but perhaps not enough to assess the coming threat of foreign competition: to quote Cyril Ehrlich, 'If there is an *annus mirabilis* in pianoforte history it must be 1853, when Steinway (New York), Bechstein (Berlin) and Blüthner (Leipzig) all commenced business'.[11] Henry Fowler would duly come to apprehend this triple threat, but he would not have the wit to counteract it. Moreover, the factory suffered a catastrophic fire in August 1856, with losses of nearly 1,000 pianos and valuable workmen's tools, which were all left on site. Despite insurance payments and various funds set up by friends of the firm, the fire and its aftermath cost Henry Fowler some £50,000 personally.[12]

After the fire, Henry Fowler took a long hard look at his business and proposed opening the partnership to non-family members. George and Frederick Rose were already loyal members of the firm and it was they who prepared the detailed plans for the new factory and organized its financing. Each was given a one-twentieth share in the partnership.[13] Nevertheless, the rebuilt factory housed old-fashioned technology, in an age where traditional craftsmanship in woodworking would be no competition for the cheaper, mechanically produced American pianos.[14]

Family Life

Although established at Lyne, the family did not forget its Scottish connections. Henry Fowler, whose natural element seemed to be more at home hunting and fishing with friends than strolling round the factory floor, chose to spend his summers at Melrose until taking over Lyne in 1864. He rented 'The Pavilion' at Melrose from Lord Somerville for over 20 years.[15] He had married Juliana Birch,

---

[8]   David Wainwright, *Broadwood by Appointment* (London: Quiller Press, 1982), p. 130.

[9]   Obituary, *Musical Times*, 34 (1893): 474.

[10]   Wainwright, *Broadwood*, pp. 131–2.

[11]   C. Ehrlich, *The Piano: A History* (Oxford: Clarendon, 1990), p. 27.

[12]   Wainwright, *Broadwood*, p. 173.

[13]   Ibid., p. 178.

[14]   Ibid., p. 180.

[15]   Shearme, *Recollections*, p. 275.

daughter of Wyrley Birch and Katherine Sarah Reynardson, of Wretham Hall, Norfolk, in 1840. His closest Cambridge friend, Robert Pryor, eventually married Juliana's sister Elizabeth, and the two families remained closely associated for many years.

Pryor, a barrister, was also part of a wealthy trading family and was a frequent guest at Melrose where he and his old friend enjoyed salmon fishing in the cold waters of the Tweed, a short walk from The Pavilion. The family spent their summers there, but for the rest of the year their base was in London, at 46 Bryanston Square, where Juliana supervised the household, recording general household details as well as family trips and events in a pocket diary.[16] Daughters followed in quick succession: the oldest, Katherine, was born in 1841, followed by Augusta Barbara (1843), Edith Juliana (1844), Bertha Marion (1846) and Henrietta Jemima (1847). This idyll quickly changed to sorrow, though, in 1849, with the loss of Henry's mother Margaret to breast cancer and, even more tragically, the deaths of two daughters, Augusta, aged six and Henrietta, aged two. Having lost Augusta in April, Juliana had to confront the illness and death of the 'bright and joyous' Henrietta while at Melrose in August:

I sat up with my darling child all night at four clock in the morning she seemed much worse and very soon after our Heavenly Father took her from us. His will be done for and in us.[17]

Henrietta was buried at Melrose after Henry had been summoned from London. The subsequent services later that year to pray for the end of the cholera epidemic suggest that both daughters might have succumbed to the disease, though Juliana's description of their final hours does not fit the symptoms usually associated with cholera. Juliana was advised by Henry not to attend the 'day of humiliation' services at Melrose, and remained unwell.[18] The threat appeared to be over by November, when thanksgiving services were held for 'the cessation of cholera'. The Broadwoods lost no more children to the disease.

Almost as if to offset the gloom of that year, and as a gesture of optimism about the future, two more daughters were born in quick succession: Mary Stewart in 1850 and Evelyn Charlotte in 1851, both of whom were healthy and thrived into late adulthood. The succession of daughters seemed to be inevitable with the birth of Amy Murray in 1853, but the following years saw the long-awaited arrival of two sons and heirs, James Henry Tschudi in 1854 and Henry John Tschudi in 1856. In retrospect Lucy's birth seems somewhat of an afterthought: by this time Juliana, now in her early forties and busy with many things, had little time to note much in her journal; the one for 1858 is noticeably sparse in its entries, and there is nothing about this last birth. Indeed, having borne 11 children, Juliana was developing

[16]   Diaries of Juliana Birch Broadwood, 1849–1872, SHC, 6975/3, no. 1.
[17]   Ibid., 10 August 1849.
[18]   Ibid., 18 October 1849.

health problems and was content to leave much of the job of running such a large household to her older daughters.

Growing up as a Broadwood

During the 1850s the family became especially close, enjoying a rich cultural life in the capital, punctuated by idyllic summers north of the border, where the children amused themselves by compiling a family newspaper. Called 'The Fragmentary Miscellany', the paper was a satirical look at local life and afforded an opportunity for the children to exercise their literary skills.[19] Katherine, the oldest, was particularly skilled at this and probably influenced her younger siblings. The paper was above all funny, and trenchant in its observation. Begun in July 1857 with the motto 'Copiously supplied then most enlarged; Still to be fed, & not to be surcharged', it was a family affair, replete with limericks, stories, advertisements and observations. The fishing exploits of their father and grandfather were duly recorded with pride:

> Mr Broadwood of the Pavilion caught today 4 seatrout & a 7 pound salmon in the Tweed. Wyrley Birch Esq left the Pavilion today after having caught a salmon of 14 lb besides other smaller ones.

Local horror at the truncation of the fishing season ('in consequence of the new Tweed Act') was duly noted, as were the comings and goings of their father and various relations during the hunting season. There was a classified section: an advertisement for a 'gentleman tutor' to a 'small private family' consisting of 'two boys of the respective ages of 12 & 14' and '3 young ladies aged 10, 13, 16' asked for 'instruction in the rudiments of Latin and for good references, the application to be made to A. Jollycove, Livewell House, The Bull Commons, Goodborough nr Melrose'.

As the eldest, Katherine was probably the chief organizer and, as an enthusiastic writer, she was the chief contributor of various verses and satirical commentary on various events in the locality. We get a glimpse of her vivacious personality in the following:

> Cacoethes Scribendi by a young Female Sufferer!
> Oh dear I am seized with a mania for writing!
> My brain is on fire! I'm all effervescing
> This disease Cacoethes Scribendi's delighting
> I really must just put my thoughts down while dressing.
> Oh Simpkins you're pulling my hair without mercy
> Don't torture me so with that horrid hair-pin!

---

[19]   SHC 6975/3/26.

...

But ah! While my poetry I've tried to rehearse
I find all the time I've been writing in verse!
I thank thee, kind Muse who attended unseen
I declare this shall go to the new Magazine
Yes child of my brain to—Broadwood I'll send ye
And tell him to head you Cacoetheses Scribendi![20]

However, the most salient remarks were made by Juliana herself, who as 'Materfamilia' [*sic*] inveighed against the corruption of her children by current music-hall favourites, presaging her as yet unborn daughter's career in encouraging traditional music of a past era:

> I write you these few lines to bring before your notice a great evil of this, & to this present generation i.e. the redundance if I may so speak of Comic songs so called, vulgar witless jingles to my mind. But Sir so these foolish rhymes take the public taste, so are they now hummed & drummed throughout our domestic circles that even tender branches that have scarce seen six summer in lieu of having their young ideas taught how to shoot with 'Twinkle twinkle little star' or 'Come when you're called, do as you're bid' maybe heard lisping out 'Villikins & his Dinah', 'Bobbing round" etc. Sir, what a boon would it be to our families, were some verses suitable to children written to the airs of the street ballads that from their liveliness are so apt to catch infant ears. I need not say how great a favour it would be to [signed] Materfamilia.[21]

The year 1858 had been a typically busy year for the family: a governess, Harriet Ainger, was hired in January to teach the girls and, to judge from Bertha's atrocious handwriting and spelling, was much needed. Large and plain but clearly bright and kindly, she was nicknamed 'Aingie Mangee'. The drab days of the new year were enlivened somewhat by attendance at Michael Faraday's lectures, which Juliana duly supplemented with a book on electricity. As part of their education, the girls were taken on educational visits to the British Museum and the Kensington Museum, and occasionally to Lyne to practise their sketching. Being Broadwoods, their musical education was not neglected, and, as well as having music lessons, they attended concerts regularly. As was their custom they went up to Scotland for the summer, setting out in mid-April. Their father took them on the usual fishing trips, but also provided unusual entertainment such as mesmerizing one of the roosters, though it is not clear from Bertha's diary exactly what this involved.[22]

In July, late in Juliana's pregnancy, the family went on extensive travels in the Highlands, though Kathy and Miss Ainger returned to help Juliana on 8 August,

---

[20]   Ibid., August 1857.
[21]   Ibid., no. 9, September 1857.
[22]   Bertha Marion Broadwood Diaries, SHC 2185/BMB/5/13, 3 June 1858.

just in time for the birth of 'little Lucy' the following day at 2 pm. Her birth was recorded by Bertha, but not by Juliana in her day book. Henry did not return from the Highlands until about a month later. A nurse, Mrs Baker, was brought in to assist, and Lucy was christened on 17 September. For Bertha at least, lessons resumed with Miss Ainger a few days later.

Towards the end of her life, Lucy wrote of her earliest memories of her father, whom she portrayed as a benevolent *paterfamilias* with a fine voice. Although she did not return to Melrose until long after her childhood, she remained close to her Scottish roots. 'Sound' played an important part of her early life:

> I was sitting astride a trousered leg and looking into a pair of wonderfully bright brown eyes. And I thought the eyes like the colour of the river Tweed, near which we lived for part of each year. There was a head of rich black-brown hair. An exquisite noise came from a mouth belonging to the head. It was a noise that I loved, and yet tears poured down my cheeks. Since I associated crying with being naughty this puzzled me.

> As time went on, I learned that the leg, eyes, head and voice – a beautiful baritone – were parts of something called 'Papa', and that my earliest musical impression had come through his singing of 'The wee little croodlin Doo', a Scottish version of the ballad 'Lord Randal', sung to him in his childhood by his mother; the words of which conveyed nothing whatever to me at that baby age when the tune made havoc with my emotions.

Lucy's eyes were as astute as her ears, though; the Broadwoods also had a fine art collection, and Lucy's appreciation of painting began early:

> Someone – was carrying me slowly on an arm round the drawing-room of our house in Bryanston Square, pausing silently before the many big pictures on the walls. As if I were being fed something altogether new, delicious and satisfying I drank in rich blends of mellow browns, reds, greens, greys, blues, that seemed to soak into my little being, to remain there for ever. ... Later again I came to know that Boucher, Fragonard, Lancret, Watteau, Cuyp, Ruysdael, Teniers and others had made the pictures which had filled a baby soul with supreme content.[23]

In London, family life was a whirl of musical, artistic and intellectual events. During Lucy's first year, her older siblings resumed their usual round of educational visits to museums and concerts. Unusually, they did not go up to Scotland until July, but took a brief holiday in newly fashionable Ryde, where the girls were able to try their hand at sailing. Their grandmother, Juliana's mother Katherine, died in October 1861. The following year, her namesake, the spirited Katherine, married Edmund Craster, whose position in the Bengal civil service

---

[23]   SHC, 'Youthful Memories', 2185/LEB/10/117, typescript, 1927.

took them to India, from where Katherine continued to write sparkling poetry for her younger siblings.

Juliana herself was not well as she suffered from severe asthma, and with the departure of her oldest daughter she increasingly left the supervision of the family to Edith, then 18, and Bertha, who was 16. The beloved Miss Ainger left, to be replaced by Miss Susanne Murphy, who became a great favourite and was probably instrumental in educating the younger girls to a high standard.

While in London, the Broadwoods entertained some of London's most outstanding musicians, both for business and pleasure. The Manchester pianist and conductor Charles Hallé was a frequent guest. The Broadwoods regularly attended his concerts as well as those of the German emigré Ernst Pauer, whose series of Historical Recitals marked an innovative experiment during the 1863 concert season. The older girls were taken regularly to concerts with Miss Murphy, hearing violinists such as Joachim and Vieuxtemps, the cellist Piatti and the pianist Arabella Goddard, an old favourite. Bertha, often underwhelmed, began to write fairly trenchant reviews in her diary and was clearly developing a critical ear. Already a concert habituée, she objected most to those who attended concerts merely for their social cachet, especially if royalty was present:

> May 4 We missed Pauer's concert today which I was very sorry for. In the evening Miss M, Evelyn & I went to the Philharmonic we had made up our minds to be vulgar for once & go as alas, most English people are ready to do, not to listen to the music but to see (or stare at) the grandees there who today were the Prince & Princess of Wales. Except when they came into the room there was nothing to be seen of them but the backs of their heads for they sat in the very front row, the worst place for hearing the music … we were in what is called the Royal box but which is never used as such. The room was crowded & therefore very hot oh dear! … The concert was very long & dry, first of all portions of Beethoven's opera of 'Egmont' performed by a full orchestra the music was very grand & would have been imposing if it had not been too loud for the place, & besides between each part a nasty little man Mr A Matthison got up & read in bad stage voice a descriptive poem by one Bartholomew. The only [thing] I really cared for was the slow movement in Bennett's concerto in F minor which Miss Gaddard [sic] performed magnificently.[24]

Visits were still made to Wretham, their mother's old home, and Bertha and Mary attended a ball there early in 1863, staying for 10 days, much enjoying the music played by four men from Norwich on fiddle, double bass, flute and harmonium. The latter was a sort of one-man band, as he used his spare hand to play various types of percussion, marking the time exceedingly well. Bertha noted with satisfaction that 'it was quite a pleasure to dance to his music & this I did with all my might'. They visited with their cousin, Rebecca Wyrley,

24   SHC 2185/BMB/5/14, 4 May 1863.

who joined Mary in playing waltzes in the evening after dining with 25 guests. Arriving home, Bertha wrote rather plaintively that her stay there marked 'the pleasantest days I have ever spent (all together) in my life'.[25]

Upon her return, the whole family was forced to take dancing lessons with a Miss Lennox in preparation for more lavish balls to come. The 'pleasantest days' at Wretham might well have been equalled by a visit to Uncle Tom in Holmbush, not far from Lyne, where Bertha spent her seventeenth birthday. The trip took two and a half hours from London by train and was obviously a pleasant family day trip. She went fishing for pike in the millstream with her father, while her younger siblings (not great anglers) ran about gathering flowers. The forest and wildness of the area reminded Bertha of the Highlands – but they were only 30 miles from London![26] Henry Fowler also took the opportunity to visit Lyne, occasionally taking his daughters with him. Bertha recorded in her diary of 1863 the pleasant times she had there with her Aunt Charlotte and Uncle John when she and her sisters were children, with free run of the estate and opportunities to play with the children there.[27]

Family life continued apace, but Juliana was often indisposed, still subject to severe asthma attacks and often remaining in bed for most of the day. She was dispatched to relations at High Elms, near Watford, for a rest cure. It is at this stage of her life that Juliana is reminiscent of Austen's Mrs Bennet in her chronic indisposition combined with an unfailing interest in everything around her, especially the activities of her daughters. Her letters reveal a loquacious person who noticed everything and who no doubt knew all the eligible young bachelors in the area. Her youngest daughter enjoyed robust health and was now included on visits to the Pantheon and to the British Museum, usually accompanied by Miss Murphy and some of her sisters. She also managed a long walk around Belgravia and Kensington Gardens on a May outing with her father and sister Mary. 'The little creature came back as fresh & merry as a grig.'[28] Miss Field, Lucy's nurse, a simple but kind person according to Bertha, became the sixth servant to leave in as many months, followed by the beloved Miss Murphy, who had decided on the radical venture of moving to Australia with her mother and sister. Bertha was much pained:

> I really feel quite low at having to say goodbye to her. Poor thing she grumbled a good deal when first she came to us ... but lately she has quite changed & only the other day she told Mamma that this was one place in a thousand for comfort & kindness. She has always been most good natured & nice & very patient with

25   Ibid., 28 January and 7 February 1863.
26   Ibid., 27 March.
27   Ibid., 17 June.
28   2185/BMB/5/15, 17 May.

poor troublesome stupid me. She has done me an immense deal of good & who
I am to finish myself of without her I can't guess.[29]

Edith took over the teaching of Mary and Lucy during the summer in Scotland.
The family did not return to London until December. Just before Christmas, Henry
Fowler entertained his family with his fine singing of German student songs he
had learnt while in Heidelberg. 'His voice came out almost as clear & strong as
ever; of course he gained immense applause'.[30] A new era was about to begin.

Moving to Lyne

The year 1864 dawned with the usual dances and an invitation to a ball at the
Hollands, 'who had taken a fancy to our looks', wrote Bertha.[31] News of Uncle
John was not good, though, and on 20 January the family friend and doctor,
Dr Jones, reported that he had been down to Lyne 'to see poor Uncle John who has
had some kind of paralytic stroke & is very much worse'. This meant declining the
Hollands' invitation, much to their disappointment. Five days later the Reverend
John Broadwood died at Lyne, survived by his widow Charlotte. Henry returned
from Lyne, and the month ended on a sombre note as the family went to Harvey &
Nichols to envelop themselves in black crepe; even Lucy was not spared. Henry
Fowler's formidable unmarried sister, the intrepid Susan Monteith Broadwood,
came to dinner in preparation for the trip down to Lyne.

The funeral over, and after a decent interval during which Aunt Charlotte
presumably arranged her departure, plans were made to move down to Lyne.
Bertha and Edith joined their father and Hillyer, one of the servants, on the
bright spring morning of 21 March on the trip down by train, arriving just before
luncheon to inspect the entire estate, which included several farms and idyllic
fairy-like spots such as Rhome Wood. Henry Fowler had been down previously
to discuss the proposed railway line through Osbrooks farm, and had also cut
down some trees in order to clear walkways, enlarging and tidying the garden and
improving the farm road to Capel so that it would be 'made fit for carriages'.[32]
Bertha noticed a local fox hunt. On the following day they went for a walk along
the proposed railway track and talked to some of the tenants and comforted Aunt
Charlotte, who was to leave Lyne for Winchester at the end of April, leaving the
house free for the large family of Broadwoods.

In the meantime Bertha went to Paris, finding the innovations of Louis
Napoleon somewhat distasteful, but enjoying the sights of the city for the first
time. On her return, her two brothers were dispatched to a Mr Seager's private

29   Ibid., 3 July.
30   Ibid., 19 December.
31   Ibid., 25 January 1864.
32   Ibid., 19 March.

school at Stevenage, which would prepare them for entry to the major public schools of Harrow and Eton. The family moved down to Lyne on 29 April. Plans were being made to sell the house in Bryanston Square, which Henry Fowler had altered in order to accommodate his large family; he was already planning how he could enlarge the accommodation at Lyne.

Moving the entire family and entourage was a great undertaking, though Bertha declared that as they had been so used to travel, they performed the operation 'without the smallest rout or bustle in a way that would astonish most people'.[33] The situation was helped by there being little furniture, which would arrive when the Bryanston Square house was sold. Various servants were also left behind, including the footboy William who was in bad health. Bertha spent the afternoon planting ferns and watching the summer house being turned into an aviary for the children's canaries. Bertha herself kept hawks.

The older sisters set about making the place their own, rearranging some of the furniture in the library and drawing room 'so as to make things more as they used to be in old days'. Their pianos arrived from London in the evening, along with a yellow mastiff with a black muzzle for Edith, named Twist after their father's old dog.

May Day dawned on a Sunday and was 'just like the old May days one reads of'.[34] The family attended the service at the local church in Rusper, with Edith driving Juliana to church in a little old pony cart drawn by one of the new ponies recently bought from Wales by Henry Fowler. The next couple of days were spent ranging around the estate, working out accommodation for the various servants. Henry Fowler went up to London for business early on the Wednesday. The family began to settle in, taking the little girls to Rusper for slates and pencils. Singing lessons with a Miss Macirone (possibly the composer Clara Macirone) were resumed. Pictures were hung, rooms decorated, and with a croquet party at the Pellys in nearby Warnham Court, where the family 'met all the neighbourhood', they truly began to settle in.

They did not leave for Scotland until early August, when the brothers went off to school. Though sad to leave, their stay in Scotland would allow time for the many alterations to be made. Lucy celebrated her sixth birthday shortly after their arrival and before her father departed on his annual trek to the Highlands, this time taking Bertha with him.

By 1867 the domestic scene was possibly stable enough to afford Juliana a health and rest cure, since she and Edith took an eight-month jaunt around Europe. Leaving London for Paris in early March, they went on down south to the Alps, arriving in Geneva on the 7th. From mid-August they stayed in Mainz, Cologne and Antwerp, returning to London on 15 October.[35]

---

[33]   Ibid., 29 April.

[34]   Ibid., 1 May 1864.

[35]   SHC, Juliana Broadwood 6975/3, Diary 1867.

Illustration 1.2   Portrait of Lucy Broadwood, aged 8, 1866
Source: Copyright of Surrey History Centre.

Juliana returned from her trip to continue with running the new household at Lyne, with alterations still continuing and many visitors. Lucy was taken on holiday to Freshwater, Isle of Wight, with Bertha, their cousin Marion and one of the servants.

In 1870 the family rejoiced at the return of their oldest sister Katherine, who was pregnant with her third child. She in fact bore twins, only one of whom survived. Christened Barbara, she was born in January 1871 and was a sister for Bertram and Katie. Katherine stayed until March and then returned to India. Harry and James were at Eton, and a Miss Koeppel had been hired to teach and look after Amy and Lucy, the two youngest girls; during the winter both Juliana and Lucy caught mumps. Although they still had a London home, the Broadwoods considered Lyne their principal residence, and Lucy was soon playing with the children of the neighbouring Lee Steere family. James went up to Trinity College Cambridge in 1873, which afforded pleasant family visits to his 'spacious, bright, nicely furnished rooms';[36] Harry proceeded to Jesus College two years later.

The Broadwoods Abroad

Juliana's asthma was beginning to severely restrict her social life and ability to travel up to London. Worried about needing help at night and disturbing others, she felt herself to be a 'hindrance and an obstacle' to her family, and resolved 'to go away and be made better, or done for!'. She hoped that Lucy, Evelyn, Mary and Miss Koeppel might accompany her and her husband, leaving the rest of the family free to lead their lives. She would return restored and able to lead the vigorous life her husband liked.[37]

They set out in July, heading for the Bavaria Hotel, Louisenbad, Reichenhall. The salt springs of Reichenhall were the grandest in Germany, with 15 springs feeding the surrounding area. Under the supervision of a Dr Liebig, the family's health was monitored. Mary was thought to be too delicate to climb the hills due to a weak heart and lungs, much to her distress. The spa had no English or American visitors and, though she loved the scenery, Juliana clearly felt uncomfortable amid the many Germans there, many of them Jewish. Despite her anti-Semitism, typical of her time, her description is a valuable account of life in a mid-nineteenth-century spa with its rigid conventions:

> The place is quite charming but the company as far as we have yet seen, not so. Your sisters & I were to have been up & dressed & at the Kursaal (they drinking cups of goats whey) at 7 a.m. today but it was nearly 7.30 before we got to the place. We must be more structured another time. Many hundreds of persons very few looking like invalids come & drink out of long cups each one

36 SHC 2185/BMB/4/2, no. 6, letter from Juliana to Bertha, 25 February [1873].
37 Ibid., no.15 [?1874].

numbered from one to several hundreds and reserved for the use of the drinker whose name & number are inscribed in a large book. You are abonné for a month or 6 weeks or whatever time you choose, & pay your abonnement at the end of your course of drinking ... Some of the many Baronesses Rothschild will I hope vacate tomorrow the rooms that I wish to possess. We shall then have a piano & all that we can desire to make us comfortable.[38]

Katherine was not well and wrote that she hoped to return for good in 1875, despite Edmund's promotion to the judgeship of Patna. Meanwhile she was justifiably concerned about the health of her daughters Katie and Barbara, and felt that they could not survive another hot season in India. She proposed that they sail to England at once and take a house in Rusper, with a lady to take care of it. Juliana wrote to suggest a cottage in nearby Pleystowe.[39]

Arrivals from India

The two girls duly arrived in 3 May 1874 on board the P&O steamer, *Peshawar*. Juliana went with a maid, Cooter, to meet them, amidst 70 or 80 children and their *ayahs*. The girls were accompanied by their Irish teacher Mrs Kerr, who had cared well for them during the long voyage. The children had been well behaved and were very shy and weak on arrival. In contrast to her healthy sister Katie, Barbie was ailing; she would not speak or look at anyone and clung pitifully to Cooter. Juliana thought her backward at first, but evidently she improved after a few weeks at Lyne.[40]

There would be more difficulties to face. Juliana responded to birthday wishes from her absent husband with resignation: 'I am so very very weary of always feeling as if I ought to do more than it seems possible for me to do'.[41] There would indeed be much more for her to do. She received the tragic news of her eldest daughter's death shortly after her birthday. Katherine herself had been unwell in India, and from one of her last poems there is a poignant indication of her dissatisfaction with her life:

The Modern Doctrine
Religion for man is a curse 'tis said,
It cramps his heart, it addles his head,
It checks his aspiration.

---

[38]   Ibid., no. 9, 21 July 1873. Further information on the baths can be found in Edward Gutmann, *The Watering Places and Mineral Springs of Germany, Austria, and Switzerland* (London: Sampson, Low, Marston, Searle, & Rivington, 1880), pp. 112–13.

[39]   Letters to BMB 2185/BMB/4/2, no. 8, 14 July 1873.

[40]   Ibid., no. 12, 5 May [1874].

[41]   Ibid., no. 16, [June 1874].

But for woman a sham of much use & grace,
It gives her a bland & a smiling face,
And keeps her down in her proper place
At the feet of the Lord of Creation.[42]

Here was a spirited, bright young woman whose life had been snuffed out far too early. Her death hit the family hard, for they loved her humour and high spirits. The effect of her death on her young children is incalculable and placed an enormous burden on Juliana, whose health was not up to raising three young grandchildren. She would have to rely on her other daughters to help her through the next years. Bertha was the bossiest of them all, and one can only hope that Juliana did not take her advice on relieving her asthma:

I rejoice to hear that you have taken to smoking! Mary Arthur recommended those Stramonium cigars so strongly as the only thing that relieves Mrs Meade's asthma that I bought a box of them for you. ... They are from Kingsford of Piccadilly, the only chemist who sells the genuine article in England. Mary A said that one whiff is quite nought, or rather one draught of smoke, which you should swallow & then put out the cigar & keep it for another time ... Are you getting on with yr walking & have you ventured upon a drive yet?[43]

Bertha had already assumed a powerful position among the sisters and appeared to be a more dominating personality than Mary or Edith. She was clearly critical of her father's running of the firm and was possibly already taking an interest in its management. Juliana sprang to his defence:

You could not have thought it possible that I imagined that you liked commanding & leading ... In the same way in your father's business He having more knowledge & energy than any of the other partners must command & lead, though he would be too thankful if the others could & would act independently in some particular lines; & if they were persons of nearly but not quite equal talent & energy they might have worked well with him & have asserted themselves; as it is they could not do it. Your father most nobly & generously did his best to put all the partners on an equal footing with himself but the fact remains that he is & must be the leader.[44]

Bertha also felt that her younger siblings should have more independence and freedom, and take more responsibility. Once again, Juliana reacted defensively, but, more importantly, her letter reveals interesting tensions within such a large family and also Bertha's characteristic questioning of the status quo:

---

[42] SHC, LEB Miscellany, 2185/LEB/10/9–14. Poem dated 15 February 1873.

[43] SHC, Letters to BMB 2185/BMB/4/2, no. 17, 16 May 1875.

[44] Letters to BMB 2185/BMB/4/2, no. 25, 11 October 1877.

I am pained very much that you should think for a single instant that I have ever thought that you wished to 'play first fiddle' ... I know as well as possible that your wish is to stir up your brothers & sisters to independence of action – but in my letter I wished to point out to you that what you as an elder sister can do, the younger ones cannot do – and I pointed out that it would be thought an impertinence in one of them to order the carriage & go off on some scheme they must take orders & must defer to the convenience of their elders, yr father would not allow Evelyn, Amy or Lucy to have the same amount of liberty of ordering that you & Mary have – as if James or Henry ordered carriage or horses without asking permission you know ... that your father would be displeased ... I know that you would not find fault & that you would be glad if your brothers asserted themselves more & that your great desire is to push them forward. James is very anxious to do the least that can be done for heating Rusper Church ... what I said about Lucy was to allow that you had reason in thinking that the younger sisters did not do all that they might. I think ... that a good deal is done for her amusement. Mary so perpetually gave up everything to her in London & she has had more pleasant amusing outings than almost any of the sisters have had. I don't think that my fault is to under value my goslings – I am always laughed at [for] my great admiration of them.[45]

Such questioning was typical of Bertha's character, and her energy was formidable, as she would demonstrate in her future family and professional commitments. Possibly her father's favourite (after all, she was the one he took fishing), she must have clashed with her mother who favoured the quiet and domesticated Mary, who was musical and played the organ at church, setting an example for her younger sisters. Sounding once again like Mrs Bennet, Juliana wrote somewhat admonishingly to Bertha:

I hope and pray that Amy & Lucy may be like [her] indeed & may help her & you more than they have yet done. Amy is helping in the practise of the oratorio & will be of great use with her clean true voice. Harry Steere, the Kennedys & Mrs Gore are very good about the practising and the choirboys take great interest – young Kimber is to come back from W. Houthly to stay at the Pickards ... M has covered herself with credit as pro.tem organist at Capel during Mrs [?] absence & now that she has come back poorly & nervous Mary will play again two days – but she is doing too much. She has somehow not had the heart to touch her painting since she came home but I hope she will take it up again. She is a capital housekeeper – she is the most punctual & orderly member of the family ...[46]

---

45   Ibid.
46   Ibid., no.33, 17 October 1879.

Life in London

Things were going better for Amy and Lucy. The family had moved to 52 St George's Square in Pimlico, which was a valuable base for London activity. Lucy was allowed to attend parties, but only if chaperoned. In May 1877 Juliana took her to dinner with some old friends in Bryanston Square and then on to a ball at their friends, the Stopfords. It was Lucy's 'first appearance in the London world', aged 19; she knew but few people there, but danced a good deal. The crowd, mostly young and high-spirited young people, danced polkas all night, which Lucy found much too violent and romping, but she eventually fell in with the 'dancing, fling and whirling about'; Juliana had nothing to find fault with and thought 'all the arrangements so nice and pretty', with the hostess 'very nice and good natured & attentive & anxious that all the guests should get dancing & enjoy themselves'.[47]

Lucy was indeed enjoying herself. She had London (and Cambridge) yet to explore. Her older sisters Edith, Evelyn and Mary were married; the formidable and organizing Bertha was away, travelling. Just after her twenty-first birthday in August 1879 she was busy at Lyne entertaining various friends and relations, commenting on the harvest in an exuberant letter to Bertha. She had attended a meeting of the Primrose League with Amy in nearby Ockley and, amid the dancing and merriment afterwards, had been 'induced to become a Primrose-dame' for seven and sixpence. She was longing to go up north to see 'the kiddie-widdies', Bertram, Katie and Barbie, who must have seemed like younger siblings, and for whom she had great affection.[48]

But the older siblings must have had even more influence. Her mother and sisters had already shown what could await her, and for a woman of her class there were probably few options to contemplate: would she follow Edith and Evelyn into a life of marriage and motherhood, or would she follow Bertha's independent and headstrong example? Would she remain a 'Primrose-dame' Conservative, comfortably ensconced on a country estate? Would she be political at all, as her society changed and women began to take more of a share in it? Was she possibly envious of the Cambridge education her brothers had been able to take for granted but which, for her, was impossible? Now off travelling on the Continent, they looked forward to an assured future; at the very least there would be positions in the family firm, but never for the women of the family, able though they were. Always fond of Jane Austen, perhaps Lucy pictured herself as an Elizabeth Bennet or possibly Emma Woodhouse. Literate, witty and sparkling in company, and musically gifted, she had had a taste of cosmopolitan and sophisticated London, its concerts and its social whirl, and had much enjoyed it, even when under the watchful eye of a chaperone. Lyne and Sussex would always be close to her heart, but for the moment there were other places to explore and boundaries to test.

[47]   Ibid., no.21, 10 May 1877.
[48]   2185/BMB/4/24/2, Lucy to Bertha, 16 August 1879.

Chapter 2

London

By the 1880s the family was growing up and dispersing, and Henry and Juliana wanted nothing more than a quiet life at Lyne. Both were in declining health, and Henry's worsened considerably after an accident with a falling blind in September 1884, which left him with reduced sight and confined to a wheelchair.[1] He had retired from the firm three years previously at the age of 70, leaving his 23-year-old son Harry as a newcomer on the factory floor, though he himself remained a partner and kept in touch with the London showroom and factory. The firm had benefited from a healthy injection of capital from Henry's half-brother Thomas Broadwood Jr, who died in the same year, leaving £424,000.[2]

On the home front, the older members of the family were marrying and moving away. In 1881 Mary became the fourth daughter to marry, choosing the affable clergyman John Shearme, who had a living at the newly formed parish of Holmbury St Mary's, near Dorking. They were married at Newdigate Church on 1 February by the Reverend Francis Holland of Canterbury, Mary's cousin by marriage. A daughter, Mary Dorothea, was born in January 1883, and Lucy was invited to be her godmother and presented her with a coral necklace at her christening.[3] Mary, previously robust and healthy, soon became ill, and the baby was chronically unwell.[4] Edith had joined the ranks of the Anglo-Irish, having married the Irish landowner Robert Conway Dobbs; the couple's two sons, William and Henry, were of school-age by the 1880s. A daughter, Alison Charity, was born in 1885 at a time when the spectre of Home Rule was agitating families like theirs, and they were greatly relieved when Gladstone's bill was defeated.[5] Evelyn, married to barrister William Forsyth, had a daughter, Jean, in September 1879 and a son, Hazeldean, shortly thereafter.[6] Her husband, who had been working in India, returned in 1881. She and the family were living in Haslemere, where

---

[1]   Surrey History Centre (SHC), Diaries of Lucy Broadwood, LEB 6782 (hereafter Diaries). For ease of reference I will refer to the diaries by year. Compare the entry for 18 September 1884 with David Wainwright, *Broadwood, by Appointment* (London: Quiller Press, 1982), p. 224, who states that this incident happened in 1888.

[2]   Wainwright, *Broadwood*, p. 203.

[3]   Diaries, 20 January 1883.

[4]   SHC, Letters to BMB, 2185/BMB/4/2/no. 47, 16 May 1884. Juliana wanted the Holmbury water tested as both Mary and the baby had been so poorly.

[5]   Alison was born on 23 December 1885 and was christened at Woking on 4 May. Lucy was a godmother, along with Alice Broadwood. Diaries, 4 May 1886.

[6]   Hazeldean eventually moved to India and died in a military accident there in 1910.

she was a neighbour of Tennyson, the poet laureate, and his family; Lucy met the distinguished man after a local concert in November 1883 and subsequently in September 1884, forming an instant rapport. Evelyn, meanwhile, was preparing for publication an edition of a sixteenth-century Romance by Griffith Boan, *Ye Gestes of Ye Lady Anne*, illustrated by Anna Hennen Broadwood, the American wife of her uncle, Thomas Capel Broadwood, who had emigrated to New Orleans in 1847. The book was published by Leadenhall Press, which specialized in producing high-quality books, exemplary for their illustration, printing and typography.[7] Eventually, Evelyn took a flat in London, in Carlisle Mansions, Victoria.[8]

Bertha had virtually taken over the management of Lyne. Far from overseeing just household staff, she had inherited her grandfather's interest in tenant welfare and the responsibilities of landowners. Concerned about the medical welfare of the rural poor, many of whom dwelt not far from the grand house, she rallied support from the wealthier families of Surrey to organize local nursing services and home helps to care for those who otherwise would have had no access to medical services. As the foundation for district or cottage nursing, her 'Holt-Ockley' system gained support throughout Britain, and she travelled widely recruiting nurses, setting up homes for them and lecturing on her system. Eventually, her operation comprised 800 cottage nurses, 4 per cent of whom were certified midwives.[9]

Bertha's domestic life would become inextricably entwined with that of her younger brother James, who seemed to be a 'late developer' to judge from his mother's letters, and who was uncertain about his future career. His lack of interest in the family firm must have been a disappointment to both parents. After coming down from Cambridge in 1877 he became a member of Lincoln's Inn and was called to the Bar in 1882. He visited Lyne amid continental travels, eventually marrying Evelyn (Eve) Fuller Maitland in a lavish ceremony at St Andrew's Church, Wells Street, in December 1884.[10] His sisters Lucy and Amy were two of eight bridesmaids, and three priests officiated. The marriage produced three children, but ended tragically with the death of Eve upon the birth of her third child, their only son (christened Evelyn) in 1889. James, who must have been devastated at this event, thereupon moved from his home in Malvern down to Lyne, where Bertha took over the raising of his young family while he occupied himself with the running of the estate. He became a partner of the firm in 1889, but only after obtaining mortgages on the Lyne estate and ploughing £30,000 into the company.[11]

Shy, stuttering Harry, meanwhile, was struggling with his new duties in the family firm, having taken his degree in 1879. An inexperienced and unwilling

---

[7]   Diaries, 22 May 1884. The book was published in November; see entry for 11 November 1884.

[8]   Diaries, 25 February 1888.

[9]   Wainwright, *Broadwood*, p. 225.

[10]   Diaries, 11 December 1884.

[11]   Wainwright, *Broadwood*, p. 226.

recruit, he had much to learn from the vastly more experienced and older members of staff, notably the Rose brothers, and his own father. By 1881 he had developed a romantic interest in his neighbour and childhood sweetheart, Ada Heath, but was not in a financial position to propose marriage. Ada was the daughter of Admiral Sir Leopold Heath, who had distinguished himself in the Crimean War and was ADC to Queen Victoria. His son Cuthbert, somewhat isolated in childhood owing to chronic deafness, had been a good friend who later made a successful career in business. The relationship between Harry and Ada occasioned much correspondence between the families, centring on the other financial responsibilities of the respective families (in Broadwood's case, the necessity of providing for three unmarried daughters) and their inability to offer much help to the young couple.[12] In the end, the loyal Bertha weighed in to resolve the wrangling, and the couple were married on 26 August 1886 in Holmwood Church. The ceremony was much more austere than James's wedding two years previously, with Amy (33) and Lucy (28) again taking part as bridesmaids. Ada proved to be a formidably efficient wife and mother, who was perhaps constitutionally stronger – or just luckier in terms of her medical care – than her less fortunate sister-in-law, and she produced a daughter, Marion, the next year, followed by Stewart (1888), Leopold (1890) and Janet (1895). All survived to maturity.

The Broadwoods in London: St George's Square

Lucy's position in the family as youngest daughter meant that she was often paired with her sister Amy, who was five years older and also on the marriage market in the 1880s. Like Lucy, Amy had a clear singing voice, but her mother despaired of her ever being assertive enough to run a household and was reluctant to let her take any such responsibility at 52 St George's Square.[13] One wonders if both sisters envied their two brothers their unchaperoned freedom as they left home for Eton and then Cambridge, where they received their sisters in their spacious rooms. Meanwhile both sisters divided their time between country life at Lyne and the social whirl of London. The crumbling old family house at 52 St George's Square, Pimlico, afforded a convenient base during the season, and it was not long before Lucy felt comfortable in the London scene. London also offered some intellectual activity, and in 1884 she began exploring the library of the British Museum, combining a visit there in November with fittings at the dressmakers in preparation for her brother's wedding.[14] Life in London made her aware of how

---

[12] SHC, BMB 2185/4/50–54.

[13] Juliana to Bertha, 2185/BMB/4/2/ no. 45, 6 March 1884.

[14] Diaries, 24 November 1884. Lucy examined various publications of the Percy Society, including Dixon's *Songs of the Peasantry*, and Christmas carol collections of Sandys, Gilbert and Gauntlett.

stifling life in Rusper could be, and she resigned her choir-directing duties there after Christmas in 1883.[15]

Eva James

Though Lucy was reasonably close to her sisters, her closest female friend was undoubtedly Eva James. Eva enjoyed music too, and the 'at homes' at 52 St George's Square afforded the perfect opportunity for performing. Eva was an accomplished pianist who was happy to play for entertainment, as well as to accompany others. Born in Watford, Eva had studied in London with Edward Dannreuther, who also numbered Lucy's cousin Herbert Birch Reynardson among his pupils, which was probably how the two women met. She and Lucy were extremely close, and on one occasion she stayed over and co-hosted a breakfast 'levee' the following morning to welcome in the new year of 1883. When Eva came down with measles the following month, Lucy produced a poem in her honour, reminiscent of, and possibly inspired by, her older sister Katherine's efforts many years before in Scotland:

> Here lies poor Eva hot & measly,
> Let her be glad she's got 'em eas'ly,
> She's not allowed to read in bed
> She has already too much red –
> Her eyes (a daily joy to some)
> Alas, have weekly now become
> Deep speckle-ations, hid till now,
> Are now all read upon her brow –
> No friends can get a glimpse of Eva,
> For why? They are afraid of fever,
> So let us hope it soon will leave her
> And that cool draughts may now relieve her![16]

The Broadwood name was the passport to some of the most significant musical events of the decade. Surprisingly, Henry Fowler left for Scotland a week before Franz Liszt's visit to England in April 1886 after many years' absence. Lucy travelled up to London in the morning to stay with Eva. They enjoyed a brief concert of their own, playing with a young violinist identified only as 'Mr Sutton', before going to the reception for the composer at one of their favourite haunts, the Grosvenor Gallery. Sutton was performing in *Angelus*, for 23 strings; Lucy noted some women among the players, notably Winifred Robinson and Emily Shinner. Liszt's protégé (and host for this event), Walter Bache, played the *Bénédiction de*

---

[15]   Diaries, 28 December 1883.
[16]   Diaries, 14 February 1883.

Dieu. A choir of female Royal Academy students sang the chorus of angels from *Faust*, and tenor William Winch sang three songs from *William Tell*. Liszt himself consented to play and improvise on the last movement of Schubert's *Divertimento hongroise* and then on Hungarian dances. With relief, Lucy noted that the piano (a Broadwood, 'our best') had never sounded better under the touch of the master: 'His touch was wonderful, execution beautiful and his use and *not* abuse of tempo rubato delightful'.[17] Four months later the composer was dead.

Eva's engagement in September and subsequent marriage in December of 1886 to the worthy but austere cotton magnate and MP Thomas Gair Ashton came as a severe blow to Lucy, possibly because she had secretly hoped or expected that her friend would make a more romantic match (possibly with Sutton, who seemed to be a favourite) or – more likely – because her marriage would affect the closeness of their relationship. Unlike Evelyn and James Broadwood's lavish wedding two years before, Eva's wedding in Ennismore Gardens, Kensington, on 2 December 1886 was a decidedly subdued affair, with only one clergyman officiating and no bridesmaids. Eva herself wore just a plain brown dress and bonnet.[18] Could it have been that her parents disapproved of her relationship with Sutton, a talented but impecunious musician with working-class roots, and forced the marriage with Ashton upon her? Fortunately the marriage, which was long-lasting and seemed to be happy, did not end the friendship. Soulmates of a kind, the two women remained in contact throughout their lives, with Lucy often visiting Eva at her home, Vinehall, in Robertsbridge, Sussex. But though she kept up some of her music, any hopes of a real career were eclipsed by the domestic responsibility of being wife to a respectable businessman and eventually mother of four children. No more was heard of the young Sutton.

Social Life in Sussex

Small wonder that one of Lucy's favourite authors was Jane Austen, when there was the Sussex social scene to consider. The new year was invariably ushered in with balls, which Bertha had so much enjoyed some years earlier. Now she was Lucy's chaperone to the Horsham hunt ball, where Lucy danced polkas with neighbour Harry Lee Steere, one year her junior and a great admirer, and also with William Bence-Jones, son of the local doctor Archibald Bence-Jones and, like James, studying for the Bar.[19] The Dorking county ball was a more elaborate affair, at which William Bence-Jones was also present amid the blazing diamonds of Lady Bathurst and Lady Henry Somerset, niece of the photographer Julia Cameron.

---

[17] Diaries, 8 April 1886.
[18] Diaries, 2 December 1886.
[19] Diaries, 2 January 1883.

Illustration 2.1   'The Ball' as seen by Lucy Broadwood
Source: Copyright of Surrey History Centre.

Lucy was besieged with partners and was introduced to Hugh Charrington by William, and thereupon found herself invited to the Charrington's fancy dress ball at Bury's Court.[20] Lucy decided to go as Henrietta Maria of England, in a sumptuous white satin period costume, complete with pearl stomacher and decadent puffed sleeves undercut with tulle.[21] Her hair hung in ringlets and, sporting her mother's ruby pendant, Lucy as Henrietta presented a strong figure indeed – an ideal preparation for her presentation to royalty along with Amy, sponsored by their friends, the Clark Kennedys, who invited them to rehearse for the event at a 'curtsey party'. On 21 May Lucy and Amy, their hair specially done by Charenté of Brompton Road, were formally presented to some 10 royal personages, both bejewelled in their court dresses. Somewhat belatedly (she was now 25) Lucy was now officially part of the London scene as well as that of rural Sussex.[22]

While the balls offered some entertainment, everyday life at Lyne forced young women into genteel but frustrating confinement. Off-season, Lucy kept herself occupied by playing the organ and taught a group of unruly boys on Sundays at the Rusper church. She also read voraciously and maintained a regimen of piano and vocal practice that would have challenged the most diligent conservatory student. With fine company pianos at her disposal – a fine new one arrived at Lyne in September 1884, which she inaugurated with Bach and Beethoven – she practised regularly, finding a kindred spirit in her friend and neighbour Anne Parbury, a mother of three whose husband was often away. Lucy and she played duet arrangements of symphonies by Mozart and Beethoven.

Mrs Parbury had been a pupil of the composer William Sterndale Bennett and passed on some of his wisdom to a sceptical Lucy, who had little patience with his casual approach to teaching. Practising was not to be 'overdone', and composition was 'as simple as anything – can be all written on a sheet of notepaper!' to which Lucy wrote in her diary, 'why didn't he, then?' after struggling with a harmony textbook.[23] She did not care much for his compositions, but had been invited to sing in Bennett's oratorio *The Woman of Samaria* in Dorking. She found the work tedious and resented the hours of practice she had to devote to it, but in the end enjoyed the actual performance where she was joined by a number of professional and competent amateur soloists. The concert had been organized by the Beneke family, and also included Handel's *Acis and Galatea*. Lucy pronounced the performance a success; it was well received and, for her, marked an auspicious start as a singer.[24] She soon engaged a professional teacher, a Signor Zuccardi, in 1883, but after a few lessons switched to the sought-after and fashionable William Shakespeare, taking her first lesson in May 1884.

---

[20]   Diaries, 5 January 1883.

[21]   Diaries, 9 January 1883.

[22]   Diaries, 21 May 1883.

[23]   Diaries, entries for 13, 14 November 1883.

[24]   Diaries, 19 December 1882.

Singing and Other Pursuits

Shakespeare was only nine years Lucy's senior but had already established himself as a performer and conductor in London, where he also taught at the Royal Academy of Music.[25] A career teacher as well as an active performer, he promoted a particular method, which he eventually published; meanwhile, his eager pupil soaked up everything he said and took copious notes.

As was the case for many young women in country houses with time on their hands, crafts took up a proportion of Lucy's time, but surely painting bellows, arranging flowers and making peacock fans could not have satisfied her for long, though she was commissioned to paint a Japanese umbrella with Greek designs to be used in a production of Aristophanes's *The Birds* in Cambridge. Her cousin Frank Pryor was involved in the production, and the umbrella was used by Prometheus – played by another relation, Harry Cust – to hide himself from the other gods. The production, with music by Parry and conducted by Stanford, was directed by Charles Waldstein, director of the Fitzwilliam Museum. With such academic backing, *The Birds* created a small sensation and was reported in the press as a landmark production, though Lucy was not credited with her artwork.[26]

Lucy had not had the benefit of a Cambridge education, but her family surroundings had provided her with a keen appetite for the arts. Having been educated in true Victorian style with governesses and access to a large library and art collection which included works by various great masters, her education now served her reasonably well, and she read voraciously in both English and French. She found role models in Madame de Staël and George Sand, but Jane Austen remained a staunch favourite. Her appreciation for art stayed with her for life, and she was a frequent visitor to London art galleries, finding much pleasure in the exhibitions in the Grosvenor Gallery, which also served as a concert hall. Not restricting herself to fiction or biography, she read widely, including *Some Modern Difficulties* by the prolific Devon clergyman, Sabine Baring-Gould. Her interest in religion went far beyond the Christian theology she taught to her class of boys at the Rusper church and extended to the mystical and spiritual. Indeed, her readings in comparative religion might well have made her an extraordinary teacher, for how many young women of the time were familiar with Edwin Arnold's *Light of Asia*, or could discourse on Buddhism?[27] Likewise, while in London she frequented St Peter's Church in Vere Street especially to hear the Reverend William Page Roberts, whose unconventional and non-literal approach

---

[25]   Obituary in *The Musical Times*, 72 (1931): 1137.

[26]   See 2185/BMB/4/24, no. 4, 5 December 1883, from Haslemere.

[27]   Diaries, 11 December 1882 The book was under discussion by the women of family, who had read an article on comparative religion two days previously: 'We women chatted & discussed in the drawing-room whilst the men went a-shooting. I also sang, whilst Cousin Eleanor read aloud E. Arnold's "Light of Asia". An animated discussion took place on Buddha therefore at luncheon'.

to Christianity greatly appealed to her.[28] Though she had a penchant for visiting churches, as much to hear the sermons as to look at the architecture, while in London she also visited the Jewish synagogue in Upper Berkeley Street and was much impressed with what she heard.[29] Similarly, on a visit to Walsingham she was entranced by a Gregorian service which featured the singing of an old hymn from the Sarum rite.[30]

The London social scene, with its many private parties, offered many opportunities to widen her social circle: Lucy had met the Potter family, particularly young Beatrice and her married sister Mary Playne, visiting them occasionally at their home in 47 Princes Gate.[31] She referred Signor Zuccardi to Mary as a singing teacher. The social whirl included numerous private parties, complete with musical entertainment. Friends of the family, such as Charles Hallé, included Lucy on their guest list. The Stopfords, relatives and neighbours in St George's Square, invited composers such as Maude Valérie White to perform her songs, which she did 'with rather too much sentimentality of gesture'.[32] Lucy also had a valuable contact in John Alexander (Alec) Fuller Maitland, a trained musician with an interest in the harpsichord whom she had known since the 1870s and from 1882 was a critic for the *Pall Mall Gazette*, later moving on to the *Guardian* and *The Times*. He had studied with Pauer, Rockstro and Dannreuther before going up to Cambridge in 1875.[33]

The 1880s marked a decade of self-discovery for the young Lucy. Not always inclined to genteel, ladylike activity, she took to tennis, crossbow shooting and bicycling at various times, with varying degrees of success. Clearly someone (possibly a rejected suitor?) noticed these masculine tendencies and sent her a letter purporting to be from a tailor in Regent Street, offering to make her a masculine sporting costume.[34] Still supported by her father, who acknowledged her growing independence with an official 'allowance' from 1882, which he increased from time to time, she was relatively free to explore London from the

---

[28]   Diaries, 8 April and 1 June 1884. Page Roberts was critical of the 'bigotry and narrow-mindedness of Christians past and present'. She was also interested in spiritualist literature and had read Carpenter on Spiritualism (see 18 March 1883). Page Roberts's book, *Liberalism in Religion and Other Sermons*, was published by Smith, Elder & Co. in 1887.

[29]   Lucy attended an evening service at the synagogue in Upper Berkeley Street on 30 May 1884 and went again on 7 June, impressed by the beautiful language and singing, though not with the sermon.

[30]   Diaries, 27 April 1884.

[31]   Diaries, 17 May 1883. For more on the Potter sisters, see Barbara Caine, *Destined to Be Wives: The Sisters of Beatrice Webb* (Oxford: Oxford University Press, 1986).

[32]   Diaries, 27 June 1883.

[33]   Jeremy Dibble, 'Maitland, John Alexander Fuller (1856–1936)', *Oxford Dictionary of National Biography* (Oxford: Oxford University Press, 2004) at: http://www.oxforddnb. com.ezproxy.library.yorku.ca/view/article/34838 (accessed January 2009).

[34]   Diaries, 11 July 1883.

family base at 52 St George's Square, where she was getting to know her new neighbours.

Back at Lyne, Bertha increasingly dominated the household, advising on allowances and finances and eventually controlling them; most of the family held her in awe, if not terror. Businesslike to the core, she was fully involved not only with her Nursing Association, but also with the piano business. Probably wishing to be even more involved, she kept a beady eye on her younger brother and despaired of the business acumen on the male side of her own family. The company was entering a new and troubled phase as competition mounted from other countries, such as Germany, and was simply not keeping up technologically. Harry was at the helm but, despite the continuity provided by longstanding employees such as the Rose brothers and Alfred J. Hipkins, the company was foundering. But Hipkins also represented an innate conservatism which now beleaguered the firm, and proved to be its downfall.

Alfred J. Hipkins

Never a partner but very much the *éminence grise*, Alfred J. Hipkins had joined the firm as an adolescent apprentice piano tuner in 1840 (the year of Henry's marriage to Juliana), working on equal temperament and the standardization of pitch, and ultimately tuning instruments for Chopin on his visits to England.[35] Academically as well as musically inclined, he swiftly rose to become one of the firm's chief advisors on pianos and was involved in exhibiting the company's instruments in the Great Exhibition of 1851. He possessed an encyclopaedic knowledge of pianos and early instruments, and published *A Description and History of the Pianoforte* in 1896. As a Fellow of the Society of Antiquaries, he was also much interested in early and non-Western instruments, and was an advisor to the musical section of the Inventions Exhibition in 1885, held in the Albert Hall. Three years later he published *Musical Instruments: Historic, Rare and Unique*.

By that time he had become an avuncular figure to young Lucy, with whom he shared an interest in folksong. In 1885 he invited her to the Exhibition, which she referred to in her diary as a 'private view of musical things in Albert Hall', giving her and her cousin Marion Birch Reynardson a guided tour. The exhibition was indeed a collector's dream, especially if the collector was musical: Lucy marvelled at a fifth-century book of Gregorian chant lent by the monks of St Gall, but the real treasure was a fifteenth-century clavicytherium, a kind of upright harpsichord with a 2½-octave keyboard and an intriguing soundboard 'made to look like hills and forests inside some sort of painted carving and at the top like a house, with perforated windows'. There were some other old instruments: a tromba marina,

---

[35]   Anne Pimlott Baker, 'Alfred James Hipkins', *Oxford Dictionary of National Biography* (Oxford: Oxford University Press, 2004) at: http://www.oxforddnb.com. ezproxy.library.yorku.ca/view/article/33890 (accessed September 2007).

a portable spinet, some square pianos by Zumpe, a Kirkman harpsichord, as well as instruments by Lucy's ancestors Burkhardt Tschudi and John Broadwood. Scotland was represented by a Celtic harp which was said to have belonged to Mary Queen of Scots and a set of early bagpipes.[36]

Hipkins did not only collect early instruments; he also played them and effectively began (with Arnold Dolmetsch) the early music movement in England, often giving private performances on the clavichord and harpsichord. Lucy was a constant visitor to his home in Warwick Gardens, which he shared with his wife, daughter Edith and deaf-mute son John, a talented wood-engraver. A man of many interests, Hipkins also had an interest in folk music and began corresponding with Lucy on various tunes, wondering if their modal quality was the same as he heard in plainchant. With some prescience he encouraged her to write down 'the old Sussex airs' as he feared that 'in these days of rapid change, many good airs will be lost that ought to be preserved'.[37] The idea of 'collection' was attractive to the Victorians, and Hipkins represented just one of its aspects. What, indeed, was the motivation for collecting? What kind of person collected? Were Hipkins's old instruments merely an objectification of the past? After all, the instruments remained silent; nobody played them. Who could sing the early chant from St Gall? Above all, the emphasis was on objects, not people. Was folksong any different? If Lucy recorded the songs, would they remain dormant in a book, or would 'the folk' (whoever they were) still sing them? Or would they endure a transfer into a class who could sing but no longer understand them?

Both Hipkins and Lucy had been influenced by William Chappell's *Popular Music of the Olden Time*, which had been published in two volumes between 1855 and 1859.[38] Essentially a collection of English vernacular song from Anglo Saxon and medieval times to the nineteenth century, Chappell's work built on the efforts of earlier scholars such as Percy, Ritson and Rimbault. Both scholar and sleuth, Chappell mined printed and manuscript collections of song, arranging them chronologically with simple harmonic accompaniments devised by George Macfarren. Realizing the importance of both music and text, Chappell performed the complex task of fitting them together, for often they had become separated. But Chappell's work was, above all, a collection of tunes in print. Might it be possible to find tunes that were still being sung, but were not in Chappell's book?

---

[36]   Diaries, 2 June 1885. Many of the instruments described here, notably the clavicytherium, are now housed as the Hipkins collection in the Museum of Instruments, Royal College of Music, London.

[37]   Letters to Lucy Broadwood, SHC 2185/LEB/1, no. 3, 25 October 1884.

[38]   Chappell's work was later revised, not altogether successfully, by the artist and musical antiquary H.E. Wooldridge, as *Old English Popular Music* in 1893. For detail on Chappell's work and Victorian song-collecting generally, see E. David Gregory, *Victorian Songhunters: The Recovery and Editing of English Vernacular Ballads and Folk Lyrics, 1820–1883* (Lanham, MD: Scarecrow Press, 2006), pp. 157–96.

Charity Concerts

While Hipkins represented the scholarly side of musical life for Lucy, she was determined to make her way as a singer, at least in an amateur capacity. As part of a family which took its social responsibilities seriously, she could not have failed to notice the 1880s preoccupation with social welfare. The publication of the Reverend Andrew Mearns's pamphlet, *The Bitter Cry of Outcast London* in 1883 had drawn attention to the plight of London's dispossessed and, although Lucy did not rush to join the Fabians when they started up in 1884, she leapt at the opportunity to participate in charity concerts, in which 'good music' (usually the chamber variety) was brought to the working classes. As the settlement movement took hold in London, spearheaded by Toynbee, Passmore Edwards, Barnett and others, she was curious to visit one of these communities and in June 1886 she went with Fanny Birch to St Augustine's Stepney where the resident clergyman, Harry Wilson, showed them round the various club buildings, the clergy house (which Lucy compared to 'a hovel') and mission house. Situated in the Jewish area of East London, St Augustine's had been consecrated as recently as 1879 and, with its crusading clergy, swiftly sought to ease life for the immigrant Jewry fleeing the pogroms of Russia and Poland. Lucy noted the many Polish Jewish women in the settlement, presumably Orthodox, as they all wore wigs.[39]

St Augustine's Stepney had become a venue for the People's Entertainment Society (PES), also founded in 1879, one of several organizations at the time that sponsored concerts featuring skilled amateur and semi-professional performers in locations outside the fashionable West End. Early in 1885, prior to her visit to St Augustine's, Lucy had been invited by the PES to participate and accordingly appeared in Stepney in May, singing light music to an enthusiastic crowd, observing that a quarter of them were 'confirmed drunkards and pickpockets'. Nevertheless she recorded that she had 'enjoyed it thoroughly', underlining the sentiment, even though her party had got lost on the way in such an unfamiliar part of London and had arrived a quarter of an hour late.[40]

Bolstered by this positive experience, six months later Lucy volunteered to sing in another concert with her cousin Herbert and the music antiquary H. Ellis Wooldridge in attendance. This time she was joined by the young violinist Susan Lushington, one of a well-known Kensington musical family, who was already involved in promoting the charity concert movement and who was roundly applauded.[41] The PES began to find other venues, penetrating into areas south of the river such as Battersea, where in early 1886 Lucy and the other performers had an even better reception than they had had in Stepney. While all this was encouraging and permitted her to air her own songs and arrangements to an

---

[39]   Diaries, 17 June 1886.
[40]   Diaries, 12 May 1885.
[41]   Diaries, 17 November 1885.

indulgent audience, she was still an amateur, the concerts of course did not pay, and in many cases she was forced to find her own expenses.

London Concert Life

London concert life at this time offered a dazzling array of solo, orchestral and chamber concerts in addition to opera. The 'Popular Concerts' begun in 1859 by Thomas Chappell and continued by Samuel (both brothers of William Chappell and also partners in the music publishing firm) were weekly chamber concerts in St James's Hall, featuring established favourites such as Charles Hallé and his wife the violinist Wilhelmina Neruda, as well as the inevitable procession of pianists such as Clothilde Kleeberg, Fanny Davies and Agnes Zimmermann. The light classics of the 'Pops' attracted a middle-class audience, many of whom became members of groups like the PES, which in turn offered similar repertoire to the working classes, who, when lured from the more decadent delights of the music halls, proved to be appreciative audiences. A combination of the 'Pops' and 'Ballad' concerts, the latter featuring not folk ballads but sentimental parlour songs, the charity concerts spelt respectability for both audience and performer.

The death of Wagner in 1883 precipitated a frenzy of Wagnerism in London, though he already had many devotees owing to the championing of his music by the conductor Hans Richter. German music of both the symphonic and operatic variety was the staple of the season, and Lucy herself had gone three times to see Beethoven's *Fidelio* conducted by Randegger at Covent Garden. For light relief, audiences turned to the Savoy operas of Gilbert and Sullivan, which Lucy adored, finding much amusement in *Iolanthe* in 1883, and taking in *The Mikado* as well as the Japanese Village in Knightsbridge in May 1885.

The season was alive with violinists and pianists from both the Brahms and Lisztian camps. The violinist Joachim dominated the stage with his performances of his friend and mentor Brahms, and the glamorous Liszt pupil Sophie Menter enthralled critic George Bernard Shaw and others as she pounded her way through the 1883 season, much to Lucy's disgust. Various Clara Schumann pupils, including the exuberant Fanny Davies, made their debuts, fresh from their studies with 'die Frau' (as Hipkins called her) in Frankfurt. The reserved but diligent Agnes Zimmermann, who had remained in England to study, was unusual in combining composition with performance and was also prolific in this decade. Max Pauer, son of Ernst Pauer, a friend of the Broadwood family, who had pioneered historical recitals in London decades earlier, made his debut, while established pianists such as Anton Rubinstein made regular visits to the capital.[42]

---

[42]   For more on the London concert scene at this time see D. de Val, '"Legitimate, Phenomenal and Eccentric": Pianists and Pianism in late 19th-century London', in *Music in Nineteenth-century Britain*, eds, J. Dibble and B. Zon (Aldershot: Ashgate, 2002), pp. 182–95.

But the pianist who most fascinated audiences throughout the decade was the Odessa-born Vladimir de Pachmann. Deliciously foreign and exotic, with high shoulders and flowing raven-black hair, the clean-shaven Pachmann fascinated audiences with odd facial distortions accompanying his idiosyncratic performances of Chopin, with whom he had a special affinity. At a time when there were still a number of people (including Hipkins) who remembered the composer, their critical acclaim of his style gained him much ground. A Pachmann performance was not just a musical experience, it was a theatrical one, as he blew kisses to the audiences and indulged in various quaint mannerisms. Lucy heard him play in 1883, having been provided with insider information from her father that the pianist's fingers were 'so short he needed to have the black notes lowered to suit him'.[43] He was not a conventional virtuoso, unlike the other lions of the London concert stage. Lucy went to several of his concerts throughout the 1880s but soon tired of the mannerisms, though she was 'struck by his marvellous execution and liquid touch', but still thought him wanting sometimes a little in breadth'.[44] Chopin was his speciality, though he played other composers as well. Tending to superstition, Lucy became depressed on hearing him play Chopin's Sonata No. 2 (which includes the Funeral March), brooding that it always brought misfortune. Sure enough, the sad news of the death of her niece and god-daughter, Mary Dorothea Shearme, came the next day. The little girl had never been well and died after a week of illness.[45] Such premonitions would plague Lucy throughout her life, so much so that she, like many of her time, took to various aspects of spiritualism and fortune-telling, occasionally consulting psychics. Though never stated, it is possible that she thought of them as a kind of inherited Scottish-style 'second sight', for it often manifested itself in that way. On another level it was a source of entertainment: mind-reading and 'visualizing' became popular parlour-games in future years, but they were played with serious intent beneath the light-hearted exterior.

A European Grand Tour

Despite this busy and sociable life, Lucy tended to depression and melancholy at various times. This condition remained with her throughout her life, and she was often incapacitated by illness which kept her in bed for days. She often felt tired and ill and prone to what would now be called seasonal affective disorder. By the time she reached her late twenties, she was also watching all her old friends marry and move away. She had been feeling weary and hoarse throughout the autumn of 1886 and was dreading the winter. In January 1887 she was back in Lyne, where family members came and went and friends came to shoot. Her nieces

---

[43]   Diaries, 10 May 1883.
[44]   Diaries, 12 May 1883.
[45]   Diaries, 3 March 1890.

Katie and Barbie Craster were at school far away in north London, so there was only the relentlessly busy Bertha around for company. A visit to London to see an art exhibition probably exacerbated a bad throat which she had endured since the previous September, and a prolonged period of bitter cold did not help matters. Her doctor prescribed the unpleasant-sounding remedy of strychnine tonic in cod-liver oil, and her cousin Marion sent over some 'Muriat of Ammonia' lozenges, which do not sound much better. She settled into a biography of Charlotte Bronte with some relief.[46]

Perhaps this was not tonic enough, though, for the next diary begins abruptly with the decision to join her mother, sister Amy and one of the servants on a grand tour of Europe. Would this be the ideal escape? They took the usual route from Victoria to Dover and then crossed to Calais the next morning, making their way to Marseilles and then on to their destination, Hyères.[47] The contrast with dreary England must have been striking and, hopefully, palliative. At Hyères they found their Aunt Susan Broadwood awaiting them at the Hotel Continental, where various English people were staying. Lucy went out walking with Amy, noting with approval the colourful green dresses of the local women, with their pretty bodices and petticoats. The town was perfect for visiting churches and sketching. On the following Sunday, at church, she was overjoyed to come across her old friend Eva James (now Ashton), who was staying at another hotel with her husband. Eva, also happy to reconnect with her old friend, presented her with a lovely blue and white 'Arab' wrap and a brooch from Tunis. They were all supremely happy.[48]

Their happiness was short-lived. Two days later, on the morning of 23 February, the first tremors of a massive earthquake began, affecting most of the Riviera coast and northern Italy. Mentone suffered the most damage, with Nice and Monaco also badly hit. It soon became clear that this was a natural disaster of huge proportions, and the area was soon full of people fleeing the wrecked villages. Hotels swiftly emptied, leaving frightened and haggard-looking staff. Survivors slept outdoors: even the wealthy Rothschilds confined themselves to a carriage in the street. The aftershocks continued for the next few days. People continued to camp out, sleeping in improvised tents and railway carriages.[49] Exhausted and fearful for their safety and health, the Broadwoods doggedly kept to their itinerary and proceeded to the devastated Genoa and then away from the disaster area down to Pisa and Florence, where, with some relief, Lucy and Amy took refuge in the major art galleries.[50] Not surprisingly, their mother was 'tired and bilious'.[51] On 8 March, after an intensive tour of the major art galleries and churches, the Broadwoods left for Rome early in the morning, meeting their

---

[46]   Diaries, see entries for January 1887.
[47]   Diaries, 10–12 February 1887.
[48]   Diaries, 21 February 1887.
[49]   Diaries, 23–26 February 1887.
[50]   Diaries, 24–25 February 1887.
[51]   Diaries, 1 March 1887.

Uncle Thomas Broadwood at the Hotel de Paris. Again, they took in various sights, declaring themselves 'not disappointed' with St Peter's Basilica.[52]

The ordeal was not over, however. As they travelled down to Naples and Amalfi, Lucy was beginning to feel ill, and not even a cream tea at an English pension in Ravello could restore her. The party spent Easter in Naples, then returned north to Rome and Siena, marvelling at the distinctive black and white stonework of its cathedral. Then it was on to Bologna and Venice, where Lucy still felt 'bad and feverish'. On 2 May an English doctor, Dr Menzies, was called in, and diagnosed malaria. The group remained in Venice while Lucy dosed herself with quinine, becoming weaker and thinner by the day. A few days later she was able to tolerate some sweetbreads and spinach, and then began a grim-sounding course of arsenic and iron. Out in a gondola, she felt 'tottery, weak and absurdly thin'.[53] By the end of the month she was feeling well enough to celebrate Juliana's seventy-third birthday *en famille* on the 31st, but it was clear that she had been very ill and that everyone should go back home. On 1 June they began to pack for the long journey home through Switzerland, arriving back at Lyne on 7 June. A week later Lucy once again became an aunt with the birth of Harry's and Ada's daughter, Marion.[54]

Return to Lyne

The after-effects of the malaria were severe and continued to plague Lucy for the rest of her life. The immediate effects were more catastrophic: the cocktail of arsenic and iron which she had taken while away had caused her to lose her hair, and by her twenty-ninth birthday on 9 August she was nearly bald. Special shampoos were supplied and wigs made up while she waited for her hair to grow back. It is a measure of her strength that she seemed little deterred by all this, and a week later was back at the Primrose League, where she took out a membership. In September she and Bertha were invited to tea at nearby Abinger Hall, seat of Sir Thomas Farrer (1819–99) and his second wife Katherine Euphemia Wedgwood, whom he had married in 1873. Katherine was a distant relation, and the company at tea included her distinguished sister, the writer Julia Wedgwood, and a Miss Gaskell, daughter of the writer Elizabeth Gaskell. Lady Katherine enjoyed music so this meeting was only a beginning, and the company was joined on another occasion by another relation, Ralph Vaughan Williams.[55]

---

[52]   Diaries, 3–11 March 1887.
[53]   Diaries, 19 May 1887.
[54]   Diaries, *passim.*, entries up to 16 June 1887.
[55]   Diaries, 20 September 1887.

Mary Wakefield

Having recuperated somewhat, Lucy felt strong enough to take the train up to Kendal to visit her friend Mary Wakefield.[56] Like Lucy, Wakefield was a trained singer, but she also conducted and had a superb gift for organization, which led to the establishment of the competitive music festival, designed as a showcase for local choirs and singers. Also like Lucy, she had a real interest in local folk music and wanted to provide an opportunity for everyone to perform and hear it. The festival had already grown from its modest beginning two years earlier, and had begun to attract press attention, mainly because of its competitive feature and its departure from the usual Victorian festival such as the Three Choirs choral display.

Lucy did not stay long, but travelled on to see her brother-in-law Edmund at the family seat, Craster Tower, in Beadnell, Northumberland. After Katherine's death in 1874, Edmund Craster had met and married Barbara Stewart Lee, the daughter of a Welsh clergyman, in 1878. The birth of Herbert a year later tragically claimed his mother's life. Edmund remained at the family seat to raise Herbert, and Lucy found them well on her visit. She travelled back home by way of her friend Lily Beaumont at Swannington House in Leicestershire, and then back home via London and Haslemere, stopping off to see various family members. Perhaps the northern air had done Lucy good, for on visiting the Tennysons she found herself in good voice, stronger than before. There was also the good news of the birth of James's and Eve's second daughter Audrey Julia at their home in Kingsfold.[57] It was a quiet end to a busy year, the effects of which she would feel for the rest of her life.

A Trip to Holland

The new year (1888) opened with still more health problems, as Lucy nursed a sore foot and sat out the usual new year dances. She made her usual trips up to London, however, taking in concerts and visiting friends. Though still feeling 'bilious', by April she felt well enough to join her friends Isobel Manisty and Gertrude Sichel (among others) to sing some madrigals by Wilbye and Farnaby, the latter recently discovered by Barclay Squire. They performed them a few days later to an audience of over 140. She also indulged her concert and theatre life, with a visit to hear Grieg play his piano concerto at the National Gallery and an enjoyable evening at the play *David Garrick*.[58] Her singing lessons with Shakespeare continued regularly up until June when, despite the disastrous experience of the previous year, she began preparing for another trip with Amy to visit their Dutch friends, the Plantengas, in July.

---

[56] Diaries, 22 September, 1887.

[57] Diaries, 3 November 1887.

[58] Diaries, entries for April and May 1888.

WINDOW & GROVE,   63ᴬ BAKER ST LONDON,

Illustration 2.2   Portrait of Lucy Broadwood as a young woman, 1880s
Source: Copyright of Surrey History Centre.

Eventually arriving in Scheveningen, they took in an excellent orchestral concert in a café setting and observed some English and American bicyclists who must have been touring. The Scheveningen women looked quaintly Dutch in their elaborate lace headgear and wide, full petticoats, silk aprons, shawls and low shoes. Travelling to Leyden, they noted the old brick gabled houses with their ancient doorways and luxuriant flowerbeds. The high point was a visit to the Mauritshuis Museum to see Rembrandt's painting, *The Anatomy Lecture of Dr Nicolaes Tulp*, the detail of which Lucy found 'wonderful, though ghastly'. Lucy was evidently charmed by the young Pieter Plantenga, ('*very* nice') with whom she danced a Dutch polonaise in Delft, and she began learning Dutch. She left Holland with much regret.[59]

Even the delights of this trip could not chase away her old illness and she marked her thirtieth birthday with fever and a chill. Relieved at the protracted absence of Bertha, who had gone abroad, and still infatuated with Pieter Plantenga, she scoured the family library for books in Dutch (alas, most were in German) and resolved to learn the language. There was some correspondence from Mary Wakefield, who was interested in her Sussex songs. There was no recovery, however, and by November she was subjected once again to an odious cocktail of arsenic and soda, despite the disastrous results of the previous summer. The doctor also advised a homeopathic remedy of aloes, nux vomica and belladonna pills. Told she was suffering from 'bloodlessness' and general disorder, she was advised to avoid cold and damp, keep her chest warm, and to eat as much fat and cream as possible. Clearly her condition was serious, borne out by the doctor's verdict that the previous summer's illness was none other than a dangerous mixture of typhoid and malaria.[60]

Cousins

But there was much to get on with. Deprived of the affections of Pieter Plantenga, Lucy settled for a genial relationship with her cousin Herbert Birch Reynardson, in whom she found a musical soulmate, if not a romantic partner. The Birch Reynardson cousins – William, Marion, Aubrey and Herbert – were constant visitors, and also entertained the Broadwoods at their home, Adwell, in Oxfordshire. In Victorian fashion, there were flirtatious exchanges of funny poems and cards between the cousins, and Lucy became quite close to all three of them. Herbert, who was still studying with Edward Dannreuther, shared her musical interests and proved to be an excellent duet partner, and sometimes composed his own.[61] He also had a penchant for songs, mostly in *lieder* style, which inspired Lucy to attempt some composition herself, though she was more

---

[59]   Diaries, 24 July 1888.
[60]   Diaries, 7 December 1888.
[61]   Diaries, 19 December 1884.

attracted to English songs in a traditional style. Lucy perhaps felt more than just cousinly affection for Herbert, as she regaled him with presents, poetry and even a mock biography. He in turn wrote songs and piano duets for her, which they could play together. Herbert had the benefit of elegant rooms in London, convenient to visit and close to the British Museum, where he worked as a librarian. He had passed the exams in 1883 and was appointed Assistant to George Bullen, Keeper of Printed Books. His musical ambitions there were thwarted, though, for although he was put forward in 1885 as a candidate for Keeper of Printed Music, the position went instead to his contemporary William Barclay Squire. The rest, as they say, is history.[62]

John Broadwood and *Sussex Songs*

Lucy had meanwhile introduced Herbert to her Uncle John's collection of folksongs, which were not widely known. As noted above, the Reverend Broadwood had noticed that the songs he had heard from 'the country people' of his parish, were not in print and therefore decided to rescue them 'from oblivion'and invited his organist, Dusart, to provide accompaniments. Herbert saw the opportunity of replacing Dusart's hymn-like accompaniments with something more imaginative and fluid, and Lucy began to look for additional material, soliciting songs from local people and her father. As her father had also had an interest in local song, there were family records of the tunes and texts, and the more obscure texts could also be checked against older printed sources, with which Lucy was becoming familiar.

The preparation of *Sussex Songs*, a joint venture between Lucy and her cousin, occupied them throughout the decade. For Lucy it was both a tribute to her late uncle and an exploration into territory which she increasingly felt was her own. She was encouraged in this by F.E. Sawyer, who got in touch with her in November 1884 about his own collection of songs from Sussex. The two scholars established a correspondence, with Lucy copying tunes for him and Sawyer sharing his notes on Sussex dialect.[63] He later published a pamphlet on the subject. The collection was not simply a reworking of Uncle John's tunes. To the original 16 songs Lucy added nine new ones, namely the 'Mummers' Carol', which was an old favourite from Lyne and would reappear in her later work, as well as nos 14 to 21 ('The Nobleman and the Thresherman', the harvest supper songs, 'The Woodcutter' and 'Bango', the hunting songs 'Bold Reynard the Fox' and 'Last Valentine's Day', and 'The Sweet Rosy Morning', and finally the drinking songs 'Bowl! Bowl!', 'I've been to France and I've been to Dover') and no. 25, 'He swore he'd drink old England Dry', referring to Napoleon, and

[62]   See Barclay Squire, 'A History of the Music Room of the British Museum, 1753–1953', *Proceedings of the Royal Musical Association*, 79 (1952): 65–79.
[63]   Diaries, 25 November and 5 December 1885.

for which only the words to the refrain were provided. Notes on concordances and variants were added to most of the songs. Although the Preface claims that 'the songs, words and music, were faithfully written down exactly as they were sung by country people in the Weald of Sussex', a note on the 'Mummers' Carol' states that the words were 'put into shape from two very illiterate versions written down from memory by two of the actors', which probably applies to a number of the other songs.

The songs appear as a vocal line with unobtrusive accompaniment, doubling the vocal line in the right hand. Herbert's accompaniments are fluid and translucent, with an uncomplicated use of counterpoint. There were a few musical mistakes in the edition, which did not escape the notice of at least one German critic, much to Herbert's embarrassment.[64] Nobody asked about the original singers of the songs, though, or whether the texts had been 'corrected'. Lucy set the pattern for her later work by tracking down the origins of the tunes, checking the texts with printed sources and filling in any gaps or questionable lines with alternatives. The Preface does not reveal much, but one imagines that, if pressed about their motives for publication and their prospective audience, Herbert and Lucy would probably have protested that they had done their public a service in rescuing the old songs 'from oblivion' in her uncle's words, and making them presentable for comfortable performance in the drawing room, for both were familiar with the delights of a private musical evening – the hallmark of polite Victorian society. For the time being, this would be the pattern for Lucy's work as a collector, in terms of both research and arrangement, and it would serve her well.

Sussex Songs was bought from Herbert by Lucas, Weber & Co. in November 1889 for £25 and was published shortly thereafter with a cover price of two shillings and sixpence.[65] It bore Herbert's name on the cover but was a proving ground for Lucy, whose contribution was acknowledged only in the Preface. Perhaps no longer as self-effacing as she once had been, she had learned through the process of publication that she could collect and arrange folksongs, and play Herbert at his own game of composition: she would not make the mistakes that Herbert's German critic, Johannes Schreyer, had spotted. She could also publish. She was now ready to take to the field in every sense.

---

[64] See SHC, Letters to LEB 2185/LEB/1 no.16, 3 June 1891. The criticism had come from a Johannes Schreyer, who wrote to Lucy on 14 June 1891 from Dresden; see no.17.

[65] Diaries, 15 November 1889.

Illustration 2.3   Herbert Birch Reynardson, c. 1889
Source: Copyright of Surrey History Centre.

Chapter 3

The Collector

The publication of *Sussex Songs* on 4 April 1890 brought scant comfort to Lucy, who was not only nursing her sick father, but also dealing with her own ill-health. As the year opened, London was in the grip of a classic 'pea-souper', an intense dark yellow fog; to make things worse, she was losing her hair, and she had been advised not to winter abroad.[1] Her health continued to suffer: diagnosed with a weak heart, she underwent an exotic array of treatments which included Turkish and electric baths. The latter, while sounding somewhat dangerous today, was a fairly common treatment at this time and involved the therapeutic application of static electricity in a water medium, with protection for the patient provided by the use of an insulated platform.[2] Lucy did not complain about these treatments and indeed seemed to enjoy them: if anything, her descriptions of her medical treatments give some insight into the practice of the time, which included some homeopathy, as she was also wearing uncomfortable plasters of belladonna over her heart.[3] She was also subject to recurring bouts of depression, which were to plague her for the rest of her life. She continued to seek out Reverend Page Roberts at St Peter's Church in Vere Street and made occasional visits to synagogues, but still the depression did not relent.[4] Her interest in Roman Catholicism also persisted, and in August she found herself much moved by the requiem for Cardinal Newman in Brompton Oratory, noting not just the beautiful sixteenth-century vocal music, but also Cardinal Manning's gorgeous cope.[5]

The severity of the winter had been offset in part by the long stay of her cousin Fanny Birch (possibly to help her through her illness). The publication of *Sussex Songs* in April was cheering, as was the arrival of a new piano in May. But Lucy must have felt her single status keenly as her dear friend Eva Ashton gave birth to a baby girl in May at about the same time as her childhood friend and neighbour Harry Lee Steere married Anna Gordon Clark: Lucy excused herself from attending the wedding, pleading illness due to a cold.[6] Harry and Ada had their third child, Leopold (named after Ada's father), at the end of the month. If marriage and motherhood were not to be her destiny she could find much else to

---

[1]   SHC, Diaries, 1 and 2 January, 1890.

[2]   See Robley Dunglison, 'Bath, Electric', in Robley Dunglison and Richard James Dunglison, *A Dictionary of Medical Science* (London: J. & A. Churchill, 1876), p. 117.

[3]   Diaries, 25 January 1890.

[4]   Diaries, 1 March 1890.

[5]   Diaries, 20 August 1890.

[6]   Diaries, 27 May 1890.

do in a wider sphere. In fact, the recent deaths in the family – Eve Broadwood in childbirth, her sister's infant daughter, not to mention the premature death of her oldest sister Katherine some years earlier – might well have persuaded her that marriage carried too much risk; and in any case there were enough siblings to carry on the Broadwood line. She had been reading Sarah Grand's classic novel, *Ideala*, which took an anti-marriage stance and was one of the first novels to deal with the nascent 'New Woman' movement.[7] At the heart of the novel, the heroine Ideala – who is unhappily married to a worthless man – declares:

> The marriage oath is farcical. A woman is made to swear love to a man who will probably prove unlovable, to honour a man who is as likely as not to be undeserving of honour, and to obey a man who may be incapable of judging what is best either for himself or her. I have no respect for the ages that uphold such nonsense.[8]

It is pure coincidence that as Lucy was reading *Ideala*, she noticed the publication of *The Golden Bough* by the Scottish anthropologist Sir James Frazer. Subtitled *A Study in Magic and Religion*, the book discussed religion and myth as cultural phenomena, an approach which Lucy had already appreciated in the sermons of the iconoclastic Page Roberts. The effect of the book, which was published initially in two volumes but eventually numbered 12, was profound and controversial, and laid the foundations for modern cultural anthropology. It took Lucy beyond the confines of folk music into folklore and appealed to her breadth of knowledge and understanding. It was this book and its author which set her on a course quite distinct from the domestic one chosen by her sisters and friends, and also one which would distinguish her from some of her contemporaries who would show less breadth and awareness in their approach to folksong collecting.

Sussex Songs had attracted some attention, especially from other collectors; Lucy met Heywood Sumner, author of *The Besom Maker*, in February, when he came to call.[9] In August 1891, as she bemoaned her thirty-third birthday ('alas'), she was approached by John Alexander Fuller Maitland (usually known simply as 'Alec') and the publisher Andrew Tuer to embark on another collection. Under the imprint of 'Ye Leadenhall Press' operating from 50 Leadenhall Street, London, Tuer (1838–1900) and his partner Abraham Field were known for their high-quality books with their 'ornamental and ancient' printing and typography. A true bibliophile, Tuer was fascinated by typography and book design and was an authority on the engraver Bartolozzi. He was also an inventor and his patented 'stickphast' glue made it possible to produce elaborate editions with hand-mounted

---

[7]   Diaries, 26 May 1889: '*very* clever study of a woman character'.

[8]   Sarah Grand, *Ideala: A Study from Life* (Charleston, SC: Bibliobazaar, 2006), pp. 103–4.

[9]   Diaries, 15 February 1891.

illustrations.[10] Music was not his speciality, though he published Fuller Maitland's and Rockstro's *English Carols of the Fifteenth Century*, perhaps because of their antiquarian value. His wife Thomasine Louisa (née Louttit) was an accomplished contralto whom Lucy knew and admired.

English County Songs

It was perhaps the influence of Mrs Tuer that prompted her husband to propose a volume of folksong (which his wife could then sing); Lucy would be co-editor of a set of folksongs representative of all the counties an England, to be arranged for piano and voice by herself and Fuller Maitland. Collection of the songs was to be divided between the two editors, who were also responsible for composing piano accompaniments for the songs. Lucy had already begun writing her own arrangements of songs, beginning with 'Jess Macpharlane – An Old Scotch Air' in 1890 and was working on others.[11] This experience served her well in this regard, and she was careful to keep the accompaniments simple, preserving the character and artlessness of each song, while also making them a vehicle for singers to make an impact on their audiences. Negotiations were carried out by Fuller Maitland, though with an unsatisfactory result as ultimately both he and Lucy had to settle for reduced royalties.[12]

Keen to get started, Lucy provided Tuer with a copy of 'The Croodlin' Doo', the first folksong she had ever heard, and then set off for Blair Atholl for her Scottish holiday, taking in the Highland Games while she was there. At the same time she worked on harmonizing 'Twankydillo', 'Bristol City' and 'The Spider'.[13] Back home, she began to build a network of correspondents who could collect and send her songs, ranging from Mr Willett the baker in nearby Cuckfield, to her sister-in-law Ada in Hertfordshire. Hipkins was still a faithful correspondent, and he contributed the beautiful 'Lazarus' tune, recalled from 1861 and some material from his grandmother Helen Grant (1770–1838). Lucy also made important connections further afield, notably with the Reverend Sabine Baring-Gould, of whom more later, and with the reclusive antiquarian Frank Kidson, who lived in

---

[10]   See Lucy Peltz, 'Tuer, Andrew White (1838–1900)', *Oxford Dictionary of National Biography* (Oxford: Oxford University Press, 2004) at: http://www.oxforddnb. com.ezproxy.library.yorku.ca/view/article/27799 (accessed October 2007).

[11]   'Jess' was published by Boosey & Co., 1890; other songs included 'In Loyalty' (London: S. Lucas, Weber & Co., 1892); 'Nae Mair We'll Meet' (London: Weekes & Co., 1892); and 'Tammy' (London: Weekes & Co., 1892).

[12]   Letters from Fuller Maitland to Lucy explaining the progress of the negotiation, which was ultimately unsatisfactory and yielded the authors less than they originally anticipated, can be found in SHC, 2185/LEB/3, Letters 5–10.

[13]   Diaries, entries 16–24 September 1891. 'The Croodlin' Doo' did not appear in the published collection.

Leeds. Kidson had published *Traditional Tunes* in 1891, and Hipkins had sent Lucy a copy; early in 1893 Kidson himself sent her an annotated and interleaved copy.[14] Unlike most song collections, Kidson's presented the tunes without accompaniment and respectfully acknowledged the singers who had provided them. A true antiquarian, he took an interest in the origins of the words and gave concordances where possible, drawing on his own vast library. In all cases the tunes were original and not previously printed. Though Lucy continued to provide accompaniments to her songs, she was profoundly influenced by the scholarly nature of *Traditional Tunes* and by Kidson himself.[15]

Lucy also received material from her old friend Mary Wakefield in Cumberland, who supplied the song 'Sally Gray' for the collection.[16] She also included songs collected by Marianne Harriet Mason, whose *Nursery Rhymes and Country Songs* was published in 1877. This collection includes both children's rhymes and ballads handed down through Mason's mother's Northumbrian family, the Mitfords. (Marianne's nickname, Mitty, was a reference to her mother's maiden name.) As such, it represented one of the earliest collections of folksongs handed down orally, rather than from printed sources.[17] Some of these songs reappeared in *English County Songs*, perhaps to fill in the county gaps, which tended to constrain the collection overall and with hindsight was an unnecessarily arbitrary way of organizing the songs. Like Lucy, Mason had been educated at home and was unmarried, and somewhat resembled Bertha in that she took an interest in community matters and worked as a poor law inspector, finally gaining paid employment in this profession in 1885, at the age of 40.[18] She and Lucy later became friends, and presumably the latter sought permission to replicate the songs in her own publication.

Many of the tunes of *English County Songs* were collected by others. To begin with, Lucy restricted her own collecting to local haunts, finding in Samuel Willett a useful collector and transcriber of tunes. It is not clear how Lucy knew Willett, unless it was through a local connection, but she sent him a copy of *Sussex Songs*, which he duly acknowledged in a letter of 1 October 1890. Ever the businessman (he was a baker by trade), he declared his terms, offering to give 'a general recital of songs and music' at Lyne. He could provide copies of songs (with words and music) at a cost of half a crown. Lucy, however, was asking for 40 or 50 songs,

[14]   Diaries, 22 February 1893.
[15]   For more on Kidson, see John Francmanis, 'The Roving Artist: Frank Kidson, Pioneer Song Collector', *Folk Music Journal*, 8/1: (2001): 41–66.
[16]   Diaries, 16 March 1892.
[17]   For more on Mason and this collection, see E. David Gregory, *Victorian Songhunters: The Recovery and Editing of English Vernacular Ballads and Folk Lyrics, 1820–1883* (Lanham, MD: Scarecrow Press, 2006), pp. 362–7.
[18]   Katherine Field, 'Mason, (Marianne) Harriet (1845–1932)', *Oxford Dictionary of National Biography* (Oxford: Oxford University Press, 2004) at: http://www.oxforddnb.com.ezproxy.library.yorku.ca/view/article/48847 (accessed October 2007).

for which a fee could be agreed. To this he appended a list of songs, some labelled by Lucy as 'pathetic songs' – probably meaning 'useless' rather than full of feeling, given her ruthless approach to anything that smacked of the music hall or other 'non-traditional' fare.[19] In the end, Lucy used three of Willett's tunes as representative of Sussex in *English County Songs*. One, 'Twankydillo', became a perennial favourite and was reprinted many times as a single song; Lucy also performed it herself a number of times.

It seems that the hapless Willett was not invited to Lyne to give 'a recital of songs', though he did provide a fair quantity, some with tunes only. Writing in red ink, 'as with his life's blood', as Lucy was to note later, Willett was sufficiently musically literate to note down the tunes he heard.[20] Somewhat Uriah Heep-like in character, he combined a forelock-tugging sycophancy with a canny financial sense; Lucy always paid for his songs, whereas it is not clear that she offered payment to other singers. It seems that Lucy was fairly specific in her requirements, and that Willett was not always sure that he understood 'the process of winnowing' suggested in her letters.[21] In another letter there is a hint of exasperation about how much more he could offer, unless he penetrated into the male domains of pubs and smoking concerts, in which case he would have to tip the singers for their tunes and words. There is a sense of frustration in Willett's letters as he attempted to cross both the intellectual and class divides.[22] In the end, Lucy paid Willett a shilling a song for 27 songs. It seems that they did not keep up a correspondence, but some of his songs appeared in the Kent and Sussex sections of *English County Songs*.[23]

Another local correspondent who was musically literate was a Mr R. Bennell. Bennell, who lived in Richmond, Surrey, but had grown up in Oxfordshire, played the cornet for a living 'in all lines of the business theatrical or otherwise'. Like Willett, he requested remuneration for his efforts, though mainly for postage and minor expenses. He provided the tune and what he could remember of the words to 'The Good Old Leathern Bottle'; Lucy took the remainder from Heywood Sumner's *The Besom Maker* when she included the song in *English County Songs*. He also commented on the unsuitability of the words to many of the songs, commenting that 'our ancestors in their simplicity were rather coarse in their sentimental ditties'. Lucy was clearly pleased with his offerings, as he later submitted other Oxfordshire songs: 'Turmut-hoeing', 'The Thresher and the

---

[19]   VWML, LEB file 2, no. 71.

[20]   Lucy Broadwood, 'On the Collecting of English Folk Song', *Proceedings of the Royal Musical Association*, 31 (1904–05): 98.

[21]   VWML LEB file 2, no. 85, n.d.

[22]   VWML LEB file 2, no. 89, 15 October 1891.

[23]   Diaries, 2 July 1891. For more on Willett and Broadwood, see Vic Gammon, 'Folk Song Collecting in Sussex and Surrey, 1843–1914', *History Workshop Journal*, 10 (1980): 61–89 *passim*. Songs collected from Willett were 'John Appleby' (Kent), 'The Farmer's Boy' (Sussex), and the popular 'Twankydillo' (Sussex).

Squire' and "Twas Early One Morning'. He agreed to 'steer clear of everything published', as Lucy must have instructed, and relied on his imperfect memory for the tunes. Lucy must have been pleased to receive 'The Thresher and the Squire' with its similarity to the 'Lazarus' tune provided by Hipkins, and which was later used in *The English Hymnal* with a different text. Here was a tune which 'the peculiar quaintness and minor tendency' of rural district songs, which he and others clearly favoured; by 'minor' he might well have meant 'modal'.[24]

The purpose of *English County Songs* was to present new (meaning unpublished) songs by provenance, ordering by county. The latter aspect posed some difficulties, in that many songs transcended borders and some counties were richer than others in terms of song. Some counties were completely unrepresented, notably Monmouthshire, Huntingdonshire and Bedfordshire. Both editors felt the lure of the field, though Lucy must have chafed at the constraints imposed upon her as a single woman; she would later rue the advantages of the male collector, who 'could make merry with songsters in the alehouse over pipes and parsnip wine, or hob-nob with the black sheep of the neighbourhood'.[25] Sabine Baring-Gould noted in a letter to Lucy in 1892:

> I can understand the men being shy of singing to a lady, they think they are being laughed at, or else are simply shy as they would not be before a man, moreover they want grog to unlock their hearts, and refresh their memories, & a lady can hardly stand grog for them.[26]

Though she started by relying on local informants for songs, Lucy eventually overcame the problems of the 'lady collector' and went into the field herself. Usually invited by a friend or relative who knew some local singers, she would travel to the area and arrange to meet the singer at an agreed location: this could be either at the host's or singer's house or garden. For example, her sister-in-law Ada Heath introduced her to a local carter, a Mr Grantham, who had grown up in Sussex and was living at Holmwood. Grantham lost his initial shyness when Lucy provided an improvised piano accompaniment to one of his songs. Wearing an old-fashioned smock, and with piercing blue eyes and a shock of white hair, he sang many songs and claimed to know many more which, because they were 'outway rude', he could not sing to a lady.[27] Some years later, Lucy mentioned her regret at having to forgo 'the rescue of the most promising old ballads' as a consequence, though they would have undoubtedly been bowdlerized on publication; both Baring-Gould and Sharp altered the texts of songs without compunction.

---

[24]   SHC, Letters 2185/LEB/1, no. 438 dated 10 November 1891, 439 dated 23 November and 440 dated 3 December.

[25]   Broadwood, 'On the Collecting of English Folk Song', p. 95.

[26]   SHC, Letters, 2185/LEB/1, no.21, 30 May 1892.

[27]   Broadwood, 'On the Collecting of English Folk Song', p. 101.

Illustration 3.1   Lucy Broadwood with J.A. Fuller Maitland at Abinger Hall,
                    for the Leith Hill Music Festival, 1914

Source: Copyright of Surrey History Centre.

Grantham's 'Venus and Adonis' (which Lucy took to be a version of an old Vauxhall song), 'The Sweet Nightingale', 'The Painful (or Faithful) Plough' and 'Sheepcrook and Black Dog' were included in *English County Songs*. Another solution to the 'single woman problem' was simply to invite singers to Lyne, where they sang to her in the billiard room. Lucy offered encouragement by singing some songs herself, and one would assume that some refreshment was offered in addition, to induce the visitors to participate.[28]

There were many women informants, however, who might have been encouraged to sing precisely because Lucy was a woman and a singer too. Herbert Birch Reynardson's interest had not dimmed since the publication of *Sussex Songs*, and he introduced her to Clara Wilson, the wife of a local gardener in King's Langley, Hertfordshire, who, after a few nervous false starts, sang (appropriately enough) 'The Seeds of Love'. This was followed by other songs such as 'Lord Bateman'; in the end, four of them were included in *English County Songs*. On a trip to Oxford, visiting Herbert at his family seat, Adwell, she collected songs from another gardener's wife, Patience Vaisey; her husband did not approve of her singing the old songs, as he preferred *Hymns Ancient and Modern*, so the session with Lucy must have been one of complicit pleasure for both. Mrs Vaisey provided 19 songs in one day, including the haunting Dorian tune of 'My bonny, bonny boy'.[29] By this time things were moving ahead quickly – it seems that proofs of other songs in the book were already arriving – so the new material had to be arranged quickly.[30]

The Beginning and End of an Era

English County Songs was published on 1 July 1893. A week later, Henry Fowler Broadwood was dead. He died at Lyne, with the family gathered round his deathbed, where he lay comatose. Lucy spoke to him for the last time, telling him that her book had been published. If he indeed understood her, this would have brought him great joy. The funeral was held at Rusper church on 11 July. The firm was appropriately well represented by the 40 factory men who travelled down to attend, along with stalwarts such as Hipkins, Frederick and George Rose; they were joined by various relations and longstanding neighbours such as the Lee Steeres and Calverts. The aftermath of the funeral took about a month, as the family packed up their belongings and prepared for their removal from Lyne. Lucy left the old house with her mother, Bertha and the servant Atkins a day after

---

[28]   Diaries, 30 October 1892.

[29]   See Broadwood, 'On the Collecting of English Folk Song', p. 125; and Diaries, 16–18 September 1892.

[30]   For more on Lucy's collecting at this time, see E. David Gregory, 'Before the Folk-Song Society: Lucy Broadwood and English Folk Song, 1884–97', *Folk Music Journal*, 9/3 (2008): 372–414.

her thirty-fifth birthday, on 10 August.[31] They journeyed down to Ryde, where they stayed with the Shearmes.

A Trip to Devon

Feeling somewhat recovered by September, Lucy determined to visit Baring-Gould in Devon. In fact, the south-western counties of Devon and Cornwall had not been well represented in *English County Songs* as many of the songs had already been published by Baring-Gould in his *Songs and Ballads of the West*. Lucy had sent him a copy of *Sussex Songs* upon their publication; as a mark either of the clergyman's busy schedule or his opinion of the book, its receipt was acknowledged not by the man himself, but by two of his flock of 15 children.[32] Baring-Gould, the epitome of the nineteenth-century 'squarson', had taken over the living at Lew Trenchard in 1881 on the death of his uncle. A personable intellectual, his sermons drew people from far and wide, and his prolific output of books helped to pay for local improvements. Interested in folklore, he encouraged local customs and was well informed about local traditions. He began collecting folksongs in 1888. As he was not a musician, he relied on help from the flamboyant Oxford don, Dr Frederick Bussell, and fellow clergyman Henry Fleetwood Sheppard, who collaborated with him on his four-volume *Songs and Ballads of the West*, providing simple and somewhat stilted piano accompaniments to the tunes; Lucy did not like them. No sources were identified in the collection, and Baring-Gould and Fleetwood Sheppard had no compunction about making changes to the text – many were certainly bowdlerized – and music when they thought them necessary.

Lucy arrived at Baring-Gould's parsonage on 4 September 1893 in the evening after a day's travel. She spent the next day looking through his collection of traditional songs and broadsides and discussing them with him, before being taken to a folksong concert in Launceston.[33] Naturally she was taken to hear some singers, and on a visit to Milton Abbott was given tea at the rectory by Mrs Herbert Carr (her first name was Geraldine), who had a gift for finding local singers and indeed would turn out to be a valuable resource in the future. Lucy took down songs from 'Mrs Jeffrey, an old singing woman' and then travelled to Lifton (on the Devon–Cornwall border) to see a Mary Fletcher, wife of a local farmer.[34] There were also numerous social occasions, complete with 'tea flowing

---

[31]   Diaries, 1 July–10 August 1893. There are few or no entries during the period 12 July to 10 August.

[32]   Diaries, 29 April 1890.

[33]   Diaries, 5 September 1893.

[34]   Diaries, 21 September 1893.

with clotted cream' in true West Country fashion.[35] The contrast could not have been greater though, when in an eerie moment Baring-Gould (ever the folklorist) took Lucy past 'the white witch's house', a tumbledown hovel with no roof, doors or windows. The 'white witch' was in fact a mad old woman, whose only possessions were an umbrella (for shelter) and three bibles, which she knew by heart. This poor demented soul was clearly not going to be a source of songs, and it is interesting that there was no provision to help her, even though the clergyman appeared to be aware of the social strata of his parish.[36] Lucy stayed for just over a fortnight, returning via Ryde to see family members before staying with the Arthur Broadwood family in London.

Baring-Gould remained a valuable contact, and the two collectors continued to correspond over the next few years. Baring-Gould was dogged in his pursuit of singers and had a valuable informant in Sam Fone of Mary Tavy, a local man who had a vast repertoire of songs. Letters from Baring-Gould to Lucy complain of the problems of 'the best melodies ... attached to the grossest words', or the intrusion of 'vulgar modern song'; not least, Baring-Gould needed Lucy as an ally when his relationship with Fleetwood Sheppard broke down, as his associate's irritability made it 'hard working with him'. Above all, Baring-Gould believed that the songs should be published with accompaniments, stating that Kidson's *Traditional Tunes* would 'remain deathstruck till some musician takes them in hand'.[37]

We have seen that Kidson's approach to collecting was different from that of Baring-Gould and his collaborators. Lucy had in fact gone to visit him and his niece Ethel in Leeds in April 1893, staying for three days as part of a longer trip to Woodsome Hall, near Huddersfield.[38] In a long letter to Lucy, written in the final stages of preparation of *English County Songs*, Kidson set out his own methods of collection and his objections to Baring-Gould's as demonstrated in *Songs and Ballads of the West*. Writing with passion and conviction, he criticized both Baring-Gould's musical ear and his methods of collection. In Kidson's view, Baring-Gould had misrepresented both the music and the text, suppressing 'even the title or first few lines of a song. I cannot in the least believe that a simple song is here placed as it was sung to Baring-Gould'. Kidson also protested that he had 'not sat at home and received tunes already noted down by post', but had gone out 'among the people to collect my tunes'. Moreover he had identified his informants by title, using 'Mr' where Baring-Gould would have simply written 'Old John so & so very illiterate'. Kidson went on to give an example of a Mr Lolley, a bricklayer and fiddler who had helped him collect tunes.[39] As *English County*

---

[35]   Diaries, 8 September 1893. The event was a choir party and tea at the Duke of Bedford's show gardens at Endsleigh.

[36]   Diaries, 20 September 1893.

[37]   VWML, Letters to Lucy Broadwood, File 4/27, 4 February 1894. Baring-Gould's letters are nos 12–44.

[38]   Diaries, 10 April 1893.

[39]   VWML, Letters to Lucy Broadwood, File 4/100, 14 May 1893.

Songs drew near to publication, these different approaches to collecting must have influenced Lucy, though their effect became evident only after the publication of the collection. Venturing into the field herself, she knew that there were plenty of sources closer to home, though frustratingly (for us) many of them materialized after *English County Songs* had gone to press.

'The Bell-ringer of Horsham'

One of these sources was Henry Burstow. Known most often as 'the bell-ringer of Horsham', Burstow was in fact a musically-inclined shoemaker of nearby Horsham, who had learnt nearly 200 songs from his father, a clay tobacco pipe-maker, and began singing them to Lucy in the long, dry spring of 1893. The bell-ringing aspect was important: Lucy later wrote that the Sussex bell-ringers had been famous for centuries and thought musically in the numbers of their chimes. Burstow had dictated some of the tunes in this way.[40] Born in 1826 into a large family in the roughest part of Horsham, Burstow was apprenticed as a shoemaker in 1840 after receiving a rudimentary education at the village school. He augmented the repertoire learnt from his father with tunes sung by fellow workers at their benches, but many were also inevitably picked up from 'the taprooms and parlours of public houses in the Towns and Villages round, and where the words of many songs have been taught and learnt, exchanged or sold, perhaps for a pint of beer'.[41] The remainder he learnt from ballad sheets bought at local fairs, and from printed sources. A well-liked character in Horsham, he also indulged his passion for bell-ringing and could not decide whether it was singing or bell-ringing that gave him the most pleasure. Towards the end of his life, he became destitute and, to avoid the horrors of the workhouse, dictated his memoirs to William Albery, a saddlemaker. The resulting volume was published in 1911, five years before his death, with the proceeds going entirely to his support.

Burstow was 68 years old when he sang to Lucy in 1893 and had never left Horsham, 'except once for a week'.[42] He knew Lyne well and had visited it when younger; he also rang the bells regularly at Rusper. His letter to Lucy indicates a good memory and a picture of life below stairs which Lucy may have never known; the recording of the distance walked to get to Rusper was also surely added to draw her attention to his faithful service to the family:

> I often wondered w[h]ere you made your home when I thought of the time I came to Lyne to sing the old songs, I quite enjoyed it I use to go out in the

---

[40] Broadwood, 'On the Collecting of English Folk Song', p. 99.

[41] Henry Burstow, *Reminiscences of Horsham, being the Recollections of Henry Burstow*, ed. William Albery (1911; rpt Folcraft, PA: Folcraft Library Editions, 1975), p. 107.

[42] See 'Introduction', *Journal of the Folk-Song Society*, 1/4 (1902): 139–40.

kitchen and sing to Monday the butler and Worsefold. I still go to Rusper some time they have 8 bells now I go to Ring. I have been to Rusper ringing 51 years. I counted my steps once from my door to Rusper church door it was 10611 steps. Yours truly Henry Burstow[43]

Burstow had a repertoire of some 400 songs and provided Lucy with a list of them, though he certainly did not sing all of them to her, as he had done for 'a gentleman': the process had taken a month. Like Willett, he had learnt some of his songs from his father, who was also a singer with a repertoire of about 100 songs; his son remembered 45, according to his letter. As with Mr Grantham the carter, there were a number of tunes he felt he could not sing to her because they were 'unfit for ladies' ears'; as he could not detach the tunes from the words, the songs remained unnoted. Lucy noted 41 of Burstow's songs and published 21, including the text-free 'Salisbury Plain', in her article in the *Journal of the Folk-Song Society*.[44]

The Dunsfold Singers

With *English County Songs* in print, Lucy devoted herself to collecting in the area she knew best: Sussex and Surrey – and, once again, relied on her contacts to secure her suitable singers. In 1896, on a visit to see her mother and sister Amy in Midhurst, she went via Witley station to the village of Dunsfold to see Herbert and Geraldine Carr, whom she had met previously on her visit to Devon. Mrs Carr's sister, Kate Lee, was a classically trained singer who was beginning to take an interest in folksong, and Lucy knew of her at this time. Mrs Carr invited about a dozen farm labourers to dinner, mostly over 50 years old (which Lucy deemed to be 'old'), to sing. Lucy noted some 14 old tunes, several of which appeared in an article for the *Journal of the Folk-Song Society*.[45] The singers, identified as Messrs Baker, Bromham, Cooper, Ede, Lough, Rugman, Sparks and Whitington, did not hesitate to sing for a woman, and Mrs Rugman joined in as well. Indeed, the experience of folksong collecting could be dramatic as when Mr Ede, 'looking like a Viking' sang 'Oh, the Trees are Getting High', 'emphasizing the tragic points of the ballad with vicious snaps of his shears'.[46] In 1898 Lucy made another visit to

---

[43]   VWML LEB File 2, no.7.

[44]   The text to this song is given by Vic Gammon in *Desire, Drink and Death in English Folk and Vernacular Song 1600–1900* (Aldershot: Ashgate, 2008), p. 61. This is a revision of his article 'Song, Sex and Society in England, 1600–1850', *Folk Music Journal*, 4/3 (1982): 208–45.

[45]   Diaries, 4 September 1896. Lucy visited the Carrs again in September 1898. The article appeared in the *Journal of the Folk-Song Society*, I (1899–1904): 139–225. For more on the singers, see Gregory, 'Before the Folk-Song Society', *passim*.

[46]   Broadwood, 'On the Collecting of English Folk Song', p. 102.

Mrs Carr, who again invited the same group to sing, and their songs were included in the *Journal*.[47]

Lucy was unlike any of the other collectors in that she was a trained singer in addition to having a practical and scholarly knowledge of folksongs. Her own voice provided a link with the singers, and presumably she did not sing in a fully 'trained' manner; indeed, in her article on folksong collecting she described herself as 'croaking' in order to encourage a reluctant singer to perform.[48] She could also arrange the songs she collected, and such activity led naturally to the composition of her own songs. With the family's removal from Lyne, she now lived permanently in London, where her widening circle of professional music friends and the opportunities for performance must have encouraged her to keep up her performing and try her hand at composition. Through Fuller Maitland she was introduced to a circle of critics, scholars and composers, including Charles Graves, Barclay Squire and Hubert Parry. Music-making was a catalyst for making new friends such as fellow singer Isobel Manisty, daughter of a wealthy Scottish family, and the violinist Susan Lushington.

William Rockstro

In 1890 Lucy began singing lessons with the eccentric and elderly William Rockstro, a distinguished and prolific contributor to the first edition of Grove's *Dictionary of Music and Musicians* and a friend and teacher of Fuller Maitland, who had brought him out of an impoverished retirement in Torquay to London, where he taught privately and at the Royal College of Music.[49] Rockstro visited Lucy at 52 St George's Square for a series of 16 lessons, evidently enjoying his visits (which seem to have been rather chatty affairs) very much.[50] Rockstro had established a reputation as an expert on ecclesiastical modes, harmony and counterpoint, and was known for his work in early music – surely an attraction for Lucy. In addition to writing manuals on harmony (1881) and counterpoint (1882) he was also a composer and taught counterpoint and plainsong at the RCM.

Although Rockstro might well have advised Lucy on composition, she had already found a kindred spirit in Arthur Somervell, whom she met in October 1890. An accomplished songwriter himself, Somervell had an affinity with vocal style and was a kind and constructive critic. Likewise, the singer and composer Liza Lehmann also became an ally. Lucy knew Liza from visits to her artist father's home and from her many concerts in which she often sang her own songs. As an established performer and composer, Lehmann must have been an important

---

[47] See *Journal of the Folk-Song Society*, 1/4 (1902): *passim*. Many of these songs appeared in Lucy's 1908 collection, *English Traditional Songs and Carols.*

[48] See Broadwood, 'On the Collecting of English Folk Song', p. 99.

[49] J.A. Fuller Maitland, *A Door-keeper of Music* (London: John Murray, 1929), p. 107.

[50] SHC, Letters 2185/LEB/1, no. 16, 14 May 1891.

role model for Lucy as she began writing her own songs. Lucy was especially pleased when Lehmann, a trained singer, agreed to sing 'When Trees Did Bud' and 'Nae Mair We'll Meet'. Upon her marriage, Lehmann retired to Pinner, where she kept up some composition but gave up her professional career; she wrote to Lucy thanking her for a present she had sent and hoped she would keep in touch.[51]

Though plagued with throat problems, Lucy resumed her lessons with William Shakespeare after the period with Rockstro and was soon enthralling the factory girls of Lambeth at People's Concert Society concerts with her own traditional-sounding strophic songs such as 'Nae Mair', 'Tammy' and 'Annie's Tryst', all simple but effective settings with a Scottish flavour, both in words and music. She had agreed to become an executive member of the People's Concert Society (not to be confused with the People's Entertainment Society, another charitable group) in January 1892.[52] This was professional activity in which she could indulge without fear of censure and, doubtless influenced by her cousin Herbert, she successfully hawked 'Tammy' and 'Nae Mair' to Weekes & Co. The agreement, dated 14 May 1892, was parsimonious: there was an upfront payment of £5 5s for each song, plus 50 copies, but then came the typical publisher's twist of the knife in that the 3d royalty per copy would not apply to the first 500 copies sold. There was also a 'baker's dozen' clause in which 13 copies would be sold as 12. The copyright was signed over to the publisher.[53] This was a brave foray into independent earning for a young woman on a slender private income, but Lucy's earnings from her published works would never be substantial.

Harry Plunket Greene

Although Lucy sang her songs for the People's Concert Society, similar material dominated the programmes of the Ballad Concerts, and the performers were usually singers of merit, such as Sims Reeves, whom Lucy heard on 12 March 1890. A few days later, on St Patrick's Day, she donned a shamrock and went to an Irish Ballad Concert, joining an enthusiastic audience for an evening of song and harp music.[54] The featured performer was Harry Plunket Greene, a handsome young Irish baritone who had had some success in oratorio and opera from 1888, but was turning more to accompanied song and ballads – much in the same vein as Sims Reeves. Lucy encountered him later at the Three Choirs Festival in Worcester, where Plunket Greene sang in Parry's oratorio, *Job*, and then again at a private musical party at Abinger Hall. Plunket Greene, much taken with Lucy's performance of 'Jess Macpharlane', immediately sought her out and asked her

---

[51]   Ibid., no. 32, 27 February 1894.
[52]   Diaries, 9 January 1892.
[53]   See letters re publishing SHC 2185/LEB/3, no.1 from Weekes, 1892.
[54]   Diaries, 15 [*sic*] March 1890.

to send him a copy. Could it be published? The pair stayed on to play some of Herbert's new songs and some Irish tunes by Stanford.

Harry Plunket Greene knew a good song when he saw one and, once the summer was over, began to pester Lucy about publishing 'Jess Macpharlane' as a royalty ballad. The Ballad Concerts, held in St James's Hall until 1894, when they were moved to the Queen's Hall, were begun in 1867 by John Boosey, uncle to Lucy's publisher, William Boosey, as a popular alternative to Chappell's Popular Concerts. The concerts were long (often three hours) and featured sentimental songs sung by the most popular singers of day. By 1890 Sims Reeves, 'the star turn' of the series, had made a great hit with Balfe's 'Come into the Garden, Maud'.[55] William Boosey had joined his uncle in the firm in 1880 and, with a nose for success, by the end of the decade had introduced Harry Plunket Greene to the Ballad Concerts, where he made a hit of 'Off to Philadelphia'. Plunket Greene joined a host of other popular performers, singing ballads by composers such as Molloy, Adams and Hope Temple with great success. The concerts became a means of selling sheet music – always a popular industry in London but by this time much more calculating and commercial, particularly as music hall had begun to have mass appeal. In the royalty arrangement, Boosey took a percentage of each copy sold, with the remainder going to the performer and the composer. Lucy began to work on an accompaniment which would appeal to a musical amateur. Cousin Herbert made some suggestions and on 13 November Plunket Greene and Lucy climbed the stairs to Boosey's office in Regent Street to perform – and pitch – it to the hard-nosed publisher. Lucy had much to learn about negotiating with publishers (not that she ever admitted it in her diaries), but Plunket Greene was well versed in the art. Not least, the song would make a good number for his upcoming concert at St James's Hall early the next month.

'Jess' was an ideal vehicle for Harry Plunket Greene, whose rich baritone and flawless diction fitted perfectly with the song's heartfelt text, its refrain of 'Oh! this love, this love!' and its alluring melody. Plunket Greene was cordial but at the same time somewhat patronizing (particularly in suggesting that Herbert Birch Reynardson might assist), which must have been irritating: at his suggestion, Lucy varied the accompaniment for each verse, altering the harmonies slightly and moving from a straight chordal texture to a more fluid accompaniment, filling out with full chords towards the end. Plunket Greene had written:

[Boosey] says he will give you a Royalty of 2d per copy sold & me a royalty for signing it. I hope this doesn't sound dreadfully professional! We agreed not to put very heavy royalties on it because the song being small & light and there being no real copyright of it it wouldn't do to over-weight it. We also thought too that, as the verses were all the same, the accompaniment should be altered in style & perhaps harmony where possible, to suit the character of each verse.

55   See William Boosey, *Fifty Years of Music* (London: Ernest Benn, 1931), p. 17.

If you did not feel inclined to do that yourself, perhaps Mr Birch Reynardson would do it for you.[56]

Boosey accepted the song, but in a few months was asking for a simplified version to sell to a pianistically challenged public whose taste in music was that of an 'ignorant and uneducated fool'.[57] It is not clear how Lucy took this, but on the same day she wrote in her diary that 'Boosey begged hard for a second and simplified edition of Jess'; Plunket Greene continued to get substantial mileage (and royalties) from singing it in London and Glasgow, where a disgruntled critic questioned its authenticity, much to Lucy's annoyance. Lucy sang it herself, notably at the farewell banquet for Charles Hallé, sponsored by the Westminster Orchestral Society, a notable occasion which she attended with Ada and at which many of her friends were present.[58] A Mr Notcutt of the central press agency asked to see 'Jess' and 'was highly pleased with it'. The success of 'Jess' spurred Lucy on to her own composition, and she completed 'Nae Mair' and 'Tammy' in short order. Plunket Greene found the tunes 'simply lovely' and he accordingly made plans induce the commercially-minded Boosey to publish them.[59] By the end of 1892 Lucy had made over £15 on 'Jess' alone.[60] Plunket Greene eventually took over some of the songs from English County Songs, notably 'Twankydillo', 'I will give you the Keys of Heaven' and 'The Golden Vanity', asking for minor adjustments to make them into performance pieces.[61]

Arnold Dolmetsch

Lucy's clear voice was ideal not just for popular traditional song, but also for early music, and in 1892 she joined a chamber choral group called The Magpies. Directed by Lionel Benson, The Magpies sang English madrigals, which were enjoying some popularity due to the efforts of scholars such as William Barclay Squire. Through Fuller Maitland, also in the vanguard of the nascent early music movement, she met the pioneering Arnold Dolmetsch and sang a Henry Lawes song to his lute accompaniment. On a cold day in February, she joined an illustrious group of people to sing, play and listen to music for viols, harpsichord and lute. Her friend Cecilia Hutchinson was rehearsing as she arrived. The concert began at 9.30 in the evening and was listened to attentively by a knowledgeable and critical audience, including Lionel Benson, Plunket Greene, the American baritone David Bispham, Liza Lehmann, Arthur Somervell and Charles Stanford.

---

[56]   SHC, Letters to Lucy Broadwood, LEB/2185/1, no. 8, 19 September 1890.

[57]   Ibid., no. 11, 5 January 1891.

[58]   Diaries, 14 March 1891.

[59]   SHC Letters, 2185/LEB/1, no. 11, 5 January 1891.

[60]   Diaries, 2 February 1892.

[61]   Letters, 2185/LEB/1 no. 27, 27 September 1893.

Lucy was enraptured by the full and mellow tone of the viols and found that they complemented her clear soprano.[62] Mrs Hutchinson, the other soprano whose voice was similar to Lucy's but stronger, was becoming well known in London and abroad. She became a friend and singer of Lucy's own songs (notably 'Nae Mair We'll Meet') and eventually sang *Old World Songs*, arrangements by Lucy and Fuller Maitland of songs by eighteenth-century composers; Lucy arranged songs by the French composer Jean-Benjamin de la Borde (1734–94), which were favoured by Hutchinson and Plunket Greene.

The success of his 'at home' concerts launched Dolmetsch on his idiosyncratic career. He was immediately attracted to Lucy's voice (and possibly to Lucy herself) and deemed it ideal for English music up to and including Purcell. Late in 1893 Lucy travelled down to Dolmetsch's new home in Dulwich, aptly named 'Dowland', to hear the viols and lutes, as well as a performance of an anthem by Henry VIII for three male voices, organ and viols.[63] Dolmetsch was nothing if not ambitious: he invited the concert pianist Fanny Davies and Fuller Maitland to join him in a performance of the Bach triple harpsichord concerto in one of his concerts, to which he invited a distinguished audience.[64] Still entranced by Lucy's voice, Dolmetsch invited her to sing more songs to his lute accompaniment and some works of Bach with his daughter Hélène playing a viol da gamba; Hélène later played a viol da gamba in a 'stupendous' performance of the *St Matthew Passion* as part of that year's Bach Festival, which included Bispham as Christ and Shakespeare, standing in for an indisposed singer, as the Evangelist, though Lucy felt that her former teacher was 'not the right man' for this part; the soprano solos were sung by the German singer Marie Fillunger (who with Fanny Davies was part of the Clara Schumann set), and Joachim played the violin obbligatos.[65]

Lucy continued to sing despite continuing problems with her throat, for which the 'cure' sounded far worse than the condition (it involved 'burning' the throat with electricity), and she sang songs by Lawes in another Dolmetsch concert, this time featuring Dolmetsch's second wife, Elodie, playing the virginals and Dolmetsch the lute, viola d'amore and a newly built clavichord. Later her throat problems turned to hay fever, for which a cocaine spray was prescribed, again another indication of the peculiarities of late nineteenth-century medicine.[66]

Although Dolmetsch continued to praise her voice and musical style, Lucy demurred when it came to joining the ranks of professional singers and turned down his invitation to sing at a public concert in December 1895; her realm was the drawing room and charity concert hall. Dolmetsch's disappointment was palpable:

---

[62]   Diaries, 24 February 1892.

[63]   Diaries, 16 December 1893.

[64]   Diaries, 22 May 1894. This was probably a private concert. Arthur Balfour and Mrs William Morris were in the audience, and a number of Bach's works were played on period instruments.

[65]   Diaries, 2 April 1895.

[66]   Diaries, 27 May 1895.

I am very sorry that you cannot sing at my Purcell concert; but it is a public one, and I see your reasons – I regret it all the more, as you sang the Purcell songs so exquisitely last Friday! ... It is very nice of you to be singing 'in spirit' at my Purcell concert, but I wish you were singing for good; it will be difficult for any singer to please me in these two Purcell songs now that I have heard you; you really sang them with admirable expression and taste. Lots of people have good voices, and know how to use them; but, the understanding of that music is not given to everyone![67]

Lucy's part in the Purcell concert was taken by Helen Trust, and it seems that her decision not to pursue public singing was final. It is difficult to discern whether this was because her age (she was in her late thirties at this time) and chronic throat problems made such a career uncertain, or whether her sex, background and class were determining factors in her refusal of a professional career, when clearly she had been training seriously as a singer for some time. Certainly her contemporaries Helen Trust, Cecilia Hutchinson, Thomasine Tuer and even Liza Lehmann did not seem to suffer socially from being professional singers, but Lucy might have felt that she could not compete with them vocally. One cannot help but think that the refusal of Dolmetsch's invitation was a missed opportunity to explore professionally a repertoire which was eminently suited to her voice and which she could have continued to sing for at least a decade.

Lucy's decision not to sing Purcell seems particularly unfortunate as his bicentenary year of 1895 (commemorating his death) would have afforded many opportunities to perform publicly. Lucy attended the commemoration concert on 21 November in Westminster Abbey, where the *Te Deum* and a number of anthems were performed by a choir of some 90 boys and nearly 200 men and women. The English Establishment was there in full force, and Cummings, Parry, Barclay Squire, Stainer, Mackenzie and Stanford placed wreaths on the composer's grave. The following evening the Philharmonic presented the *Ode to St Cecilia* and the 'Golden' Sonata which, to Lucy's horror, was 'shamefully padded out by two pianofortes and wind instruments'. The Royal College of Music gave a performance of *Dido and Aeneas* at the Lyceum Theatre, conducted by Stanford; Lucy found the additional accompaniments by Charles Wood 'wicked', though it is hard to tell whether she actively disliked them or merely thought them a bit too modern and innovative for the period.[68] Her association with Dolmetsch had clearly influenced her perception of how Purcell's music should be performed, and the lack of period authenticity in these performances must have been anathema to her.

Despite veering away from a professional singing career, Lucy's engagement with this music must have been evident to her contemporaries, and only a few weeks later she was invited by William Barclay Squire, president of the Purcell Society, to edit 'some songs' for the Society on a visit to a special collection of

---

[67]   Letters, SHC 2185/LEB/1, no. 42, 2 December 1895.
[68]   Diaries, 20 November 1895.

pictures and autographs of the composer at the British Museum where he was Keeper of the Music Collection. The 'songs' turned out to be *Amphytrion* and *The Gordian Knot Unty'd*.[69] Lucy duly consulted with Fuller Maitland and returned to the British Museum to look at the music. If her career as a singer was waning, she could take up scholarship instead. She could certainly avail herself of the best editorial advice from Fuller Maitland and Barclay Squire.

'An Era in One's Life': Visiting Bayreuth

Amidst all her activity in early music, Lucy remained avidly interested in the London concert scene and saw Saint-Saëns conduct his own symphony concerto 'for many curiously combined wind instruments as well as strings, organ and pianoforte' in June 1894.[70] The summer of that year was taken up with a pilgrimage to Bayreuth to immerse herself in Wagnerian opera. She arrived in the afternoon of 1 August, observing the quaintness of the town and its houses, which resembled those in Nuremberg. The following day she called on 'Mme Wagner' (presumably Cosima) at 'Wahnfried' as prearranged, but 'found her out'. After meeting some of her friends, including the violinist Emily Liddell, at the theatre, a fanfare of trumpets playing the 'Grail' motif from *Parsifal* summoned them into the theatre where Lucy noted the raked seating (and compulsory removal of hats) with approval. The audience revelled in the wonderful playing of Richard Mühlfeld, Brahms's favourite clarinettist, and in the 'magnificently managed scenery'. As in all opera, disbelief had to be suspended somewhat: Parsifal was ugly and Kundry was fat, but good on stage. The next day she took in *Lohengrin* – its first performance at Bayreuth – performed without cuts. This was followed by a day of sightseeing, taken up in part with visits to the graves of Liszt and Wagner. A return visit to *Parsifal* on 5 August with a different cast (Marie Brema sang Kundry) was 'more sublime' and an interesting comparison to the previous performance. The last day was disappointing: the performance of *Tannhäuser*, with its 'indifferent singing' and lacklustre orchestra, left her unmoved. On 7 August she left for Nuremberg and endured a rough crossing home.[71]

On her return Lucy plunged back into her own musical life, translating and arranging songs by de la Borde, and singing them to Chappell in an effort to persuade the firm to publish them; she eventually received £6 6s from him for three.[72] At about the same time she became involved in the English Ladies' Orchestral Society, of which her friend Mary Venables was a leading member.[73] This was an era of women's instrumental ensembles, given their exclusion from

[69]   Diaries, 29 November 1895.
[70]   Diaries, 7 June 1894.
[71]   Diaries, 1–8 August 1894.
[72]   Diaries, 19 October and 19 November 1894.
[73]   Diaries, 17 October 1894.

established orchestras; in December Lucy attended a concert given by the Moberly Ladies' String Band, in which her friend Gertrude Sichel was playing. At the same concert she heard her arrangements of the de la Borde songs sung by Cecilia Hutchinson; she must have declined to sing them herself. Given this reticence, it is surprising that she agreed to sing Elvira in production of *Don Giovanni* organized by Mrs Augustus Hughes-Hughes, wife of the Keeper of Music Manuscripts in the British Museum, in November. This connection was surely not accidental as Lucy already knew Barclay Squire, and her cousin Herbert also worked in the library. The allure of this invitation must have been the fact that this was an amateur production, taking place at Holloway Hall where Lucy also sang vocal solos in charity concerts. Unperturbed by the role, which is a demanding one, Lucy clearly took everything in her stride, as she noted nonchalantly in her diary that she 'trimmed a hat' before the performance.[74] She must have enjoyed the experience, though, as she accepted when Mrs Hughes-Hughes asked her to sing Dorabella in *Così fan tutte* in January.[75]

The Folklore Society

The decade of the 1890s marked an exciting period in Lucy's life, as she was able to participate fully in both the art and folk music sides of her life, taking up opportunities to compose, perform and research. The publication of *English County Songs* attracted the interest of none other than Sir Alexander Mackenzie, Principal of the Royal Academy of Music, who enlisted her help in preparing material for a lecture on folksong. Lucy would also sing the musical examples.[76] Her folksong work also attracted the attention of several members of the Folklore Society. Founded in 1878 by a group of anthropological folklorists intent on understanding primitive man from contemporary folklore, the Society attracted a scholarly elite headed by Laurence Gomme, Alfred Nutt, Andrew Lang, Edwin Sidney Hartland, Edward Clodd and William Alex Clouston. All had worthy professions by day: Gomme, its first president, was Clerk of the London County Council and wrote prolifically on the early history of the capital; Andrew Lang, a Fellow of Merton College Oxford, left Oxford to become a freelance literary journalist in London; Clodd was a banker with an interest in evolutionary theory; and Alfred Nutt, who had Celtic interests, was highly respected as a publisher. Hartland was a solicitor and mayor of Gloucester for a term; Clouston was a journalist. Alice Gomme, wife of Laurence and, with Charlotte Burne, one of

---

[74]   Diaries, 14 November 1894.

[75]   Diaries, 9 January 1895. As Lucy does not record any rehearsals for this, and writes that she sang in only the first half, this must have been an amateur or 'read-through' performance.

[76]   Diaries, 26 December 1894. Unfortunately Lucy was not able to illustrate the lecture owing to illness.

the few women in the movement, became a major figure in her own right as a folklorist, suffragist and theatre historian.[77]

Though committed to 'scientific' folklore – in Richard Dorson's words 'the scientific study of the survivals of archaic beliefs, customs, and traditions in modern times',[78] few of the folklorists engaged in any sort of fieldwork and instead encouraged others at home and abroad to collect data for them, much in the way that Lucy and Fuller Maitland had done for much of *English County Songs.* Nor did they restrict themselves to England, but took an interest in Ireland, Scotland and Wales as well.[79] Lucy's interests included folklore, and, as we have seen, she was familiar with the latest researches in the area as exemplified in James Frazer's *The Golden Bough.* Might she have something to offer the Society, and could they help her? She began attending meetings in 1892, and in May went to the Eyre Assembly Rooms to see the Burne family dance Oxfordshire morris dances.[80] Lucy did not become involved in dance research herself, but she must have recalled this event when the morris dance became a prominent feature of the folkdance revival and a subject of some controversy. All the avatars of folklore research were there, including Charlotte Burne, the Gommes and the folk-drama specialist T. Fairman Ordish.

Gomme was at this time two years into his presidency, which he combined with his day job in London. London was not his only interest, though, as he also took an interest in English villages, as did the folksong collectors.[81] His wife, Alice, had even more connection with the folksong revival in her work on children's singing games. Lucy began to go to the Society's meetings regularly, usually taking a sister or female friend. Early in 1893 she heard Ordish's paper on 'Primitive Drama', which must have interested her in its tracing of the Mummer's play of St George back to its supposed roots in Scandinavian mythology. Ordish illustrated his paper with photos of costumes from Hampshire and Shropshire.[82]

---

[77]   See Robert Gomme, 'Gomme, Alice Bertha, Lady Gomme (1853–1938), *Oxford Dictionary of National Biography* (Oxford: Oxford University Press, 2004), online edn May 2006 at: http://www.oxforddnb.com.ezproxy, library.yorku.ca/view/article/38616 (accessed October 2007). See also Georgina Boyes, 'Alice Bertha Gomme, 1852 [*sic*]–1938: A Reassessment of the Work of a Folklorist', *Folklore*, 101 (1990): 198–209; and idem, 'Alice Gomme' in *Women and Tradition: A Neglected Group of Folklorists*, eds, C. Blacker and H.E. Davidson (Durham NC: Academic Press, 2001), pp. 65–86.

[78]   R.M. Dorson, *The British Folklorists: A History* (London: Routledge & Kegan Paul, 1968).

[79]   Ibid., pp. 202–65.

[80]   Diaries, 3 May 1892. Lucy went with Fanny Birch.

[81]   See Robert Gomme, 'Gomme, Sir (George) Laurence (1853–1916)', *Oxford Dictionary of National Biography*, Oxford University Press, 2004 at: http://www.oxforddnb.com.ezproxy.library.yorku.ca/view/article/38353 (accessed October 2007).

[82]   Diaries, 15 February 1893. The paper was noticed in *Folkore*, 13 (1902): 296–7.

Clearly there were shared interests between the folklorists and folksong enthusiasts. Much of their approach was the same, including the antiquarian aspect of digging for origins. But the fieldwork aspect was different. Lucy's own work demonstrated that it was preferable to do one's own collecting in the field than to rely on the work of others, valuable though those efforts were. Collecting songs directly from Burstow's singing had been far more satisfactory than relying on the red ink of Samuel Willett, and Mrs Carr's singers in Dunsfold had produced a harvest of songs. Moreover, Mrs Carr's sister, Kate Lee, was interested in singing some of the *English County Songs* and rehearsed them with Lucy. Kate, a singer who had tried a professional career in London had, like Lucy, turned to folksong and joined the ranks of the charity concert singers, performing selections from *English County Songs* at a People's Concert Society concert in December 1897.[83] At their rehearsal, where Lucy accompanied Kate, they must have discussed folksong and their common interests. Should they join forces with the folklorists? Or was folksong important enough to be the subject of its own society?

[83]   Diaries, 7–8 December 1897.

Chapter 4

The Folk-Song Society

On a cold day in January 1898 Lucy went to meet her fellow folklorists at the premises of publisher David Nutt and his son the Celtic scholar Alfred Nutt, then President of the Folklore Society, to discuss folksong in the context of folklore.[1] The last meeting of the Folklore Society had been desperately boring, and she had virtually slept through Nutt's address.[2] Could the Folklore Society include folksong in its researches? What were their respective aims and approaches? Was there enough difference to warrant forming a separate society? Although Lucy was a vital link between the two groups, it seems that each had distinctive interests which were best pursued separately. The ebullient Kate Lee must have made her feelings clear to Lucy in their rehearsals and indeed she had visited a few days previously to say that there should definitely be a society devoted exclusively to folksong,[3] but Lucy, with feet in both camps, wished to discuss the matter with her colleagues, especially Alice Gomme and Marion Roalfe Cox, and, of course, Alfred Nutt himself. Alice Gomme had combined music with her folklore research in her *Traditional Games of England, Scotland and Ireland*, a collection of some 800 children's games complete with tunes, which was published in two volumes in 1894 and 1898. Lucy, influenced by this, collected several games at Embleton in 1895.[4]

The meeting in fact was a prelude to another one which took place later the same day at the rooms of the Irish Literary Society further along the Strand at 8 Adelphi Terrace. Alfred Graves, an authority on Irish folksong, was the host at this subsequent meeting and was joined by Kate Lee, Fuller Maitland, Barclay Squire, the Hungarian-born composer and singer Francis Korbay, Edgar F. Jacques and the Manxman W.H. Gill. Clearly there was some disagreement between the folklorists and the folksong collectors about methodology and approach, as Alfred Graves spoke of 'restoring' folksong. It is not entirely clear what he meant by this, but it was countered by Lucy, Fuller Maitland and Kate Lee, who all spoke in favour of establishing a continuous tradition through active fieldwork and collecting.[5] The idea was probably to move away from Chappell's

---

[1]   SHC, Diaries, 27 January 1898.

[2]   Diaries, 18 January 1898.

[3]   Diaries, 15 January 1898. For information on Kate Lee and her role in the founding of the Folk-Song Society, see C.J. Bearman, 'Kate Lee and the Foundation of the Folk-Song Society', *Folk Music Journal*, 7/5 (1999): 627–43.

[4]   VWML, LEB file 2, no. 36.

[5]   Diaries, 27 January 1898.

model and adopt a more active approach. There was also to be no 'faking'. Lucy's diary entry is characteristically terse on what happened at the meeting, but a note in the Folk-Song Society minutes in May records that the negotiations with the Folklore Society were 'abortive' due to an initial misunderstanding.[6] A subcommittee was struck to deal with the practical considerations of establishing a new and independent society.

Founding the Folk-Song Society

On 8 February, less than a week later than this unsuccessful meeting, Lucy returned to Nutt's premises in 270 Strand to find Frank Kidson, who had travelled specially from Leeds, joined by 'regulars' Fuller Maitland, Edgar F. Jacques and W.H. Gill ready to discuss the new society, with Alfred Nutt in the chair. Lucy recorded even fewer details about this meeting than the previous one, but it seems that the fledgling society was about to take flight. On 23 March the committee met again, not at Nutt's but at Forsyth's (another publisher) in Regent Street, this time with Kate Lee, Alfred Graves, Jacques, Fuller Maitland and Lucy present. Nutt was no longer involved, and with his departure the folklore influence was absent. Afterwards they repaired to celebrate over lunch at Pagani's, the famous Italian Swiss restaurant nearby.[7]

After this, the society began to gain momentum. Lucy was able to attend a committee meeting of the Folk-Song Society on 4 May, again at Forsyth's in Regent Street, but not the crucial one held on 16 May, which was held at the premises of the Royal Agricultural Society at 13 Hanover Square, where one of the members, Sir Ernest Clarke, had a connection. Formerly the home of the Duke of Roxburgh, the house boasted fine Adam decoration throughout. This time the folklorist Alice Gomme was present and the core subcommittee was joined by a number of new members, among them Sir Ernest Clarke and Sir Alexander Mackenzie.[8] Fuller Maitland chaired. It is ironic that Lucy was not present at this seminal meeting, for reasons discussed below, as she would later become a crucial member. The meeting discussed the need for an annual income of 100 guineas, to be derived from membership fees. It was pointed out that rural members would be less likely to be able to attend meetings, so should pay a reduced rate. Meetings would include the performance and discussion of songs, and there would be publication of proceedings and collections. Frank Kidson, no doubt with his own circumstances in mind, pleaded for a reduced membership fee for those in the north.

---

6   VWML, Minutes of the Folk-Song Society (hereafter Minutes), 16 May 1898, reporting on the preliminary meeting of 27 January.

7   Diaries, 23 March 1898.

8   VWML, Minutes, 16 May 1898.

A set of rules was drafted, which formed the basis for the revised set which appeared in the first volume of the *Journal*. The name of the new society was significant. It was not the *English* Folk-Song Society but, like the Folklore Society, its remit would include 'British and foreign' music. This was revised later to read: 'The Society shall have for its primary object the collection and preservation of Folk Songs, Ballads and Tunes, and the publication of such of these as may be advisable'.[9] Throughout its existence the Society resisted an English or British designation, though this was often raised by some members as a desirable option. After some discussion, the membership fee was set at 10s 6d, payable on 1 January. The affairs of the Society would be managed by the president, vice-presidents, treasurer, secretary and a committee of 12. Lord Herschell, the ex-Lord Chancellor, was appointed president after some initial difficulty in finding someone willing to serve in this capacity. Four vice presidents were chosen to represent England, Wales, Ireland and Scotland. All were pillars of the musical establishment who had demonstrated some interest in folksong: Sir John Stainer, Sir Alexander Mackenzie, Hubert Parry and Charles Stanford. The music critic Alfred Kalisch was appointed treasurer and Kate Lee became the honorary secretary. The committee of management consisted of the usual stalwarts: Mrs Frederick Beer (Rachel Beer, née Sassoon, who replaced Frederick Corder), Ernest Clarke, W.H. Gill, Alice Gomme, Alfred Graves, E.F. Jacques, Frank Kidson and Fuller Maitland; Lucy was appointed *in absentia*. The committee met again on 6 July, again without Lucy, who was away for the summer, and two weeks later the subcommittee drafted the 'Hints to Collectors' which would be published as a pamphlet for use by interested members of the public who wished to collect folksong in the field.[10] Lucy was absent yet again, busy in Dunsfold collecting folksongs. She would not make her first appearance until December.

The Society met again in October at Forsyth's and welcomed several new members, including the folklorists Charlotte Burne and Marian Roalfe Cox (both friends of Lucy, who still had a strong folklore connection), Israel Gollancz, Edward Elgar, Joachim and the blind collector Percy Merrick. A *conversazione* was planned to celebrate the inaugural meeting, along the lines of the Folklore Society's event of the same name held as part of the International Folklore Congress in 1891. Rachel Beer, by that time owner and editor of *The Sunday Times* and editor of the *Observer*, offered her handsome Mayfair mansion in Chesterfield Gardens, which she shared with her husband Frederick Beer, as a venue. Its fine Adam staircase would form a dramatic backdrop for the *conversazione*, but nothing could be further away from the world of the folk which the Society proposed to explore.[11]

---

[9]   See Frederick Keel, 'The Folk Song Society, 1898–1948', *Journal of English Folk Dance and Song*, 5/3 (1948): 111–13; see also *Journal of the Folk-Song Society*, 1 (1899).

[10]   VWML, Minutes, 20 July 1898.

[11]   Vanessa Curney, 'Beer, Rachel (1858–1927)', *Oxford Dictionary of National Biography* (Oxford: Oxford University Press, 2004) at: http://www.oxforddnb.com.

The AGM

The long-awaited first general meeting of the Folk-Song Society took place at the Beers' Mayfair home on 2 February 1899, with Sir Alexander Mackenzie in the chair. The Society now had a membership of 73 and a balance of just over £24.[12] Sir Hubert Parry delivered an imposing inaugural address which, read now, is revealing about the divide between the membership and those whose music they sought to collect. Parry abhorred the excrescences of urban life, with its gin palaces and music halls, and sought to restore a shared heritage as embodied in rural folk, a 'race' which embodied the true ideals of the English people. This was strong stuff, reminiscent of an earlier generation represented by Herder and a century of German romantics.[13] It is telling that the only folksinger members of the Society were members of the Copper family, who had been drawn in by Kate Lee. Parry's remarks were riddled with the class assumptions and divisions of the time, but they were followed by a refreshingly honest and genuine paper from the honorary secretary, Kate Lee, who spoke with enthusiasm and delight about her collecting, with particular reference to the Copper family. Again, Lucy was not there.

Family Milestones

It seems extraordinary that such a key figure as Lucy Broadwood should have missed almost all of the early meetings of the Folk-Song Society and, in particular, its first general meeting. It is ironic that she was not present at the early meetings and founding of a society in which she would play a major role, but unfortunately these events coincided with the death of her mother on 2 April 1898. The funeral was held in Rusper four days later, with many friends present. Lucy was too ill to go. The following days were taken up with dealing with the aftermath of the death and preparing for a new life ahead.

The death of her mother meant uprooting from St George's Square. Lucy began hunting for flats in South Kensington, but decided to stick to her original summer plans. This meant extensive travelling in the north of England and Scotland, before returning to the south-east to do some more collecting in Dunsfold. This was either procrastination on a grand scale, or quite possibly the best thing she could have done, but it meant not only that was she missing crucial meetings of the Folk-Song Society, but also that she was postponing her entry into a new phase of her life. Her sister Evelyn had a flat at 59 Carlisle Mansions,

---

ezproxy.library.yorku.ca/view/article/48270 (accessed November 2007).

[12]   See 'Report of the First General Meeting', *Journal of the Folk-Song Society*, 1 (1899): vi–vii.

[13]   For an interpretation of Parry's address see Georgina Boyes, *The Imagined Village* (Manchester: Manchester University Press, 1993), pp. 25–7.

a large block of mansion flats in Victoria near Westminster Cathedral. No. 84 was becoming available: would Lucy like to look at it?

84 Carlisle Mansions, SW

Weary with looking at unsatisfactory properties in the more fashionable parts of London, Lucy eventually agreed to take the flat on 16 November 1898, seven months after the death of her mother. She signed the lease the following January.[14] She moved into the bleak flat with its bare windows and floors with two servants (Paynton and Millie, presumably a cook and maidservant) on a cold day in early February 1899. On two floors, with quarters for staff, the mansion flat was spacious and would be ideal for musical parties once decorated and furnished. There was room for a grand piano and the pair of girandoles and mirror brought by her cousins Alice and Agatha Broadwood (daughters of Walter Broadwood) from their home at 3 Queen's Gate Gardens. Her neighbours were respectable middle-class professionals and a host of similar unmarried ladies of independent means, most of whom lived with a companion, a housemaid and a cook. Lucy would follow the same pattern: the two servants were ensconced upstairs, and she soon had a companion in her niece, Barbara Craster. Barbara's older sister Katherine was engaged to be married, and Barbara was living with Harry and Ada at Bone Hill, St Alban's. Already in her thirties, Barbara seemed unlikely to marry and probably relished the idea of leading an independent life in London. She moved in on 14 December of that year. A new phase in both their lives had begun.

Broadwood & Co.

Financially, things were precarious. Despite its famous name, the Broadwood piano firm had had to navigate choppy waters since the death of Henry Fowler in 1893.[15] On Bertha's recommendation, Lucy and her sisters ploughed their inheritance of £8,000 each back into the floundering firm. A year after Henry Fowler's death, Edith's son William ('Willie') Dobbs was brought in. Young and with no experience of pianos or business, he was expected to effect some sort of financial rescue. Harry Broadwood and George Rose continued to advise on the technical side of the business. But Dobbs's reserved personality was not a good fit with the factory side of life and eventually Leonard Bevan was taken on to assist A.J. Hipkins, who was still a revered elder of the company. Youthful and a gregarious foil to the taciturn Dobbs, Bevan was the Etonian scion of a wealthy

[14] Diaries, 16 November 1898 and 14 January 1899.
[15] David Wainwright, *Broadwood by Appointment* (London: Quiller Press, 1982), Chapter 8, 'The Partnership Breaks Up'.

business family and possibly harboured grand ideas of running the firm himself. He was also a neighbour of an old Broadwood friend, Marlborough Pryor.

The immediate problem facing the company was the search for new premises, as the lease on the Horseferry Road factory was due to expire in 1902. The firm was in trouble, owing to competition from Germany, outdated production methods and lack of strong direction within the company. By 1901 an old neighbour and family friend Cuthbert Heath, by this time a prosperous businessman, had been asked to step in and assess the firm. Dobbs was dismissed and Leonard Bevan demoted to sub-manager along with George Rose. Although the factory would eventually move to new premises at Old Ford in the east end of London in June 1902, the changes came with tragedy. Hopes dashed, Bevan slit his wrists and then hanged himself at the family home in Kensington on 13 October 1901.[16]

This turbulent decade in the firm's history must have affected and troubled the sisters, particulary the indomitable Bertha. Like Bertha, Lucy took an interest in the firm and was appalled by the amateurish way in which things were being run, partly a legacy from the lack of business acumen displayed by their father. Harry was not a trained businessman, and his father's death merely brought to light the management fault-lines and lack of foresight in the face of increased competition and a changing international economy. The firm's troubles would inevitably have a negative effect on the unmarried sisters' incomes. Though comfortably off for the present, none could afford to adopt an extravagant lifestyle. Lucy had taken stock of the worsening situation even before her father's death, writing in response to a letter from Bertha in 1891 that the firm was suffering from a severe lack of business sense: they were still using messengers instead of telephones, the ledger system needed updating, and the quality of the instruments had declined. Brother Harry was an inventive piano-maker, but had had no training in accounts: 'he should ... have been put through the account-work as a youth, as a preparation ... [he] was never enlightened as to the workings at all'.[17]

Despite all this, Lucy managed to continue with some folksong collecting. Her friend Geraldine Carr had moved to Bury, a picturesque village in Lucy's home county of Sussex, and once again she invited Lucy to hear some songs over supper. This time there were four singers: quarryman John Searle, aged about 70, his sons Walter and Edward, and a labourer named Mr Hoare, who was in his sixties. Among the songs they sang to her were 'Poor Mary in the Silvery Tide', 'The Cobbler and the Miser', 'The Bob-tailed Mare', 'The Young Servant-man' and 'The Rich Merchant and Daughter'.[18] She sent off all the songs she had collected – from Burstow, the Dunsfold singers and the Searles – to Alfred

---

[16]   Lucy recorded this sad event on 14 October 1901, registering shock at the tragic death of the 25-year-old Bevan. She sent a wreath to his mother and later received some of his songs from his sister on 25 April 1902.

[17]   Wainwright, *Broadwood*, p. 229.

[18]   *Journal of the Folk-Song Society*, 1 (1899–1904): 216–23. See also Diaries, 3 October 1901.

Kalisch early in 1902 for publication in the *Journal*.[19] She was also in touch with H. Ellis Wooldridge about her collection, and continued her activities with folklorists, visiting a Miss Salmon in Reading to listen to some singers and to collect some games.[20] She also became closer to Vaughan Williams, who sought her advice on folksong. Like Mackenzie before him, he invited her to sing musical illustrations to his lectures.[21]

The Ritchies

Lucy's pleasant singing voice was still attractive. Richmond Ritchie, the husband of Annie Thackeray (daughter of the novelist), met her in 1896 and evidently found her (and her voice) charming. The two found several occasions to meet privately. Seventeen years younger than his wife, Richmond was only four years older than Lucy and was entranced by her wit and her singing voice; he was also known to have a roving eye, and it is clear he was attracted to her. A brilliant scholar educated at Eton and Trinity College Cambridge, Ritchie had also enjoyed glittering successes in sport and debating; he was above all a keen lover of music. The couple held salons in their home, 'End House' in Berkeley Place, Wimbledon, in which musicians played a prominent part: Lucy was in demand as a vocalist, not least to the ministrations of Richmond, who, as a Christmas present in 1896, bribed her with a box of 'eatables' to sing at a home concert the following March. The programme, devised by Richmond with amusing comments about how the event would run, complete with intervals, refreshments and 'congratulations to the Voice', began with Ritchie's favourite Bach aria ('Patron, Patron, das macht der Wind' from the secular cantata *Geschwinde, ihr wirbelnden Winde*, BWV 201) and concluded with Purcell's 'Expostulation' and 'Dido's Lament'.[22] The two obviously had much in common, including a robust sense of humour, and Ritchie, clearly totally captivated, must have enjoyed his visits to see Lucy in London for dinner and even the occasional concert.[23]

By 1898 the Ritchies felt the need to live in London, so they let End House and rented a flat in Kensington Court Gardens, spending summers at End House. By this time Richmond was a high-flying career civil servant in the India Office, serving as private secretary to a succession of under-secretaries of state between 1883 and 1892. By the time he met Lucy, he was private secretary to the then secretary of state for India, Lord George Hamilton, a position which he had held since 1895.

---

[19]   Diaries, 26 February 1902.

[20]   Diaries, 18 March–10 April 1902.

[21]   Diaries, 17 November 1902. Vaughan Williams, now a MusDoc, gave a lecture to 112 people at Boscombe, where Lucy sang 10 songs as illustrations.

[22]   SHC, Letters 2185/LEB/1, no. 450, 16 December 1896, and no. 451, 22 March 1897.

[23]   Diaries, 20 October 1897. Lucy and Ritchie attended *La Périchole* with Amy.

Illustration 4.1   Sir Richmond Ritchie standing under a portrait of Charles
                    Lamb at the India Office

Source: Copyright of Surrey History Centre.

In 1898 he was made a Companion of the Order of the Bath, an event which Lucy celebrated with him at the home of her friend Edith Sichel.[24] His prestigious career did not come without problems, however; in 1893 he had become ill with Menière's disease, a problem with balance that might have been caused by overwork and/or anxiety, and he predeceased his wife by seven years.[25]

Was the marriage happy? By the time Richmond met Lucy it had probably stabilized, but he must have delighted in the company of the younger woman and her musical gifts. Like Annie, Lucy was an excellent hostess and enjoyed entertaining, but her quiet, even temperament matched Richmond's introspection more than his wife's extrovert personality. Despite her husband's obvious attraction to Lucy, Annie remained warm; she was used to her husband's flirtations and tended to turn a blind eye, though a previous affair with the widow of Lionel Tennyson had hurt her deeply. There is no evidence of a sexual relationship between Richmond and Lucy, but clearly for its short duration their friendship was a close and affectionate one. In any case, Annie had a successful career as a writer and she was also mother to two children, Hester and William. She was also the daughter of a famous author, and by 1896 she was hard at work on an edition of her father's works, which must have taken up all her time and energy.[26]

Edward Clifford, Art and the Church Army

Annie shared with Lucy a love of art, and both were friends of the artist Edward Clifford, who was also honorary secretary and treasurer of the Church Army, which had been founded in 1882 as an Anglican counterpart to the Salvation Army. Clifford led a double life, combining his charitable work caring for the indigent and dispossessed with a successful career as a portrait painter of the wealthy and aristocratic. A rather mannered man, he lived with a male friend and was probably a closet homosexual. He counted numerous duchesses among his friends – and they in turn doted on him – and frequently held elegant parties for them in his home in Kensington Square.[27] Characteristic of Clifford's spontaneity and generosity was an occasion, described by Lucy, when on a visit to her friend

---

24   Diaries, 22 May 1898.

25   Chandrika Kaul, 'Ritchie, Sir Richmond Thackeray Willoughby (1854–1912)', *Oxford Dictionary of National Biography* (Oxford: Oxford University Press, 2004) at: http://www.oxforddnb.com.ezproxy.library.yorku.ca/view/article/35764   (accessed November 2007).

26   For biographical information on the Ritchies, see Winifred Gérin, *Anne Thackeray Ritchie: A Biography* (New York: Oxford University Press, 1981).

27   In *Three Houses* (Oxford: Oxford University Press, 1931), p. 39, Angela Thirkell reminisced that her family, the Mackails, knew Clifford's male friend as 'the giant'. She also commented on 'his funny affected voice, and his strange mixture of romantic snobbism and religion, his kindness and capacity for friendship'.

the violinist Susan Lushington in Kensington Square, the two women were interrupted by an excited Clifford rushing in to ask Lucy to go to his studio to meet Lady Eileen Wellesley, daughter of the Duke of Wellington, 'painting very cleverly'; an invitation to dine on 18 January was extended for her 'to meet the rest of the family'.[28] Lucy accepted, and performed with Lushington at an informal dinner party in the family's honour; Clifford rewarded her with two green and white porcelain plates.[29]

Like Richmond Ritchie, Clifford was immediately captivated by Lucy's singing and character, and Lucy just as quickly felt an affinity for him. The two became close friends, and upon his death in 1907 Lucy confided to her diary that the funeral was so moving that she 'had never felt more moved or more sad at the death of anyone and was overcome all day'.[30] Unfortunately, he did not paint her portrait, but he did present her with paintings as gifts and constantly invited her to his home, where she often performed in his musical parties. It was through Clifford that she met Frances Balfour.[31]

Frances Balfour was Lucy's exact contemporary and wife of Eustace Balfour, youngest brother of Arthur James Balfour, who was First Lord of the Treasury at the time. Frances Balfour was an outspoken advocate for women's rights and had been part of the suffragist movement from the 1880s onwards. With her Scottish background and social status it is not surprising that she warmed to Lucy, who must have shared the same views and must have felt equally frustrated at not being able to have a career on an equal footing with her male contemporaries. And, like Frances, Lucy deplored the militant side of the suffragist movement. At the time the two women met, Frances Balfour was on the executive committee of the National Union for Women's Suffrage Society and was president of the London Society for Women's Suffrage. She was extremely influential in her efforts to influence British politicians in the interests of the cause, and her wide range of contacts made her a formidable figure in the world of women's suffrage.[32] In some ways Frances Balfour was rather like Lucy's older sister, the formidable Bertha, whose work in nursing was becoming well known: in May 1899 Lucy was invited to attend one of her meetings at 10 Downing Street, and the following summer she went with Barbara Craster to a tea party held at the same venue.[33]

---

[28]   Diaries, 17 December 1901.

[29]   Diaries, 18 January 1902.

[30]   Diaries, 23 September 1907.

[31]   Diaries, 22 March 1899.

[32]   Joan B. Huffman, 'Balfour, Lady Frances (1858–1931)', *Oxford Dictionary of National Biography* (Oxford: Oxford University Press, 2004) at: http://www.oxforddnb.com.ezproxy.library.yorku.ca/view/article/30554 (accessed November 2007).

[33]   Diaries, 30 May 1899 and 4 July 1900.

James Campbell McInnes

Influential people were important, but in the end it was not they but a young baritone from Lancashire who made the most impact on Lucy's personal and professional life. By chance, the meeting with James Campbell McInnes coincided with her move to 84 Carlisle Mansions, which was also a significant event in her life; she met him just before she signed the lease on 14 January 1899. McInnes, a young singer of Scots background from Lancashire, had come to London to study at the Royal College of Music with William Shakespeare. Possessed of a superb natural voice and a magnetic raw masculinity which appealed to both men and women, McInnes was proudly working-class. Tall, moustached and with a shock of pomaded dark hair, he cut a striking figure and was welcomed on the private concert circuit. Lucy first met him at tea with Ethel Robinson, where she provided a piano accompaniment to his singing.[34] They met again a couple of months later at a private party given by Fuller Maitland, featuring the violinist Achille Rivarde and pianist Leonard Borwick. Lady Radnor and Edward Clifford were present; McInnes sang.[35] The following weekend he joined Lucy at her new flat to go over her songs and thereafter was a fixture at all her private parties – many given to showcase him as a singer. He was also a constant private visitor to Carlisle Mansions, where he came to rehearse, eat and have long discussions with Lucy, who was evidently a sort of confidante, or possibly more.

The 16 years' difference in their ages (McInnes was born in 1874) might have precluded any romantic relationship, but there was a similar age gap in the Ritchies's marriage, which seemed to be happy overall. Sexual or not, this relationship was to be the most important in Lucy's life: if she was not his lover she was certainly an intimate friend, mentor and vocal coach for his raw talent. As a fellow Shakespeare pupil she was familiar with the technique and was able to provide a wealth of musical background to help the young singer in his interpretation. Such talent needed more finessing, though, and study abroad was recommended. The Belgian baritone, Jacques Bouhy, was teaching in Paris, but McInnes would need sponsors to go there. By October 1900 Lucy joined with her friends the Vernon Lushingtons, Fuller Maitland, Gertrude Sichel and Barbara Craster to send McInnes to Paris with £60 in his pocket. Lucy fell ill shortly afterwards and, much to her chagrin, was unable to sing with McInnes in a performance of *Elijah* in Newbury, but she joined him in a party at the Ritchies in early December. Afterwards Lucy gave him a farewell supper in her flat at which, of course, singing was required.[36] McInnes left for Paris on 9 December and three days later sent an enthusiastic letter about his first lesson from 12 Rue Vernier. We know from the diaries that cards and letters followed every two days. None survives in the archives.

---

[34] Diaries, 8 January 1899.
[35] Diaries, 15 March 1899.
[36] Diaries, 7 December 1900. The 'farewell supper' at Lucy's flat seems to have been a private occasion.

Illustration 4.2   James Campbell McInnes rehearsing with Lucy Broadwood at
84 Carlisle Mansions, c. 1904

Source: Copyright of Surrey History Centre.

Summoned back to England on the death of his father in March, McInnes remained in Britain, performing regularly and maintaining contact with Lucy. They were together at the Westmoreland Festival in April, where McInnes introduced her to Samuel Coleridge Taylor, the composer of *Hiawatha*. Back in London, the musical parties continued, featuring McInnes and other guest performers. In July Lucy and Barbara began their usual summer peregrinations; McInnes went to Ireland, returning to join them in August at Beadnell, where Lucy and he practised Bach cantatas. Finally, Lucy and Barbara had a chance to visit Paris at McInnes's invitation in September, setting off on the 20th of the month. They were disappointed not to be met by him, as planned, but travelled on to their comfortable American-style hotel in the Champs Elysées. On the following day, a Saturday, they took in the Italian galleries of the Louvre and then met McInnes for a grand tour 'through many gay streets' of most of Paris's attractions; this was only the beginning of a whirlwind tour lasting 10 days. On Sunday they heard plainsong at St Gervais church and then walked the streets of the Marais quarter before climbing the Arc de Triomphe to enjoy a 'wonderful view'. They went to Versailles by tram and by the end of the day were satiated with palaces and gilding, though they met some Polish and Algerian ladies with whom they had dinner.[37] The high point must have been sitting in on a lesson with Professor Bouhy at his home in Rue Vernier; McInnes sang four 'old French opera arias' for Bouhy, whom Lucy found 'very serious and simple and kind'.[38]

McInnes returned to London in October, and he and Lucy began rehearsing Bach cantatas in preparation for a concert at the Ladies' Musical Club in Oxford where Lucy went to stay with her friends Edith and Mary Venables. The concert was evidently a success, and the two stayed on to visit other friends.[39] On their return to London, McInnes sang to Charles Lidgey's accompaniment at a People's Concert Society (PCS) concert, joining a distinguished cast of performers, including Leonard Borwick and the Wessely Quartet in a performance of the Schumann Piano Quartet Op. 44 and singing by Mrs Speyer Kufferath.[40] By December they were looking for an agent for McInnes, who was about to return to Paris for more lessons. Ethel Robinson, Lucy's old friend from the PCS who had now set up an agency, seemed to be an ideal candidate.[41] At the end of the year, Lucy wrote a merry little verse in her usual style to her 'singing friends', recorded in her 1901 diary:

In the year one-nine-nought-two
May both friends and voice prove true,
May they both improve and grow,
Notes & friends, both high & low.
May the faults of both each day
Lessen till they fade away.
Perfect Heart and perfect Art
Be the goal for which we start
And, as we jog along the course
(On auto-car, or legs, or horse)
May we rejoice that each good friend
Is aiming at the self-same end-
And with a cheerful nod & smile
May every one his next beguile.
These wishes, doggerel as you see,
In earnest come from
LEB

---

[37] Diaries, 25 September 1901.
[38] Diaries, 20–30 September 1901.
[39] Diaries, 5–10 November 1901.
[40] Diaries, 16 November 1901.
[41] Diaries, 24 December 1901.

Even more telling, though, is the printed passage pasted into the cover of the same diary, which might be the best indication of her own thoughts on McInnes:

> To be really understood, to say what she likes, to utter her innermost thoughts in her own way, to cast aside the traditional conventions that gall her and repress her, to have some one near her with whom she can be quite frank, and yet to know that not a syllable of what she says will be misinterpreted or mistaken, but rather *felt* just as she feels it all – how wonderfully sweet is this to every woman, and how few men are there who can give it to her! Who shall describe that wonderful gift of intimacy, that miracle in human intercourse, that rare blending of subtle intelligence, of exquisite tact, of wonderful sympathy? There are men who have it; and when a woman's acquaintance with such a man is only half an hour old, she will be telling him of things that she has never told to brother or sister or mother or husband or even to her nearest woman friend.

After Victoria

This excerpt appears in a diary in which McInnes features on almost every page. The years following the founding of the Folk-Song Society were full of concert activity, much of it inspired by McInnes. The death of Queen Victoria on 22 January 1901 was noted by Lucy, who had recorded the last illness of the monarch not only for personal reasons, but also because of her brother-in-law John Shearme's connection with her as her pastor. She continued to attend the sermons of Reverend Page Roberts at St Peter's church, Vere Street, and commented on his 'beautiful address' on the life and character of the queen. The congregation was 'extraordinarily moved', and there was a feeling of personal loss among those present. The afternoon service at St Paul's Cathedral was packed, and thousands were turned away as the bells rang muffled peals.[42] She watched the funeral from Bertha's Nursing Association office in Buckingham Palace Road, paying her 'for the benefit of the nurses'. Vast crowds watched quietly as the coffin, simple in its white pall, went by.[43]

Meanwhile she continued to enjoy a busy social and musical life in the capital, often performing herself. She joined Edith Clegg, Gertrude Sichel and McInnes in a musical party at her flat, at which McInnes sang some Purcell and Vaughan Williams played two of his Dorsetshire folksongs.[44] Drawing from her circle of friends, she hosted a party featuring McInnes and Lidgey and her friends Jeanne and Louise Douste, who sang the first act of Humperdinck's *Hansel und Gretel*.[45]

---

[42]   Diaries, 27 January 1901.

[43]   Diaries, 2 February 1901.

[44]   Diaries, 15 March 1901.

[45]   Diaries, 5 June 1901. The programme also included songs by Gluck, Beethoven, Brahms, Lidgey and Lehmann, plus one of Lucy's folksong arrangements.

There were almost too many concerts to choose from, but she frequented those by the Schumann/Brahms circle – Joachim, Davies, Borwick, Mühlfeld – while also taking in the young Ernő Dohnányi and Sapellnikoff. She met Joachim at a party at the Freshfields, where she met the rest of his quartet, who were joined by Leonard Borwick for a performance of the Brahms Piano Quintet. Soprano Marie Fillunger sang two Brahms songs.[46] She began to give McInnes German lessons, to help him with his many performances of Bach cantatas.[47]

The Broadwood Concerts

The Broadwood firm, now on firmer ground, gave a foretaste of its concert series with a 'Partners' Concert' at 33 Great Pulteney Street in June, with a jumble of 'everybody musical and unmusical there' to hear Donald Tovey, Marie Brema and other performers;[48] they would launch a more formal series of 12 'Broadwood Concerts' at St James's Hall in November, featuring Kreisler and Dohnányi.[49] Lucy disapproved, but to no avail: the series was the inspiration of the company's new director William Leslie, whose father was the musician and conductor Henry Leslie.[50] On the same evening McInnes was performing with Lidgey in Paris in the Philharmonic concert series and was 'rehabilitating Brahms' in that city.[51] An Indian event was given at the Imperial Institute, featuring 'strange and picturesque dresses', though there is no mention of music.[52]

There were also plenty of new, exciting composers to hear at the Royal College of Music: Stanford's first Irish Rhapsody was performed with Holst's *Scena* and Vaughan Williams's *Heroic Elegy*; a new star had appeared in Charles Wood, whose ballet music Lucy found 'admirably clever and fresh'.[53] Vaughan Williams sought her opinion of his 'Willow-Wood' and asked if it would be appropriate for performance at the Broadwood concerts.[54] Ethel Smyth's opera *Der Wald* was performed at Covent Garden.[55] Lucy's circle of friends was expanding to include literary and artistic figures as well as musicians, and the latest novelty was to

---

[46]   Diaries, 30 April 1901. Lucy had attended the first of the Joachim Quartet concert series in St James Hall on 25 April; the quartet played in the middle of the hall. She sat with Richmond Ritchie and his daughter Hester.

[47]   Diaries, 19 May 1901.

[48]   Diaries, 21 June 1902.

[49]   Diaries, 6 November 1902.

[50]   Diaries, 2 August 1902: 'Wrote to James and Harry most strongly against Mr. W. Leslie's concert plan.'

[51]   Diaries, 7 November 1902.

[52]   Diaries, 7 July 1902.

[53]   Diaries, 11 July 1902.

[54]   Diaries, 2 October 1902.

[55]   Diaries, 18 July 1902.

consult a soothsayer, Mrs Wilkins.[56] Her own musical parties were not only social occasions but musical salons, with performances from musicians ranging from her young protégés to established musicians, such as the pianist Fanny Davies; often they were teas with mostly women attending. Such musical events inspired others, who often invited Lucy to sing. These occasions provided a perfect platform for the publicity-shy Lucy, who still possessed a good voice and was an efficient and sympathetic accompanist.

McInnes the Protégé

Lucy was following McInnes's career in minute detail. The lessons with Bouhy had been a success, and those who had sponsored him noted the improvement with approval.[57] Paris was perhaps the most exotic trip, but in April 1901 McInnes had accompanied Lucy to Kendal in the Lake District, where she had been asked by Mary Wakefield to adjudicate for her festival; they enjoyed long walks together.[58] Wakefield had given up the direction of the festival the previous year, and Lucy noted a falling off in the number of competitors.[59] At the same festival, McInnes introduced her to Samuel Coleridge Taylor, whose 'Death of Minnehaha' (from his *Hiawatha*) was being performed with McInnes as baritone soloist. Lucy pronounced herself 'delighted' with both the composer and his work. McInnes also sang two of Lucy's songs. The two travelled back from Carnforth together on the train, standing in the corridor and talking throughout the journey back. McInnes stayed to dinner on the same evening.

McInnes and Lucy had much to share musically and personally. As he approached 30, McInnes was probably working through his own personal life: he was a country boy new to London and was heady with cosmopolitan life and his success within it. His powerful gravelly baritone was a draw for composers, and by 1901 he had found a companion and accompanist in the composer Charles Lidgey, who wrote a number of songs for him. Whether Lidgey was also his lover is moot, but it is possible that McInnes was discovering his bisexuality at this time. It seems unlikely that he would have discussed such a personal matter with Lucy, but clearly the two had a fairly frank relationship and through their many discussions – and the constant presence of Lidgey, who was also her friend – she might have guessed the truth. By 1902 the two were inseparable, though the relationship had taken on a cerebral tinge. For McInnes had discovered his inner philosopher, engaging Lucy in 'speculative and philosophical talk' for several

---

[56]   Diaries, 16 May 1902; Lucy felt she made 'excellent shots about my occupation, principal friends and letters etc.'. McInnes visited Wilkins on 16 September 1902.

[57]   Diaries, 15 March 1901.

[58]   Diaries, 17–18 April 1901.

[59]   Wakefield had stepped down as conductor in April 1900; see 'Miss Wakefield', *Musical Times*, 41 (August, 1900): 529.

hours after a rehearsal and forcing her (and presumably Barbara Craster) to listen as he read Royce's *Philosophy* out loud and left books on ethics for them to read.[60] Lidgey had supplanted Lucy as McInnes's accompanist and was also composing songs for him, including 'Roundelay' which evidently led to some dispute when Lucy heard it;[61] but the two still sang together, often at private parties.

Lucy began to dispense 'grandmotherly advice' to the evolving McInnes.[62] Her protégé was still refining his magnificent voice and had left Bouhy for another celebrated operatic baritone, Jean de Reszke. Ecstatic letters began to arrive, describing the lessons with de Reszke, though at times de Reszke did more singing than McInnes.[63] On his return to London in March, McInnes gave a concert at Bechstein Hall with the Swedish pianist Alfred Roth (who played solos) and Charles Lidgey, who accompanied McInnes in songs of his own composition. Clearly the lessons with de Reszke had had some effect, as one of the reviews commented on the 'curious huskiness' of McInnes's voice and its resemblance to that of the French singer.[64] On the next day, Lucy took McInnes and Roth round to the Broadwood showroom to introduce them to the revered Hipkins and to try some of the pianos, harpsichords and clavichords. Later they took Roth on a tour of the National Gallery, where he admired the Turners.

The presence of McInnes seems to have inspired Lucy to continue with her own singing, for the diaries of these years detail a constant round of parties ranging from the indifferent to the elegant. McInnes's career was on a steady rise, and he never ceased talking about it. In Paris he was engaged by the Philharmonic Concerts for a season, while in London he still went to Shakespeare, who told him that he could now rival the great Bispham.[65] His concerts with Charles Lidgey were a great success, as were his performances of Brahms. Not content with furthering just his own career, McInnes introduced his sister Margaret ('Maggie') to Lucy, who began teaching her singing; she also had French lessons with Barbara Craster. The rise in McInnes's career had benefits for Lucy, who still accompanied him in all styles of music, including a gala *café chantant* in Leeds and Huddersfield in May, though it was Lidgey who played for him a few weeks later in Paris.[66]

Altogether this was a time of jubilation. The Boer War had ended at the end of May 1901 (it had begun in October 1899), and Arthur Balfour took over from Lord Salisbury as prime minister in July. The nation had had time to recover from the death of Queen Victoria and celebrated the coronation of Edward VII – postponed from May owing to the monarch's appendicitis – on 9 August, 1902,

---

[60]   Diaries, 5, 9, 11 February 1902.
[61]   Diaries, 14 April 1901.
[62]   Diaries, 16 September 1902.
[63]   Diaries, 26 February 1902. De Reszke 'sang to him for nearly 2 hours'.
[64]   Diaries, 6 March 1902.
[65]   Diaries, 29 April 1902.
[66]   Diaries, 23 May 1902.

Lucy's forty-fourth birthday. On one of her usual summer jaunts, staying with the Crasters in Beadnell, Lucy (ever the royalist) roused the household with patriotic airs on the piano in the morning and received her own birthday presents from Barbara Craster, Bertha and McInnes, who had sent a book of extracts by Robert Louis Stevenson.[67]

The death of both her parents and her move to Carlisle Mansions in 1899, coinciding with the founding of the Folk-Song Society, had clearly given Lucy a new lease on life as she entered her forties. The mansion flat was perfect not only for Folk-Song Society committee meetings, but also for the musical parties she loved to host, and in turn she was invited to so many private parties that she could hardly choose between them. Invitations to perform at these parties were most welcome, especially if they included James Campbell McInnes. They also afforded opportunities for expanding her network of female friends, mostly musical. Of these Fanny Davies, who had gone beyond her reputation as a pupil of Clara Schumann to make her own career as a concert pianist, was a favourite: like Lucy, she was single and had a sense of humour which made her good value at parties as she had a wonderful ability to imitate various performers at the piano. The violinists Emily Shinner Liddell and Mary Venables, both pupils of Joachim, also remained firmly in her circle; the Oxford-based Venables remained a firm friend throughout her life and wrote a sensitive memoir of Broadwood after her death.[68] Liddell, who often invited Lucy to play with her, died prematurely at the age of 39 in 1901. A regular at the Crystal Palace and Pop Concerts, she had been a pupil of Joachim for five years and had led Charles Williams's orchestra for the Bermondsey Settlement; she was also the founder and first violin of the all-female Shinner Quartet, founded in 1887.[69] Her death was a severe blow to Lucy, who was about the same age and had also worked for Charles Williams in the settlement. Lucy's charity work continued, and she helped to celebrate the twenty-fifth anniversary of the People's Concert Society in 1903.[70]

A New Company

Leonard Bevan's premature death in 1901 signalled a new era with the registration of a new company, John Broadwood and Sons Limited, with a capital of £100,000 divided into 99,996 ordinary shares of £1 each and four managers' shares also of £1 each. James and Harry Broadwood were directors, along with the faithful George Rose. The money invested in the company by Lucy and her sisters Bertha and Amy, as well as Cuthbert Heath (who had shepherded the firm through

---

[67]   Diaries, 9 August 1902.
[68]   SHC, posthumous material, LEB 2297/6, February 1930.
[69]   Diaries, 18 July 1901.
[70]   Diaries, 23 May 1903.

its crisis), was recognized by the issue of first and second debentures.[71] There was much to think about as the firm moved from its old premises in Horseferry Road (where the lease had expired) to the new factory being built at Old Ford, Hackney. New production methods were introduced by George Rose, who favoured a production system. Dragged into the twentieth century and trying to compete with the efficient German and American firms, the Victorian heritage of the Broadwoods died hard, as electricity was introduced to drive the latest woodworking equipment and an internal telephone exchange was installed. The factory would employ some 500 men and produce 3,000 pianos per year. But the move was not popular among the men, who preferred the fashionable West End premises.

The first sign of the passing of an era came with the death of James Broadwood who, already in fragile health, had moved to Funchal, Madeira, to seek a drier climate. James had never been closely involved in the firm, but he was a director and carried the Broadwood name. It is ironic that the obituary that Lucy clipped out of *Truth* said more about the firm than about him.[72] Lucy heard the news of his death from her old neighbour Mrs Lee Steere and from the *Morning Post*. James had never remarried after the devastating death of Eve. There were three children – Joan, Audrey and the 13-year-old son, Evelyn – who were left in the care of Bertha. But it was the death of Hipkins on 3 June 1903 that truly marked the sealing of the Victorian era. Lucy noted his 'splendid service to Art and the Firm' during his 63 years' association. Anxious to preserve his memory, she initiated a fund to establish a plaque in St Margaret's Church, Westminster, in his memory.[73] Engraved by Laurens Alma-Tadema, the brass bore the following inscription:

In affectionate memory of Alfred James Hipkins FSA. Born in Westminster June 17 1826. Died June 3 1903.

The path of the Just is as the shining light

That shineth more and more

Unto the perfect clay

Erected by his Friends in grateful recognition of his lifelong services to the art and science of Music.[74]

---

[71]   Wainwright, *Broadwood*, p. 257.

[72]   Diaries, 29 January 1903.

[73]   Diaries, 20 February 1905.

[74]   SHC Letters 2185/LEB/1, nos 424–5. There are a number of grateful letters from Edith Hipkins as well; see nos 413 and 423.

Mrs Hipkins died shortly after, and Lucy maintained close contact with Edith and her brother John. Hipkins had been inextricably linked with the Broadwood premises in Great Pulteney Street and doubtless he would have been saddened to witness the move from this historic site where the firm had been established for 160 years. Lucy and Harry were asked to go through the business documents as the building was cleared. The new showroom in Conduit Street, formerly known as Limmers Hotel, was opened on 2 May 1904.

The Folk-Song Society

But what of the Folk-Song Society? The constant socializing and music-making had meant little time for the affairs of the fledgling group, which was beginning to lapse into obscurity after the initial flurry which accompanied its founding. Lucy was still arranging songs and composing her own in a similar style. She also began working with Ralph Vaughan Williams, to whom she was distantly related and who was a neighbour at Leith Hill, Dorking, on his folksong lectures and sang the illustrations,[75] but from the diaries it appears that any committee involvement was completely eclipsed by concerts, parties and James Campbell McInnes.

Such neglect was telling. The Society was struggling to survive and could not do so without strong leadership for its band of collectors. Kate Lee, who had begun the movement with such enthusiasm, had fallen desperately ill, and without her there seemed little motivation to continue. New members such as the singer Walter Ford were in touch, but Lucy appeared to be doing little collecting herself during these years. However, there was one correspondent she could not ignore. The Principal of the Hampstead Conservatoire wrote to her early in December 1903 and went to luncheon at Carlisle Mansions two days later. He brought with him a sheaf of 40 folksongs he had collected in Somerset. Here indeed was a collector who could not – and would not – be stopped. He was courteous but insistent. He was impatient with the dawdling of the Folk-Song Society, which he considered dilettantish, and wanted to kickstart it back into action. His name was Cecil Sharp.

---

[75]   Diaries, 17 November 1902.

Chapter 5
Contemporaries: Some Conclusions

It was time to revisit the Folk-Song Society. Kate Lee, who had been a motivational force in its founding and later its honorary secretary, was an enthusiastic and indefatigable collector, but had fallen ill in 1902 and had grown progressively worse. Surprisingly nobody had taken over her duties and the Society eventually ceased to meet at all. Kate Lee was in fact fatally ill with ovarian cancer,[1] but Lucy was uncharacteristically unsympathetic and privately thought that she was a hopeless hypochondriac and that the problem was mainly 'nerves'.[2] Nothing could have been further from the truth, and the relationship with Lee marks one of the very few instances in which Lucy was uncharitable, particularly towards another woman. She may have been envious of Lee's unbridled enthusiasm and energy in her collecting in contrast to her own reserve: it did not occur to Lucy to invite her own informants to be members of the Society, for instance, whereas Lee welcomed the Coppers aboard. Lucy may also have interpreted Lee's initiative in starting the society as poaching on her territory. The two had certain similarities; both were classically trained singers and came from affluent backgrounds. But the personality contrasts outweighed the professional similarities, and the pair remained acquaintances, not friends.

Still, something had to be done. Cecil Sharp, ever the self-publicist, had arranged to be interviewed by the *Morning Post*, and described his collecting in Somerset and Devon.[3] But this was only a benign prelude to a barrage of critical and damning letters which he unleashed in the succeeding weeks. He threw down the gauntlet in a letter of 25 January, calling the Folk-Song Society 'moribund' and ineffectual, having published only 100 songs over six years. In response, a committee of the Folk-Song Society, comprising Kate Lee, Fuller Maitland and Alfred Kalisch, protested that the Society was 'still in existence, that it has published four volumes of folksongs, that a fifth volume is in the press, and that further material is in the possession of the committee, which will always be glad to receive further contributions'.[4] But Sharp was right: the Society had not met since 13 December 1901, when it had held its third AGM at 8 Victoria Road, Kensington, the home of Kate Lee. The occasion had been a somewhat subdued affair owing to the recent suicide of Leonard Bevan and the deaths of

---

[1]   C.J. Bearman, 'Kate Lee and the Foundation of the Folk-Song Society', *Folk Music Journal*, 7/4 (1999): 627–43.

[2]   SHC, Diaries, 1 February 1904.

[3]   *Morning Post*, 18 January 1904.

[4]   Ibid., 23 January 1904.

Sir John Stainer and Andrew Tuer, but Lee managed to give a short paper and sing some folksongs with two other members; Beatrice MacPherson performed some traditional dances. The attendance was not impressive: Lucy was not there and, according to her diary, was not busy on that date – she wrote that she was 'writing invitations for tea' that she was going to hold on the 17th; Ernest Clarke chaired in place of the absent president; and the treasurer, who always had an excuse for tardiness, presented accounts not yet audited, though in his defence it should be mentioned that the late Leonard Bevan had been one of the auditors.[5] The *conversazione* held in June 1901, modelled on the more successful Folklorists' event, had attracted some 200 outsiders but only 12 members of the Society.[6]

Sharp had joined the Society in 1901[7] and was therefore in a position to know that the Society had not met for two years and was probably not actively encouraging collectors in the field or soliciting publications. Frank Kidson wrote a diplomatic reply to Sharp's diatribe, congratulating the younger collector on his 'rich harvest' and adding a word of caution about his approach. Collecting songs was not all that easy, and, unless one knew the repertoire of printed songs (which Kidson, of course, knew intimately), it would be difficult to distinguish authentic folksong from printed popular music. He countered Sharp's idea of involving county councils in the collection of songs: 'We associate them more with gas, water and sewage rather than with such delicate things as old country songs'. Music festivals, such as the one organized by Mary Wakefield in Westmoreland were surely better conduits, and Kidson had been impressed by the quality of the latest one, in which he had served as an adjudicator.[8] Lucy wrote in a similar vein on the difficulties of identifying old tunes and also complaining of the lack of funds available to publish the journal.[9]

Sharp would have no truck with this. The difference of approach was stark. Sharp wanted to scour the country immediately in order to collect and publish, whereas Kidson and Broadwood wanted to research and authenticate. Sharp had no patience with such a bookish and scholarly approach and by early February was admonishing the Society either 'to clean its slate, and begin again, or make way for a new and more efficient organisation'.[10] Lack of funds was no excuse: there had been no appeal for public support and no effort to popularize the movement. Great names were not always a good thing as they led busy lives and could not devote themselves to honorary work. Sharp felt that he could speak freely because he was a member of the Society. In fact, it was the collecting in Somerset that was the catalyst for the campaign, and his bullish approach would set the tone for all

---

[5]   VWML, Minutes of the Folk-Song Society (hereafter Minutes), Friday 13 December 1901.

[6]   Minutes, 18 March 1904.

[7]   Minutes, 22 May 1901.

[8]   *Morning Post*, 26 January 1904.

[9]   Ibid., 2 February 1904.

[10]   Ibid.

his future activities. The challenge was blunt: any members who would not wake up to the urgency of the task at hand should retire and leave others – like Sharp – to continue the work.

Sharp undoubtedly ruffled a few feathers among the genteel members of the Folk-Song Society, but he was supported by Ralph Vaughan Williams, who had also despaired of getting the Society to be more effectual. Both intensely practical, Sharp and Vaughan Williams became allies, and on 6 February Lucy went to dine with the Vaughan Williamses – and to meet Sharp again. There was little to discuss except the future of the Society and 'reviving its dying embers'.[11] Later the same month, Lucy went to stay in Oxford with her friends Edith and Mary Venables. In the evening, Hubert Parry (who was a vice-president of the Folk-Song Society) lectured on the influence of audiences on music. The singing of folksongs by Seth Hughes was merely a platform for Parry to launch into his usual diatribe on music-hall songs ('depraved, rumbustious abominations'), a repetition of his inaugural lecture to the Folk-Song Society. But at least folksong was being discussed again.[12]

As spring approached, Lucy resumed her weekly tea parties, which tended to be all-women events with as many as 65 ladies attending, including the composer and conductor Marian Arkwright, folklorist Charlotte Burne, Louise Douste and Emily Ritchie. The ubiquitous McInnes was in attendance, this time with his lover, Graham Peel. Was Lucy aware of the relationship? If she was, she didn't confide it to her diary, noting merely that she and McInnes had had a 'very especial talk'.[13] Evening parties were more elaborate affairs, with music beginning after 9 pm. McInnes sang with Lidgey, and Lucy, yet again battling a cold, performed in the Bach 'Peasant' cantata. Her friend Dorothy Fletcher played Corelli and Leclair on the violin. There was a brief nod to folksong when McInnes sang some Breton songs, but the rest of the programme was resolutely classical. The attentive guests included musicians, family and friends,[14] but it is noticeable from the guest lists that, with the exception of Vaughan Williams who might have been invited because of his family connection, Lucy kept her folk and art music lives quite separate. Cecil Sharp was never a guest at her parties; nor was Kate Lee.

Lucy was in fact taking over most of Kate Lee's duties as secretary. Two days after the evening party, a committee meeting of the Folk-Song Society was convened at the rooms of Sir Ernest Clarke (he had been knighted in 1898), then secretary of the Royal Agricultural Society, to discuss the Society's future.[15] It must have been

---

[11]   Diaries, 6 February 1904.

[12]   Diaries, 17 February 1904.

[13]   Diaries, 3 February 1904.

[14]   Diaries, 17 March 1904. The guests (only 40 instead of the anticipated 59) included the Mackails, Isobel Manisty, the Spring Rices, the Aubrey Birch Reynardsons, the Vaughan Williamses, Lady Farrer, Philip Webb, the Chatham Strodes, Mr Toynbee, Edith Sichel, Emily Ritchie, Eve and Thomas Gair Ashton, her sister Amy and Graham Peel.

[15]   Sir Ernest Clarke had served in local government and on the London Stock Exchange before joining the Royal Agricultural Society; he was also appointed First

a dismal meeting. Clarke was late, so Fuller Maitland chaired the meeting at which eight stalwarts were present, including the loyal Alice Gomme. The committee accepted the resignation of Kate Lee, who was unable to attend due to ill-health, with deep regret. Lee was still astute enough, though, to recommend in her letter that 'someone with more leisure than Mr Alfred Kalisch' should eventually serve as treasurer, though the hapless critic 'begged' to continue in this capacity until the Society was on its feet again. He also 'begged' to see the fifth volume of the journal through to publication. Kate Lee was offered sympathy and was thanked for her services and hard work. Lucy Broadwood was elected honorary secretary in her place, announcing that she would serve only *pro tem* 'in view of a better secretary than herself being later available'. Whether such a self-deprecatory remark reflected her true feeling or was simply said to put Kalisch (for whom she had little time) in his place is uncertain; she was not usually so self-effacing. Sharp was proposed for membership of the committee by Lucy, and was unanimously accepted; Kalisch was designated to be the person to invite him to accept. The subcommittee (comprising Clarke, Kalisch and Broadwood) met a week later and drafted a notice to members regarding the Society's 'apparent inactivity' since 1902, and remitting all subscriptions for the year 1903. Mrs Lee's illness was given as the reason for cessation of activity, though it is surprising that nobody had been willing to take over from her. Lucy's position as honorary secretary was confirmed, and it was hoped that the Society had 'entered on a new and enlarged field of activity'.[16]

There were certainly changes. Viscount Cobham, who had replaced Lord Herschell as president on the latter's death in 1899, now resigned the position. There was a balance of just under £20 – corroborating Lucy's observation that the Society was short of funds – but there were now 133 members, including the folklorist Marian Roalfe Cox, who was a neighbour of Lucy's in Carlisle Mansions (she lived at no. 80), Edward Elgar, Francis Jekyll (brother of Gertrude, whose interest remained solely in gardens), Susan Lushington, Herbert Birch Reynardson and Mary Wakefield. At a subsequent meeting in May, Lucy brought in some of her friends as new members: the music scholar Godfrey Arkwright, pianist Leonard Borwick, singer Walter Ford, Graham Peel and Ralph Vaughan Williams, among others. The next committee meeting was held on 16 June at Lucy's flat, with Fuller Maitland chairing. Cecil Sharp was present and put forward his collecting partner, Reverend Charles Marson, as a member. Lord (Hallam) Tennyson's name was suggested as a candidate for president, with Lord Farrer, Lord Beauchamp and Lord Montagu as other possibilities. Quite what any of these luminaries had to do with folk music was not pursued, though Lucy had been a friend of the Tennyson family.[17]

Lecturer on Agricultural History at the University of Cambridge from 1896 to 1899. See obituary, *Journal of the Royal Statistical Society*, 86/2 (March 1923): 277–9.

[16]   Minutes, 18 March 1904, in Lucy's hand.

[17]   'Annual Report', June 1904; Minutes, 18 March 1904. The annual reports were usually printed in the corresponding issue of the *Journal*.

The Society's links to the musical establishment could not have been clearer when the AGM was held in the Concert Room of the Royal Academy of Music on 24 June 1904. The full committee was there, comprising Parry, Stanford, Gibson, Gomme, Jacques, Fuller Maitland, Sharp, Kalisch and Broadwood. Mackenzie, who was then principal of the RAM, sent regrets as he had to attend student recitals. Lord Tennyson was elected president, and Alice Gomme, Alfred Graves, Walter Ford, Gilbert Webb and Vaughan Williams became committee members. Members attending included the folklorists Charlotte Burne and Marian Roalfe Cox. Lucy was introduced formally as honorary secretary, and a new auditor was appointed. Sharp was already making his presence felt and had found a useful ally in the young Vaughan Williams; together they made a proposal to 'recast' the name of the Society, calling it the British or English Folk-Song Society. They pointed out the difficulty of dealing 'with foreign contributions which may be sent' and might be 'untraceable'. This was a constant plea from Sharp and Vaughan Williams, though the Society continued to resist it and indeed appointed 'foreign' distinguished honorary members. In its Annual Report of June 1904, the Society reiterated and emphasized its objective, which was to focus on music handed down orally, and Frank Kidson offered his services in tracing the history of tunes. Those derived from printed sources would be sifted from the 'purely traditional'. Sharp's voice was surely behind the injunction to go out into the field immediately: 'No time must be lost, for every day carries off some old singer with whom some precious tunes may die for ever unrecorded'.

'Recording' the songs in this case meant publication. The *Journal* would resume publication, with Sharp as the principal contributor. Songs would be presented without accompaniments and would include short comments on the singers; 'excerpts from foreign folk music journals and matter bearing on the subject of folk song generally should be accepted and included when advisable'.[18] It seemed a good moment to revise the 'Hints to Collectors'.

But whose copyright would the material be? How would the contents of the *Journal* be protected? Could there be any copyright of 'traditional' material? Was it not in the public domain? It was resolved to seek a professional opinion from a QC, one J.E. Scrutton. Scrutton eventually gave the opinion that 'a person who takes down the music and words of country songs has a property in his song or report of such songs until it is published, and copyright in his report or version after he has published it'. Publication in the *Journal* would 'destroy the common law property and create statutory copyright'. In addition, 'this does not stop any other person from taking down the same song from country singers and publishing his report of it, but he must not … copy the version of another reporter'. The following form of words was suggested: 'All versions of songs and words published in this *Journal* are the copyright of the contributor supplying them, and

---

[18]   Minutes, 1 July 1904.

are printed in this journal on behalf of that contributor whose permission must be obtained for any reproduction thereof'.[19]

Plans were going ahead for the publication of 375 copies of the next issue of the *Journal*, no. 6.[20] By January 1905 a competitive quote from Barnicott and Pearce, a publisher in Taunton, came through at £31s 10d, some £25 less than the estimate from Spottiswoode. The Folk-Song Society at last appeared to be viable once more, though ironically its revival coincided with the death of Kate Lee, recorded in the minutes of the committee meeting held in October 1904. An obituary notice would be placed in the forthcoming issue of the *Journal*.

The Annual Report of the Folk-Song Society, presented at the AGM on 2 June 1905, held at the Royal Academy of Music, boasted the recruitment of 53 new members and 74 new subscriptions since the spring of 1904. The new members included some committed collectors, among them Ella Leather, who was reaping a rich harvest near her home in Weobly, Herefordshire, and a young Australian, Percy Grainger, who had been collecting in Lincolnshire. The *West Sussex Gazette* would offer prizes for the 'best old songs, words and tunes; published'. Much to everyone's relief, Alfred Kalisch resigned as treasurer (though he remained on the committee), and his post was assumed by the efficient Alice Gomme.[21] Due to the influx of new members and subscriptions – and the favourable terms from the publisher – 500 copies of the *Journal* would be printed.[22]

By December the whole issue of folksong in schools came to a head. For some time previously, Arthur Somervell, newly appointed music inspector of schools, had approached various members of the Society to suggest incorporating folksongs into schools, especially now that the New Education Code included this provision, outlined in *Suggestions for the Consideration of Teachers* (1905), a document known informally as 'the Blue Book'. While everyone approved of this idea in principle, nobody queried what these folksongs might be and who would teach them. At a meeting of the committee on 13 December 1905, and of the Society in January, the Society resolved to send a resolution to the Board of Education, expressing approval of the inclusion of folk – or traditional – song in schools.[23]

The letter, dated 2 February 1906, addressed to the Secretary of the Board of Education, Whitehall, was drafted by Ralph Vaughan Williams and signed by Hallam Tennyson as president. It reflected the Society's (or rather Vaughan Williams's and Sharp's) differentiation between traditional folksong and 'national' song traceable to a particular composer, pointing out that 'much confusion is apt to exist between these two classes of song'. The Society registered disappointment

---

[19] Minutes, letter from J.E. Scrutton QC, 5 August 1904. Presented at the committee meeting of 13 October 1904.

[20] Ibid., 17 November 1904.

[21] AGM Annual Report, 1905; printed in the FSS Minutes.

[22] Minutes, committee meeting, 19 October 1905.

[23] Minutes, meetings of 13 December 1905 and 25 January 1906; both held at 84 Carlisle Mansions.

that the Appendix had a disproportionate number of national songs and offered its assistance in finding suitable folksongs to fill the list.

A minion at the Board of Education returned a bland, bureaucratic reply, explaining that he had been 'directed to state' that the list was not meant to be exhaustive and that it was meant 'only to give instances of the type of songs which might suitably be taught in Elementary Schools'. He thanked the Folk-Song Society for its interest and would 'carefully consider' its suggestions and offers of assistance if it decided to revise or supplement the list of songs.[24]

Sharp immediately sprang into action, drafting a circular to be sent to every clergyman in the land, exhorting them to search in their parishes for old singers and collect their songs. The prose was wheedling and persuasive as he painted a picture of a rural society populated by older, illiterate people; the idealized folk who could deliver back to England a portion of her lost heritage if only they could be coaxed into giving it:

> The extraordinary beauty and individual character of the melodies actually taken down from the lips of uneducated country people conclusively prove that English folk-music is in no way inferior to that of other countries ... We believe that the district in which your parish lies is virtually untouched. The clergy have exceptional opportunities of winning the confidence of the older people who are likely to retain the 'old songs' in their memories ... They live in the minds of the older people, and must be sought with care and tact. [25]

Sharp was desperate to find more 'authentic' folksongs in order to fill the school curriculum and exhorted the clergymen to note down the songs 'exactly as they are sung' despite 'the curious musical intervals and the irregular rhythms', and offered the help of the Society to help in transcribing should they find this difficult. Ever the publicist, he had written to the *School Music Review* in June 1906, declaring that the Board of Education's list was inadequate as there was not 'a single genuine peasant-made folksong' in it.[26]

Somervell wrote a trenchant reply in the October issue of *School Music Review*, refuting Sharp's idea that the only authentic songs could come mystically from the soil: 'I think it is time to protest against the cheap cant which assumes that no-one belongs to the English "folk" unless he is at the plough-tail'.[27] Like many Folk-Song Society members though, he did distinguish between national and popular song, associating the latter, like Parry, with the 'sentimental trash' of the detested music hall. His criteria for inclusion were not always clear however, as older popular song was deemed to be acceptable, no matter how sentimental.

---

[24]   Minutes, meeting of 10 May 1906.

[25]   Minutes, 4 July 1906.

[26]   Gordon Cox, *A History of Musical Education in England, 1872–1928* (Aldershot: Scolar, 1993), pp. 139ff.

[27]   Ibid., p. 95.

Therefore Henry Bishop's 1852 classic, 'Home, Sweet Home' would remain on the list.

Never a member of the musical establishment and also not a collector of folksong, Somervell was not only a composer, but had also succeeded John Stainer as inspector of music for the Board of Education in 1901, becoming chief inspector in 1920. Stainer was only the third appointee to this position, the first being John Hullah in 1872. His appointment surprised many, not least William McNaught, who, as Stainer's assistant, had expected to gain the position. McNaught was evidently passed over because, though worthy, he had only elementary-school experience, and this was considered to be limiting.[28]

Somervell had taught at Haileybury and brought his compositional experience to bear on his strategy for music education of the time, which was imaginative and groundbreaking. Lucy, of course, already knew Somervell quite well and admired him as a teacher and composer, though, perceived as a maverick, he was not in the Vaughan Williams or Elgar circles. Somervell had an interest in folksong, but was not a collector. He took a broad view of education, considering the arts as a foundation for life. Unlike Sharp, he did not take a dogmatic view of folksong and chose instead to include well-known 'national' songs which had printed sources and named composers, but were also fully embedded in British culture. His choice was catholic, based on the German model, and he disagreed with Sharp's ideas on the origins of folksong.

Somervell had made his views known in 'Letters to the Editor' of the *School Music Review* (the editor happening to be the embittered McNaught), beginning in February 1903 and in the *Morning Post*, where he made a case for English song, based on both folk music and national tunes, using Germany as a model.[29] Like many of his contemporaries, Somervell yearned nostalgically for the Elizabethan past, a heritage which had been snuffed out by Cromwell and the Puritans. Always ready to denigrate music hall, he blamed the Puritans and their banning of music for this lamentable lapse of taste and pleaded for a repertoire that would include both Sharp's folksongs and well-known composed tunes already in the popular canon. He also disagreed with Sharp that the tunes should be only Anglo-Saxon and argued for the inclusion of Celtic music as well, something which Sharp deplored.[30] Indeed, Sharp had already published *A Book of British Song for Home and School* (1902) which had had a mixed reception; Somervell did not mince his words in a letter of October 1904 in which he claimed that this book had been 'the hardest blow that the movement has had' owing to the less than stellar quality of some of the songs. This was strong criticism indeed for the man who

---

[28]   Ibid., p. 8.

[29]   Gordon Cox, *Sir Arthur Somervell on Music Education: His Writings, Speeches and Letters* (Boydell and Brewer Inc., 2003), pp. 119, 124–9.

[30]   Ibid., p. 128.

considered himself the Pope of the movement.[31] Sharp must have been incensed
at Somervell's championing of Bishop's 'Home, Sweet Home' (which would have
been anathema to him) as the equal of his best folksongs. For Somervell, it was
indeed a national song and it was 'the nation' – or the majority – that he had in
mind in his educational quest.

Somervell stood his ground and won. Sharp remained recalcitrant and difficult
all through 1906, during which Lucy, Somervell and Vaughan Williams discussed
what to do with their colleague. At their behest, Tennyson (as president) wrote
to Sharp admonishing him to 'be moderate in the expression of [his] views' as
they did not reflect those of the Society at large, who had no wish to destroy the
teaching of national music at the start.[32] But Sharp would not desist and eventually
seemed to have brought Vaughan Williams over to his way of thinking.

At the AGM of the Folk-Song Society on 6 December 1906, by which time
the battle had become quite heated, a motion regarding the wording of the
statement published as part of the June 1906 Annual Report was put forward
by Vaughan Williams and seconded by Sharp. The first paragraph of the Annual
Report (as included in the minutes), and which Vaughan Williams and Sharp
wished to amend, gives cautious approval to the inclusion of both national songs
and folksongs in schools:

> During the past year a very important step has been taken by the Board of
> Education, who in their Blue-book of *Suggestions for the Consideration of
> Teachers*, 1905, have for the first time recorded the importance of our National
> and Folk Songs in the musical training of our children, and urge earnestly that
> such songs shall be taught throughout our country. This scheme if consistently
> carried out, must become a powerful means towards cultivating a healthy
> musical taste, and certainly claims the support of all who believe in the enormous
> influence exercised by Folk Music upon the composers of all nations.

It then went on to include dance, with reference to the Morris dancing undertaken
by the girls of the Esperance Club under the leadership of Mary Neal:

> That Folk Songs and Dances are eagerly assimilated by children has long been
> proved beyond dispute, and lately fresh proof has been given by the enthusiastic
> way in which classes of London girls, and others, have taken to the English
> traditional songs and dances taught to them, which they have executed with an
> excellence that has surprised even the most sanguine teacher.

---

[31]   Ibid., p. 121. The 'Pope' idea comes from Francis Toye, but Sharp appears to have
referred to himself this way, in jest. See Roy Judge, 'Mary Neal and the Esperance Morris',
Folk Music Journal, 5/ 5 (1989): 586, footnote 119.

[32]   Cox, *Somervell*, letter of 6 June 1906.

It ended with the usual exhortation to go out and collect 'at once', but this time with the phonograph. English collectors were technologically challenged compared to their contemporaries such as Bartók and Lineva. The Society advised the

> ... formation of song-collecting centres in country neighbourhoods for the purpose of organised work. *Such centres it is in the power of country members to create* ... And those people who own a phonograph can put it to no better use than by following the example of collectors in America, Hungary and Russia, and other countries who have freely used it for recording folk-music and dialect.[33]

The motion to amend the first paragraph was roundly defeated, with only five members voting in favour. Sharp took it badly, and there was 'a disagreeable scene'.[34] The meeting was seen as important and included an array of folksong enthusiasts and prominent musicians, plus people Lucy must have invited specially: among those present were Ernest Clarke (chair); W.P. Merrick, the blind collector; scholar and writer William Hadow; Lucy and her sister Amy; Alice Gomme; Vaughan Williams; George Gardiner (also a collector); Cecil Sharp and Mrs Sharp; Graham Peel; Stanford; Plunket Greene; William Leslie; Frederick Keel; Lucy's friend, the singer Isobel Manisty; Mrs Joachim Gibson; Barclay Squire; Edna Walter; J.S. Curwen; auditor T. Hawkin; the publisher Hugh Spottiswoode; Fuller Maitland and a new member, Elena [possibly Eleanor] Rathbone. The Society had gained enough notoriety through the press to attract a reporter, a Mr Graham.[35]

The paper which followed was of far more importance in the history of folksong than the debacle that had dominated and disrupted the meeting. A new member, Percy Grainger, presented the results of his collecting in Brigg, Lincolnshire, using the revolutionary new technology of the phonograph. This allowed him to take down songs in far more detail than previously, and in so doing he would forever change the standards of transcription. Sharp remained to be convinced about the value of recording with the phonograph and, though he admired Grainger's work, never used the technology himself.

Grainger's inspiration had in fact been not Sharp (with whom he continued to disagree on an amicable basis for many years to come), but Lucy herself. For in March 1905 she had given a paper for the Royal Musical Association on 'the Collecting of English Folksong' in which she discussed her collecting experiences over the previous decades; her presentation included a wealth of musical examples sung by herself and McInnes, with accompaniments played by

---

[33]   Minutes, printed annual report (June 1906, printed in the *Journal*, pp. 100–3) and circulated at the meeting of 6 December 1906, RAM.

[34]   Diaries, 6 December 1906. See also Minutes, 6 December 1906.

[35]   This may in fact have been John Graham, who wrote an obituary of Frank Kidson in the *Journal of the English Folk Dance Society*; see 'The Late Mr Frank Kidson', *Journal of the English Folk Dance Society*, I (1927): 48–51.

Charles Lidgey. In her paper, she outlined the history of broadside ballads and publishers such as Such and Catnach who printed the song texts which were then sung to music. The main point of her lecture was to emphasize the importance of oral transmission; the singers she had heard (unfortunately referred to as 'illiterate peasants') had sung tunes to seventeenth- and eighteenth-century texts. Here she outlines her activity:

> The versions of these songs vary astonishingly. Even the earliest are so corrupted, and have such gaps in the text, that they were obviously not only old, but *orally transmitted*, at the time of first printing. I have, indeed, been able to supply missing sense or rhymes to sixteenth and early seventeenth century broadsides, from twentieth century versions of my collecting.[36]

Lucy then went on to discuss the tunes, describing their origin as 'a mystery, and a beautiful one'. She explained that when hunting through printed songbooks of previous centuries, as she had done with Kidson, she had discovered that although folk-like tunes could be found, they were never exactly like the songs she had heard in the field. In this she was oddly like Sharp, who claimed a similar mystical origin for songs or, as Lucy put it, 'Spects they just grow'd'. She also quoted Vaughan Williams who got the following response from a shepherd when he asked about the music: 'If we can get hold of the *words* the God Almighty sends us the *tunes*'. Lucy then went on to explain the nature of the tunes – mostly diatonic, but some modal – and provided sung examples. She then described her collecting experiences in the field, drawing on Burstow and others. One wishes that these colourful accounts had been given in the *Journal* articles and in her books. Perhaps because of its personal nature – slightly reminiscent of Kate Lee's first presentation to the Folk-Song Society – the lecture was rapturously received by a large audience and reported in the *Musical Times* and *Musical Herald*.[37] Lucy herself felt tired and nervous, and found the room overly hot. It was a relief when it was all over. She had sung 10 of the illustrations herself, McInnes 'about eight'; both had sung the first verses unaccompanied before Lidgey came in on the piano, which worked very effectively. At dinner afterwards, Lucy gave both men gifts of books, and they in turn surprised her with the first volume of the new edition of Grove's *Dictionary of Music and Musicians*.[38] The paper was published in the Royal Musical Association's journal (*Proceedings of the Royal Musical Association*) for 1905, where it has remained a classic of early folksong scholarship.[39]

---

[36]   Lucy Broadwood, 'On the Collecting of English Folk Song', *Proceedings of the Royal Musical Association*, 31 (1904–05): 91.

[37]   Diaries, 1 April 1905.

[38]   Diaries, 14 March 1905.

[39]   Broadwood, 'On the Collecting of English Folk Song', pp. 89–106.

The paper was indeed scholarly but also personal, which appealed to the young Grainger. He promptly introduced himself to Lucy, who proceeded to take him under her wing. Unlike McInnes, Grainger was already an established performer who happened to be also intensely interested in folksong – and its transcription and transmission. Shortly after the lecture and visit to Lucy, Grainger set off for Brigg, Lincolnshire, where he was to conduct his choral piece, *March of the Men of Harlech.* The newly established festival at Brigg featured a competition for folksingers, much along the same lines as Mary Wakefield's festival in Westmoreland. Indeed, Wakefield had written to Grainger in March, recommending that he join Lucy as an adjudicator at Frome, Somerset.[40] Inspired by the singers he heard at the festival, Grainger wrote to his hostess (in Brigg), Lady Winefride Cary-Elwes, indicating his plan to return on 'a sort of byke tour thro' Lincolnsh, gathering tunes'.[41] He duly returned in the early autumn to collect a number of songs which he later arranged in various settings. Two notebooks containing texts and tunes collected in Brigg in April and September survive, and are held in the Grainger Museum, Melbourne. On this occasion Grainger went without a phonograph, much as Lucy had been doing, and took down the tunes by hand, assisted by Geoffrey Elwes, son of Lady Winefride and the singer Gervase Elwes who took down the texts. Grainger duly recorded the title, name of the singer and where the performance took place, occasionally giving their age or date of birth. Intrigued by the dialect, he also made notes of pronunciation, an aspect ignored by other collectors. He also took down variants of the tune as singers went through the verses, for example in 'Lord Lovell' as sung by Gouldthorpe.

Grainger did not restrict his activities to the Manor House, but used his 'byke' to visit Brigg Union and the local workhouse. Though many of the sources were men (Dean Robinson, George Gouldthorpe, Joseph Taylor), some were women, including a Mrs Wilkinson, who sang 'Mary at the Garden Gate'; Mrs Bowskill, who sang 'I Never Knew'; and Mrs Burton, a resident of the workhouse, who sang 'The Gipsy's Wedding Day'. In other instances, he marked the vowels, indicating their length or nasality, and 'burrs' – for example, the 'r' sound as in 'heard'.

Grainger collected with a fervour and intensity that must have been exhausting, especially as he seems to have taken some time to get to know the singers a little. His desire to note details of dialect plus variants from verse to verse made the adoption of a phonograph essential. On his return to London, he visited Lucy to show her his folksongs, and just over a week later she introduced him to the British Museum, no doubt with a view to showing him the scholarly side of folksong collecting.[42] The two remained close and were invited by Gervase Elwes

---

[40]   Grainger Museum, Letter from Mary Wakefield to Grainger, 17 March. The year, though not supplied, must be 1905, as the diaries indicate that Lucy adjudicated in Frome in May of that year.

[41]   See letter of 13 April 1905 in Kay Dreyfus, ed., *The Farthest North of Humanness*: *Letters of Percy Grainger, 1901–14* (South Melbourne: Macmillan, 1985), p. 45.

[42]   Diaries, 13 and 22 December 1905.

to adjudicate in Brigg the following April. Lucy went with Grainger to collect from '8 or 10 old men' and went to a concert featuring settings by Grainger of local folksongs, arranged for various combinations of chorus, band, vocal quartet and piano. Grainger had taken what he had heard in the field the previous year and transferred it to the concert stage, combining the 'fresh, clear Lincolnshire voices' of the locality with the professional ones of Elwes, Plunket Greene and Violetta Londa Clarke.[43] He brought a whole new approach to folksong arrangement, which Lucy had kept simple: his versions were arresting, pitting an adventurous piano accompaniment against faithfully transcribed melodies, complete with dialect and variants. Still enthused, he remained in Brigg to collect more songs after Lucy had returned to London and wrote ecstatically to her about the experience of using the phonograph to record the singers:

> I'm simply <u>scooping</u> in good tunes as fast as pen & phonograph can swallow. I find the phonograph a priceless way of working; I've filled 36 blanks (blank wax cylinders for recording) & have wired for 48 more. Balfour Gardiner passed through today & was so taken by the records that he is going to get to work with a phonograph at once. Got a gorgeous tune to 'The Rainbow' & a lovely version (called 'Lord Melbourne') of yr untouchable 'Duke of Marlboro' one. You'll like a lot of the tunes I think. I'm taking down all words, dialect & all, & will hectograph both words & tunes & send them you for the F.S.S. as soon as ever I can ... All the words you write of are here, & you shall have them alright, as soon as I leave here. I've got 'Free & easy' & shall get 'Jolly Ploughboy'. A goldmine is a new man, George Wray, of Barton on Humber. [44]

Wray was indeed a good find, but Grainger also collected from singers he had met the previous year, notably Taylor and Gouldthorpe. The phonograph made a dramatic difference to his collecting, the results of which were published in the *Journal of the Folk-Song Society*.[45] Meanwhile, Sharp was keeping an eye on his young colleague. In a letter of October 1906 he expressed interest in Grainger's use of the phonograph and encouraged him to publish some of the songs in a series he was editing, an offer which Grainger apparently turned down. The letter Sharp wrote on receiving Grainger's decision is revealing:

> I am sorry to hear yr decision about not publishing. I think the great mistake that collectors in the past have made is that they have been attracted solely by the scientific and archaeological nature of their find. That the songs possess this

---

[43]   Diaries, 28 April 1906.
[44]   SHC, Letters 2185/LEB/1 87, 28 July 1906.
[45]   Percy Grainger, 'Collecting with the Phonograph', *Journal of the Folk-Song Society*, 3/12 (1908–09): 147–242.

interest no one knows better than I, or appreciate more highly than I do myself.
At the same time folk-singing ... has an immediate appeal to living people.[46]

By 1908, when Grainger was preparing his article for publication, Sharp's
attitude towards the phonograph had hardened to the point where he found its use
both limited and also possibly misleading: 'I think there is another view of the
matter from yours!'[47]

His disapproval was mingled with admiration for Grainger's work, though not
without a certain bewilderment. Grainger was so wedded to the new technology
that he invited Sharp to critique his approach. Lucy, who was editing the journal,
disagreed with Sharp's dogmatic views (she, after all, had begun using the
phonograph by this time) and refused to do this, and indeed sidelined Sharp in
the article, writing to Grainger that he should omit Sharp's version of 'Three
Dukes'.[48]

Enthusiastic and admiring, Grainger was an example of someone who respected
Lucy's pioneering work and was finding ways to take it to new levels. Sharp's
innate conservatism and resistance to the use of the phonograph is surprising and
perhaps a reflection of some insecurity in the face of new competition. Lucy, on
the other hand, generously encouraged Grainger and even adopted some aspects
of his approach. Her paper at the Royal Musical Association had cemented her
reputation as an authority on English folksong, but Sharp loomed as a formidable
and prolific competitor all through 1906. The battle lines had been drawn. Should
she continue collecting in her own country, or should she move on to other
territory? Vaughan Williams had encouraged her to do for Scotland what she had
done for England, and, as she herself was Scottish, this seemed appropriate.[49]

The Gaelic songs that Graham Peel had brought back from Skye were
intriguing and, most importantly, this was an area that Sharp would likely never
touch. Percy Grainger the iconoclast was truly inspiring in his advocacy of the
phonograph – which was especially attractive as it did not appeal to Sharp. So
it was that halfway through 1906, during all the wrangling within the Folk-Song
Society, Lucy quietly resolved to resume her collecting. But it would not be in
England.

---

[46]   Grainger Museum, Melbourne, letter from Cecil Sharp to Grainger, 3 November
1906.

[47]   Ibid., 24 May 1908.

[48]   Grainger Museum, Melbourne, undated note from Broadwood to Grainger.

[49]   SHC, Letters, 2185/LEB/1, no. 96, 24 July 1902.

Chapter 6

Collecting in Scotland and Ireland

Cecil Sharp never gave a paper for the Royal Musical Association. The Association's invitation to Lucy to do so marked an important recognition of folksong scholarship as 'legitimate' in a society devoted mainly to art music and Lucy's enviable position as someone who could cross those boundaries. We have seen that the Folk-Song Society was dominated by the musical establishment and the worlds of folk and art music coalesced to some extent, but Sharp was never accepted into the mainstream. This might partly explain his crusading attitude and low tolerance for opposition from other members of the Folk-Song Society. Lucy had gained her credentials at first through her family connection and then through her career as a performer and friendships with Fuller Maitland and Barclay Squire. Her constant haunting of the British Museum, whether in search of old tunes or editing Purcell or Bach cantatas, gained her entry into the more rarefied atmosphere of musical scholarship. As a founder member and honorary secretary of the Folk-Song Society she was part of a circle of scholars, including Sharp, who had worked out a methodology for collecting and publishing folksong; indeed Sharp's views had been crucial in this context. But it was Lucy's work as editor of the *Journal* that afforded her the opportunity to establish scholarly criteria for their articles and to add her own notes to the work of others, including that of Sharp.

Lucy herself had moved from a reliance on correspondents to actively seeking out singers herself and noting their songs, often through the intervention of friends who could provide introductions and mediate in some way. The collecting was in almost all cases rural, though not always entirely successful, as she outlined in her paper. It seems a pity that some of the colourful descriptions she gave only rarely appeared in the scholarly pages of the *Journal* and in her published collections of tunes. Editing Sharp's material for the sixth number of the *Journal* took time as it involved corresponding with Sharp and others, and dealing with proofreading and publishers. Accompanied by Graham Peel and McInnes, she visited the ballad-sheet emporium of H. Such at 183 Union Street, Borough, securing a leather portfolio known as a 'bible' in which song pedlars stored their ballad sheets.[1]

Scottish Connections

Lucy's correspondence with other collectors widened, and in July 1904 she met a Miss Evelyn Benedict of Brooklyn, New York, who had collected Gaelic songs

---

[1]   SHC, Diaries, 18 June 1904.

on Cape Breton Island. The correspondence with Miss Benedict continued into March 1905, and eventually the two women met again to discuss Benedict's collecting in the Hebrides.[2] Graham Peel, who had long ago mastered the phonograph, was also an avid collector and had recorded some songs on Skye.[3] By 1906 Lucy was fully engaged with the thought of expanding her collecting in this area and in May she invited the folksong scholar Anne Geddes Gilchrist to lunch 'to talk folksong', and a letter correspondence ensued. Gilchrist had joined the Folk-Song Society in 1905 and, though not a Gaelic speaker, nevertheless knew a lot about Scottish folksong and was willing to share information.[4] Her enthusiasm leaps off the pages of her letters as she recounts her collecting adventures. She shared Lucy's scholarly bent and was keen to find a link between old psalter tunes and folksongs, assuming that the latter came from the former. She was clearly excited by her singers and was more than ready to accept new songs created by them, even if they did not have the aura of antiquity about them. She had been collecting in Penshurst in Kent, not far from Lucy, and the letter she wrote about them is worth quoting in part to catch its spirit:

> Dear Miss Broadwood, ... I got altogether about two dozen songs during my few days with my brother at Blackham (which is a hamlet only three or four miles distant from Penshurst – the home of the Sidneys), and could have obtained more if I had been able to wait for the return of a celebrated singer named 'Billy Wickham' whom Mr Cuck took to distant brickfields at the time where, for my purposes, he ought to have been working at one quite close to my brother's cottage! I hope to capture him next time, and also to get more from old Mr Gasson – who only got started off on his repertoire the evening before I left. My sister-in-law affected to be shocked at the callous way in which I calculated chances of longevity, and settled which of my singers would be most likely to 'die on me' – as the Irish say – before I could return!

She then went on to say she had had some books from Kidson and was working on psalters and finding some traditional sounding modal tunes in them: 'There are three tunes resembling "I sowed the seeds of love", "The Pretty Girl Milking her Cow" and "The Goose and the Gander"'.[5] Dean-Smith posits that she might

---

[2]   Diaries, 12 September 1905.

[3]   Diaries, 18 March 1905.

[4]   Diaries, 23 May 1905. For more on Gilchrist, see M. Dean-Smith, 'The Work of Anne Geddes Gilchrist, 1863–1954', *Proceedings of the Royal Musical Association*, 84 (1958): 43–53. See also Lyn A. Wolz, 'Resources in the Vaughan Williams Memorial Library: The Anne Geddes Gilchrist Collection', *Folk Music Journal*, 8/5 (2005): 619–40.

[5]   SHC, LEB/2185/1/no.236. Annie G. Gilchrist, Bazil Pt, Hesketh Park, Southport, 22 June 1906.

have studied at some time with Rockstro, as had Lucy, which would explain her preoccupation with modes.[6]

Gilchrist, alas, did not 'have the Gaelic', though she had some observations on the Scottish repertoire she knew from printed collections. She was also interested in mode and was developing a theory about them:

I have not much of value in the way of collections of Gaelic music, though I have in various M.S. books a good many Gaelic tunes copied from various sources. You will have Capt Fraser's collection? Could lend if not. Some of the airs are rather spoilt by elaboration, and in many cases one need not take any notice of the second part, which is often just the first part varied, or an octave higher – like so many Scotch tunes in the printed collections (Christie's for example); which, instead of proving the great range of the Scottish voice (as some people seem to imagine), merely shows, I think, that such tunes have been handed down in violin or other instrumental copies. ('Gloomy Winter's noo awa') is an example of what I mean. And the taste once acquired for a 'second strain' editors seem to have been quite ready to comply with it.[7]

Collecting Gaelic Song

Gilchrist's energy must have been an inspiration for Lucy, so it was not long before she determined to hear the songs for herself, and soon she was on her way to Glasgow en route for the Highlands, leaving Sharp and the Folk-Song Society battles far behind. She remained a week in Glasgow, staying with Frank Pryor, though the affairs of the Folk-Song Society were never far from her mind. She spent the first days writing careful letters to Tennyson and Somervell about Sharp and dealing with their replies.[8] A few days later, on 5 June, she was driven in a trap up to Lea Falls where she was met by her host, a Mr Caldwell of Morar House, who was to introduce her to local singers. Morar House would be her base for a week.

This seemed straightforward enough, but Lucy hadn't bargained for the difficulties of collecting in a language as idiosyncratic as Gaelic, or for the lack of English in the farming population. Caldwell introduced her to a Mrs McLellan, wife of a crofter and a local singer, whose peat-stacking activities clearly precluded an immediate song session; Lucy returned to Morar House for tea and did not revisit Mrs McLellan until three days later. Though Lucy collected a few songs from this 55-year-old native Gaelic speaker, she found her songs difficult to note due to her unfamiliarity with the language and the degree of ornamentation used.

[6] See M. Dean-Smith, 'The Work of Anne Geddes Gilchrist, 1863–1954', *Proceedings of the Royal Musical Association*, 84 (1958): 44.

[7] LEB/2185/1, no. 237 from Gilchrist, dated 25 June 1906.

[8] Diaries, 1 June 1906.

She wrote later that 'she sang beating time with her foot, and varied the ornaments, etc. with nearly every verse'.[9] She turned to a local gardener and former bailiff, Sandy Macdonald, who advised her to visit Ewan Maclean, a crofter and famous local singer and teller of tales. Ewan fitted the Folk-Song Society's notion of the perfect peasant exactly: unable to read or write English or Gaelic, he spoke only Gaelic, and had been a famous singer and teller of tales in his time. Though he sang 'delightful Gaelic laments' to Lucy, he had clearly lost his former prowess, and Lucy found his rendering of them impossible to note due to his age and frailty.[10]

Ewan's daughter Catrinian, or Kate, who spoke both English and Gaelic, and who knew her father's songs, proved to be a more productive source. Described by Lucy as a 'beautiful, poetical girl', though presumably aged about 30 or older, Kate sang 18 songs against the backdrop of a sunset-drenched hillside on the next day, bringing with her two printed words-only anthologies with her.[11] Lucy described her voice as 'exceedingly true', as was her whistle. Likewise, 'her rhythm was very good and she was admirable at stopping, and repeating'. Uneducated in theory, she had learnt the songs from her father, who in turn had learnt them from boatmen, crofters, weavers and bards.[12] On the next day Lucy travelled back to London, thrilled with her adventure. The Gaelic was not an insurmountable problem, but it took time to find a suitable transcriber as so few Gaelic speakers could also write the language. Through her friend Cecilia Bowman of Arisaig, Kate arranged to have the texts written down and translated by a local girl, Annie Gillies, who was training to be a teacher. They would then be sent down to Lucy in London.[13]

Though Lucy was a seasoned collector, this experience was like no other. Here she was collecting not from old men and women as she had done earlier, but from an intelligent and musical young woman to whom she could relate. Lucy sent Kate a bedcover and tablecloth, and Kate in turn searched out books from an Edinburgh bookseller, suggesting that she was taking an active interest in researching the song texts, many of which were to be found in the collection, *Sar-obair nam Bard Gaelach* published in 1841 and containing poetry by famous bards.[14] The published texts are nearly all matches with the printed versions, when these were available.

---

[9]   Two of Mrs McLellan's songs were printed in Lucy Broadwood, Frank Howes, A.G. Gilchrist and A. Martin Freeman, eds, 'Twenty Gaelic Songs', *Journal of the Folk-Song Society*, 8/35 (1931): 280–303. The name is spelt 'McClellan' in the diaries; I have adopted the spelling used in the published article.

[10]   Diaries, 10 June 1906. Lucy originally noted his age as 70, but later revised it to '79 or 80' when writing her article.

[11]   Ibid., 11 June 1906.

[12]   Broadwood *et al.*, 'Twenty Gaelic Songs', p. 280.

[13]   SHC, Letters 2185/LEB/1, no. 249 from Cecilia Bowman, 16 July 1906.

[14]   SHC, Letters LEB/2185/1, no. 242 from Kate Maclean, 29 June 1906. Kate was also familiar with another anthology, *An t−Oranaiche* (Glasgow: Sinclair, 1879). See Broadwood *et al.*, 'Twenty Gaelic Songs', p. 280.

Lucy returned home to the Folk-Song Society struggle but, enthused by her new discoveries, regaled her fellow members, including Sharp and Grainger, with her new songs.[15] Moreover, the latest edition of the *English Hymnal*, edited by Vaughan Williams, was published at about this time, and Lucy was delighted to see a number of folk tunes collected by herself and Vaughan Williams in the collection.[16]

Travels in Ireland

The Celtic theme was clearly attractive so, two months later, in August 1906, Lucy went on another collecting venture, this time to Camphire, in Ireland. An area lying between the rivers Blackwater and Bride, Camphire was home to Lucy's sister Edith and niece Mildred Dobbs, who became her aunt's main mediator. The area was rural, consisting of about 25 farmhouses, the nearest villages being Lismore and Cappoquin. Lucy's first encounter was with Michael Geary, aged about 70, whom her niece described as 'keeping a potato patch and a pig' and found his singing extraordinary in its rhapsodic quality, but almost impossible to notate. Like Kate Maclean before her, Michael's daughter, Bridget, took over and sang 16 songs over two days, including one, 'The Blackwater Side', of her own composition. The text mourns the loss of the local population to the cities and prophetically hopes for a revival of Ireland's fortunes through independence. Little could anyone have foreseen at what cost.[17]

A number of the songs first appeared in the *Journal* of 1907, with detailed comments on not just the music, but also the singers themselves and the folkloric information they provided. Lucy consulted several experts in her preparation of the songs for publication, including the poet and nationalist Douglas Hyde, the scholar P.W. Joyce, Rose Young and Margaret Clandillon. The songs themselves appeared with variants and ornamentation, with Bridget's song, 'The Blackwater Side', given pride of place. This was one of the few originally composed songs collected by Lucy, and she noted Geary's local reputation as both a singer and composer of songs.[18]

Return to Scotland

Lucy decided to return to Arisaig in July 1907, this time accompanied by her niece Barbara Craster and taking with her a phonograph to record the songs she heard. No doubt influenced by Grainger, she had conscripted Graham Peel to help her

---

[15] Diaries, 20 July 1906.

[16] Diaries, 21 July 1906.

[17] Diaries, 15 August 1906.

[18] *Journal of the Folk-Song Society*, 3/1 (1907), pp. 3–38. More songs appeared in vol. 5, pt 2 (1915).

with the new technology.[19] Again, she recorded the voice of Kate Maclean, who sang through the previous year's songs for checking, and then sang 24 new ones into the phonograph. The whole exercise took four days.[20]

The collecting in the Scottish Highlands prompted Lucy to revisit her lowland roots, and she accordingly visited her birthplace, Melrose, in late August,[21] taking the opportunity to visit her old friend, Isobel Manisty. On 3 September a friend of the Manistys, Mrs Cunningham, drove Lucy and Isobel to her farm and introduced them to John Potts, her bailiff. The area in the heart of Walter Scott country was romantic and a perfect setting for the four ballads sung by Potts. Lucy described Leithen Water as flowing 'between wild heather hills and join[ing] the Tweed at Innerleithen', not far from Melrose, her birthplace.[22] A man of about her own age, Potts sang a group of Border songs which he had learned from his grandmother, who was part gypsy, and his grandmother's nurse. Potts had taught himself music and played the pipes and fiddle. He both sang and fiddled his tunes for Lucy. Some of the song texts, notably 'Lucy's flittin'', were well known, with words by William Laidlaw.[23] The tunes were less readily identifiable, but Lucy had already found a knowledgeable source of song information in Gavin Greig, a notable musician and collector in his own right, who had a day job as a schoolmaster in New Deer, Aberdeenshire.

Gavin Greig

In 1902 Greig had been invited by the New Spalding Club, an Aberdeen historical publishing group interested in preserving the local heritage, to investigate folksong of the north-east and, with collaborator Reverend James Bruce Duncan, had already discovered that there was an undreamt-of wealth of song in the area. A kindly and enthusiastic man, Greig was more than ready to assist, providing copious notes on Potts's songs. These appeared in the *Journal* for 1914, by which time Greig had died, though Reverend Duncan provided additional information. The other tunes collected were 'The Lass o' Glenshee', 'Rob o' the Capper', 'The Dowie Dens o' Yarrow' and 'Willie drowned in Yarrow'.

Greig, whose collaboration with Duncan yielded a result far beyond the original expectations of one volume of folksong, was as committed to Scottish folksong as Lucy was to English. Something of his erudition and generous character shines out in the following letter of 29 November 1907:

---

[19]   Diaries, 27 June 1907. 'Graham Peel brought his phonograph and taught me its use'.

[20]   Diaries, 9–12 July 1907.

[21]   Diaries, 28 August 1907. Lucy visited the farm a few days later, on 3 September.

[22]   See *Journal of the Folk-Song Society*, 5/2 (1915) p. 104.

[23]   Ibid., p. 105. For more on Potts, see Katherine Campbell, 'Lucy Broadwood and John Potts: A Collecting Episode in the Scottish Borders', *Folk Music Journal*, 9/2 (2007): 219–25.

Your letters are always delightful. (Why can't men write letters?) ... I am so glad you like the tunes I sent you, and that you remark on what I have begun to observe – the close resemblance between your genuine folk-tunes and ours. There are alike because they are the <u>natural</u> utterance of <u>one</u> people. It is very kind of you to emphasize the value of the work we are doing, and to anticipate interesting results. Your prescience will stand amply justified by-and-by. We can speak freely because the significance of the movement with us lies not in the workers but in the situation, which is considerably different to the situation on your side of the Border. With you folk-song is something practically new, falling – in the main at least – to be simply added to the musical treasures of the country. Folksong in Scotland comes like a dispossessed heir to confront the usurper, and –'there's bound to be a row!' Scottish song, I think, had been all right up to the Union. Then outside influences began to tell on it; and by-and-by appeared the noble band – prig & poetaster, fool & fiddler – who were to overhaul the native minstrelsy and bring it in line with conventional standards. But 'the folk' remained true. They simply ignored the 'book' songs, and stuck to their own true minstrelsy; and now after the lapse of generations we have to go to them to find what the Scottish song really is. Truly <u>vox populi – vox Dei</u>, and now, armed with this revelation, we turn back to re-read the history of native song. It will take some unravelling; but when the work is done, as it will be in due course, the whole subject will stand revolutionized.[24]

Greig could not help pointing out that he, and not Duncan, was 'the original man to whom the N.S. Club committed the folksong work' and that although they were 'collaborating on an equal footing', this point of history should not be forgotten. 'But pray this is so small.'

On returning some Gaelic airs to Lucy he wrote how nice it was to feel 'in the circle' and commented on the dignity in Highland music: 'And what an extraordinary thing it is that all this body of melody should have been floating about unnoted & uncaptured while composers were cudgelling their jaded brains to evolve fresh thematic materials. What fools we have been!' He also commented on his own collecting exploits, writing a couple of days later in the same letter:

Yesterday evening in came a folk-singer with whom I had made an assignation for the <u>previous</u> night. I ... bagged 18 songs. He has been my best subject, his record running to <u>considerably</u> over a hundred songs, and I don't seem to have exhausted him by a long way. Further, he is only some 45 years of age.[25]

Greig did most of his collecting himself, not always trusting those who sent tunes into him. He concluded that using correspondents was usually all right

---

[24]   VWML, LEB file 7, no. 17, 19 November 1907, from The Schoolhouse, Whitehill, New Deer, Aberdeen.

[25]   VWML, LEB file 7, no.18, 26 December 1907.

for words, but not very reliable for tunes. Having had similar experience, Lucy probably agreed, though she always tended to check words against other sources.

Return to London

Back at home, Edward Clifford was seriously ill at the age of 62. Lucy went to visit him and saw that he was dying; she sought some consolation from McInnes and Lidgey in the evening.[26] The revered Joachim likewise was ill, and died in mid-August in Berlin. Lucy was working meanwhile on her Gaelic songs. Clifford died while she was still on her northern travels; she grieved the loss of her 'unique and delightful friend, wise and humorous' and attended his memorial service on 23 September, finding it intensely moving.[27] Though his death clearly affected her deeply, she quickly resumed work. There was editing to be done, and she returned home to work on the journal manuscript, which she dispatched to Cecil Sharp four days later.

Editing the journal was proving to be a heavier task than expected, especially when combined with the duties of honorary secretary, so at the committee meeting of 16 February 1908, held as usual in her flat, she expressed a wish to relinquish her post; she would, however, continue with the editing. The minutes recorded the following tribute:

> The committee of the Folk-Song Society cannot allow Miss Broadwood's tenure of office as Honorary Secretary to terminate, without placing on record their high sense of and grateful thanks for her devotion to the Society's interests during the four years that she has held with so much advantage to this Society the post that she has now, to the great regret of the Committee, decided to relinquish.[28]

Mrs Walter Ford was appointed in her place, and Lucy was elected as an ordinary member of the committee. Her name would appear in the list of honorary officials of the Society as 'Editor of the Journal'.[29]

There was writing of her own to do, too. Boosey invited her to write another book of folksongs which she accepted after negotiating the terms. Fifteen years had elapsed since the publication of *English County Songs*, and in that time the Leadenhall Press, the original publishers of *English County Songs*, had taken new directions. After Tuer's death, it had gone from being a niche art press to one that was decidedly commercial, dealing in commercial printing and 'circular addressing' as well as exploiting Tuer's invention of 'stickphast and fixol pastes'

---

[26]   Diaries, 29 July 1907.

[27]   Diaries, 19–23 September 1907.

[28]   VWML, Minutes of the Folk-Song Society (hereafter Minutes), 16 February 1908.

[29]   Minutes, 4 March 1908.

which eventually became its sole trademark.[30] The rights to *English County Songs* were taken over by Cramer in 1907. By 1906 *English County Songs* was selling at 6s a book, down from the more expensive 12s edition. A reduced-price popular edition at 3s was considered but rejected. Several of the songs had been published separately ('Twankydillo', 'The Crocodile', 'Young Henchard', 'The Golden Vanity', 'Turmut-hoeing', 'The Keys of Heaven' etc.), and had achieved some popularity.[31] It was probably time to reconnect with Boosey, who had published her earlier songs with some success. It would also give her a chance to resume composing accompaniments to the songs: these were copyright, while the tunes were not.

English Traditional Songs and Carols

English Traditional Songs and Carols was duly published by Boosey & Co. in September 1908 and comprised Lucy's collecting from 1893 to 1901, after the publication of *English County Songs*. The title, with its deliberate use of the term 'traditional songs' and omitting all mention of folksong, reflected Somervell's influence and the debates within the Folk-Song Society. The book focused on Sussex and Surrey tunes, and there was more information on the singers, as well as the usual references to sources, this time collected in an appendix. Lucy provided translucent, sensitive accompaniments to the songs, sometimes varying them for each verse. There was some bowdlerization of text, notably in 'Died of Love', where an awkward first verse referring to a baby (presumably born out of wedlock) was omitted. The songs were drawn from the Dunsfold singers, from whom she had collected in 1896 and 1898; Walter Searle of the Amberley singers; Mr Grantham, who had since died; the gypsy Goby family; Burstow; Joseph Taylor (who had also sung for Grainger); Mrs Hills of Lincolnshire; Mrs Jeffrey of North Devonshire, who had also since died; and Margaret Scott Thorburn of Cumberland. Lucy also acknowledged assistance from old friends such as Godfrey Arkwright, Charlotte Burne, Geraldine Carr, Sir Ernest Clarke, Frank Kidson and Charles Lidgey, among others.[32]

Frances Tolmie

There remained the task of putting the Arisaig songs together. Still concerned about the underlay and translation of the Gaelic texts, she turned to Winifred

---

[30] SHC, Publishers, 2185/LEB/3 no. 11, 15 September 1906. Leadenhall Press ended up as Fixol and Stickphast Ltd, with no publishing connection.

[31] Ibid.

[32] Lucy Broadwood (ed.), *English Traditional Songs and Carols* (London: Boosey & Co., 1908), p. xi. A list of songs and descriptive information is given in the Appendix.

Parker, a Highlander living in London, who was also a member of the Folk-Song Society. Parker, who had been educated in London, Paris and Dresden, was not a native speaker and had been learning Gaelic with Dr George Henderson in the summer of 1907 in Sutherland, and turned to him for suggestions of who might help. Henderson suggested Frances Tolmie, who had collected songs in Skye; Henderson knew of her collection through his position as lecturer in Celtic at Glasgow University.[33]

Tolmie was a collector and musician herself. Born in 1840 near Dunvegan into a Gaelic-speaking family involved in farming as tacksmen, Tolmie grew up in a bilingual environment and learned a number of songs from her mother, Margaret MacAskill, who had grown up in the Isle of Eigg. She was educated in Edinburgh, where she had some music tuition and also began to learn to read Gaelic. Armed with this background, she was able, on her return to Skye in 1858, to notate the words and music of local songs, which included lullabies, nursery, dance and labour songs (including waulking songs used to accompany the beating or fulling of woollen cloth), mostly drawn from older people who remembered them from the early years of the century, before the evangelical movement had suppressed Gaelic entirely. The singers were almost invariably women and the locations mostly on Skye, though there were also singers from elsewhere in the Hebrides. From 1905 to 1915 Tolmie lived in Edinburgh, returning to Dunvegan until her death in 1926.

Tolmie was willing to help with the Arisaig songs, but Henderson was keen to find a home for her song collection, for, uncertain what to do with it, he had been holding on to it for five years. A number of the *Journal of the Folk-Song Society* would be the perfect place to publish such a unique collection, and he urged Parker to 'set the matter a-going at once'.[34] Parker complied, and barely a week later Lucy wrote to Parker about the enthusiastic reception by the committee of the 'generous offer' of the collection, and suggested that it could go in the number after Grainger's – that is, in 1909. She closed, expressing the committee's pride in feeling 'that our Society has inspired confidence from unknown Gaels!'[35]

Meanwhile, in Edinburgh, Frances Tolmie was still looking at the Arisaig songs and making suggestions, though she registered her pleasure at having her own collection accepted for publication.[36] The correspondence between Lucy and Tolmie over the ensuing weeks concerned both collections. With a proposed publication date of 1909, there was not much time to lose, so Tolmie's collection began to take priority. The 1909 date turned out to be optimistic, particularly with Henderson's involvement, for he and Tolmie disagreed on some of the Gaelic spellings (not an unusual thing in Gaelic circles). The Annual Report for the Folk-Song Society 1908–09 recorded the progress of collecting Gaelic song 'partly

---

[33]   For details, see E. Bassin, *The Old Songs of Skye: Frances Tolmie and her Circle* (London: Routledge & Kegan Paul, 1977), pp. 84, 95.

[34]   Diaries, 29 February 1908; see also Bassin, *Old Songs*, p. 97.

[35]   Minutes, 4 March 1908.

[36]   Bassin, *Old Songs*, letters of 5 and 13 March 1908, pp. 98–100.

with the help of the phonograph', naming Lucy and Tolmie among the collectors, along with Farquhar MacRae and John MacLennan, who had also been collecting and singing songs; Grainger by this time was collecting in Australia and Polynesia, 'which may stimulate other Englishmen in different parts of the Empire to record native music'. The collection of folksong was becoming 'scientific', and the Society was expanding beyond England to become a more international, boasting links with Berlin, Finland and Switzerland.[37]

Songs of the Hebrides

Lucy had escaped Sharp, but another rival stepped in to take his place in the shape of Marjory Kennedy-Fraser, who had begun collecting songs in Eriskay in 1905 and was singing them in public concerts. The daughter of the Scottish singer David Kennedy and a year older than Lucy, she, too, had been given Frances Tolmie's name as a translator, though in the end she relied on the services of the Reverend Kenneth Macleod for her *Songs of the Hebrides*, the first volume of which was published by Boosey & Co. in 1908. Having met Tolmie in late 1908, about the same time as Lucy had made contact, she borrowed 23 of her tunes outright, adorning them with decorative and busy accompaniments, and giving them poetic titles like 'Eriskay Love Lilt' and 'Sea Tangle'. Kennedy-Fraser both performed and published these songs with piano accompaniments, the Gaelic texts and non-literal English translations which were fitted to the music. She herself had very little Gaelic. Both she and Macleod provided information on each of the songs, and identified the sources. However, her desire to popularize the songs could not have been further from what Lucy wished to do.

Lucy went to visit Frances Tolmie in Edinburgh in the autumn of 1909, when she met her sister and their Gaelic servant, Mary Ross. Tolmie sang some waulking songs and shared some Gaelic folklore; Lucy found the statuesque Tolmie 'intelligent and observant'.[38] Slightly before this time, Lucy had met the two Gaelic singers mentioned in the Folk-Song Society Annual Report, Farquhar MacRae and John MacLennan, in London, noting their tunes. MacRae invited her to a ceilidh and highland dance at the Inns of Court Hotel, Holborn, which featured pipes, informal Gaelic songs, recitations and reels.[39] As president of the Gaelic Society, he also invited her to their meetings.[40]

---

[37]   Minutes, FSS Annual Report, 1908–09. The Society now had 243 members, 19 of them new.

[38]   Diaries, 27 September 1909. Lucy calls her 'Merry' Ross.

[39]   Diaries, 10 June 1909.

[40]   Diaries, 20 October 1910.

'Songs of Occupation from the Western Isles'

Tolmie's collection, 'One Hundred and Five Songs of Occupation from the Western Isles of Scotland' was not published until December 1911, as no. 16 of the *Journal of the Folk-Song Society*, by which time Lucy had resigned as editor, though she had extended her term to finish Tolmie's magnum opus. Anne Geddes Gilchrist ended up contributing a substantial article on the scales or modes of the songs, developing her theory of modal overlay on five 'gapped' scales. She also provided annotations on the tunes and subject matter. Lucy mined information from Tolmie regarding the singers themselves, maintaining her usual detached scholarly objectivity in the matter, while Tolmie subsided into the realms of reminiscence and nostalgia. Gilchrist became ill in 1910, which delayed the publication, but by May 1911 there seemed to be a drive to complete and arrangements were made with the printers Robert Maclehose & Co. of Glasgow. Lucy wrote to Anne Gilchrist on 2 September, thanking her for her detailed work and exclaiming 'Oh! what a relief it will be to all parties when this Journal is out!'[41] Tolmie had travelled down to London to stay two nights in October to correct proofs, writing later to thank her hostess for her stay at the *Grianan*, or 'sunlit house'. She was both grateful and moved at finally seeing her 'domestic songs of joyous work of a bygone time' in print and sent Lucy a Macleod tartan scarf with an Edinburgh Luckenbooth pin.[42] This was followed by another letter, dated New Year's Eve 1911, in which she expressed heartfelt thanks to Lucy.[43]

The AGM of the Folk-Song Society held on 16 March 1912 was a significant, happy event which featured a recital of both Gaelic and English songs. Held in Steinway Hall, this was a gala occasion, featuring performances of unaccompanied Gaelic songs by Farquhar MacRae and John MacLennan, who sang excellently for about 40 minutes; both singers and songs were much admired. Lucy's arrangement of the beautiful song, 'Died of Love', which had been published in *English Traditional Songs and Carols*, was sung by Margaret Layton, who also sang arrangements by Ralph Vaughan Williams, Sharp and Holst; Clive Carey also sang.[44] The Annual Report of 1911–12 reported the addition of 101 new members of the Folk-Song Society, swelling the numbers to 358.[45]

But what of Lucy's songs? She had published the Waterford songs in 1908, but the Arisaig songs, with their linguistic difficulties, would have to wait. Gaelic song dominated the rest of her life, and she brought many friends round to the cause. Unlike Kennedy-Fraser, she decided not to popularize them by providing accompaniments; the editing of the Tolmie collection had probably brought her to the more scholarly conclusion that the songs should be published in the *Journal*

---

[41]   Bassin, *Old Songs*, p. 109.
[42]   Bassin, *Old Songs*, letter of 6 December 1911, p. 111.
[43]   Ibid., pp. 111–12.
[44]   Minutes, 16 March 1912.
[45]   Minutes, 23 January 1913. 'Many Scotsmen have joined'.

in the original Gaelic with some English translations and notes. It is a mark of the constant activity of her social life that the Arisaig songs were not published until after her death, and then not in the *Journal of the Folk-Song Society* but in the pages of its successor, the *Journal of the English Folk Dance and Song Society*, with notes by Tolmie, Gilchrist and the editor Frank Howes.[46]

Sharp, Neal and English Folk Dance

Cecil Sharp, meanwhile, had changed direction somewhat, though he remained firmly in the realm of English music. Had the Folk-Song Society become the *English* Folk-Song Society, there would have been no opportunity to publish the Tolmie collection in the *Journal*. In any case, Sharp was turning his interest to dance. He had encountered morris dancing for the first time in 1899 but, as we have seen, had gone on to collect folksong instead. As in folksong, Sharp was not the first in the field, but he very soon made it his objective to be the only one, eliminating all competition. The competition in this case was Mary Neal and her Esperance Club. At an informal 'conference' organized by the zealous social reformer Neal at the Goupil Gallery in November 1908, Sharp suddenly realized that he was being overshadowed by the supporters of the Esperance Club. His statement barely disguised his discomfiture:

> I have only one grievance against the Esperance Club and it is this: before Miss Neal called upon me, I was flourishing in the role of prophet – I was prophesying in the Daily Press and the columns of the Morning Post, as to what Folk Song could do, and I received the pleasure and the emoluments attached to that position; then the Esperance Club proved me correct, and ruined me as a prophet and I have had to retire. It annoys me that I did not pitch higher, because the Esperance Club has not only proved me correct but I might have added 30 or 40 percent.[47]

Sharp had no intention of retiring. The transcript goes on to record plans to introduce morris dancing systematically into the school curriculum. Sharp called for the popularization of the dance, and, after some input from the Inspector of Schools, a resolution was passed to form a society for the further development of the popular practice of English folk music in dance and song. A provisional committee of 12 men and women was struck. It did not include Sharp.

---

[46]   The Gaelic songs appeared in the last volume of *Journal of the Folk-Song Society*, 8 (1927–31) and in the *Journal of the English Folk Dance and Song Society*, 1 (1932–34): 42–51.

[47]   'Report of the Conference held at the Goupil Gallery, 14 November 1907', p. 3. Copy in Dean-Smith MSS, VWML.

Things were never the same again, and the relationship between Sharp and the Esperance Club deteriorated swiftly from that point. Having been defeated in the bitter dispute with the Folk-Song Society over the dissemination of folksong versus national song in schools, Sharp must have found it irresistable to compensate for that loss by taking educational control of folk dance. In fact, Sharp was elected to the committee after the conference, and advocated a constitution which would achieve his aims.[48] The committee eventually disbanded, finding it impossible to reach agreement. The ever-disgruntled Sharp went on to found the English Folk Dance Society in 1911. It did not include Mary Neal, whose fledgling movement had been destroyed by this time.[49]

Lucy first encountered the Club in November 1906, when it gave a performance of morris dances and folksongs at the Queen's Hall.[50] Thereafter she maintained some connection with Neal, while patiently dealing with the fulminations of Sharp, especially as they had to work together editing the *Journal*. Her diary indicates that he came to visit her on 8 December 1910 to talk about morris and sword dances, but there is disappointingly little more.

Lucy and Mary Neal

Sharp moved ahead quickly in the realm of folk dance. He disliked Mary Neal and railed against her in correspondence with Lucy.[51] Though not exactly kindred spirits – Mary Neal's indomitable spirit, drive and enthusiasm were reminiscent of Kate Lee – Lucy and Neal became friends, possibly because they had a common enemy in Sharp. Neither wanted to be involved in the militant wing of the suffragist movement, though Neal's previous partner in the setting up of the Esperance Club had been Emmeline Pethick (later Pethick-Lawrence), who left to take an active role in the militant Women's Political and Social Union (WPSU). Neal was a Fabian, while Lucy retained her membership in the Primrose League. Hugh MacIlwaine, Neal's previous musical director, had been succeeded by the musician Clive Carey, a gifted singer and collector, with whom Lucy had something in common. She certainly must have been aware of his intense musicality. Lucy continued to support Neal, Carey and the dancers, and attended their exhibition of

---

[48]   Margaret Dean-Smith MSS, VWML.

[49]   For more on Sharp and Neal, see Roy Judge, 'Mary Neal and the Esperance Morris', *Folk Music Journal*, 5/5 (1989): 545–91.

[50]   Diaries, 15 November 1906. Ella Leather had been to visit, and Amy went with Lucy to the performance.

[51]   Diaries, 21 March and 23 March 1908. Lucy records receiving 'indignant' letters from Sharp 'about the folly of the Esperance Club'. Lucy wrote back to Sharp on the 25th, the same day that she also received a note from Mary Neal.

dances and song at Earls Court.[52] Later, Neal collaborated with Kidson on *English Folk-Song and Dance*.[53]

Neal was just one of Lucy's female côterie of fellow enthusiasts and collectors. She also knew Mrs Ella Leather, who was collecting songs in Weobley and other parts of rural Herefordshire, and who published her findings in the *Journal*, no. 14 (1910). Stalwart friends such as Mary Venables remained, and Lucy often visited her and her companion Anne Thackeray, niece of the author and cousin to Annie Ritchie, in Oxford at their home, 'Larkbeare'. Lucy's parties began to take on more of a folksong tinge than before. But the friendship that really blossomed during this period was that with Fanny Davies, who spent the summer of 1910 in Switzerland with her.[54] Fanny had already been converted to the glories of Gaelic song and shared some of Lucy's other interests, often going with her to various lectures.

The Marriage of McInnes

The 'passionate friendship' with McInnes became less intense as he settled into a relationship with Graham Peel, though the singer still used Lucy as a confidante. The two men moved into a new house in early 1911, and Lucy and Barbara were invited to a celebratory inaugural tea on 7 February.[55] However, it seems that as his career progressed, he felt a need to conform to convention and marry. Given the close relationship with Lucy, it seems likely that he confided some of his dilemma to her, and it is possible that she had some understanding of it herself for she, too, had close friendships with women, such as Davies.[56] Owing to Lucy's support and mentoring, McInnes, with his magnificent voice, was now a popular performer in the genteel drawing rooms of Edwardian society. Not surprisingly, many of his circles were the same ones in which Lucy moved, and this included the Mackails. Marrying into such a family would no doubt be advantageous to his career.

Margaret Mackail was the granddaughter of a Methodist minister, George Macdonald, and the daughter of Georgiana and Edward Burne-Jones.[57] The family was well connected through that quarter and also through Jack Mackail, a senior civil servant, but also an academic and poet. Lucy knew the family well and could well have introduced McInnes to Angela, their oldest daughter, an attractive,

---

[52]   Diaries, 16 May 1912.

[53]   Cambridge: Cambridge University Press, 1915.

[54]   Diaries, 27 September–4 October 1910.

[55]   Diaries, 7 February 1911.

[56]   For more on Davies and her relationships, see D. de Val, '"A Messenger for Schumann and Brahms"? Re-evaluating Fanny Davies', in T. Ellsworth and S. Wollenberg (eds), *The Piano in Nineteenth-Century British Culture* (Aldershot: Ashgate, 2007), pp. 217–38.

[57]   For more information on the Macdonald sisters, see Judith Flanders, *A Circle of Sisters* (London and New York: Macmillan, 2005).

strong-willed young woman. McInnes thereupon began a whirlwind relationship with the young and impressionable Angela. By April he had proposed to her, and their engagement was publicly announced on 20 April, 11 days after McInnes had told Lucy his news over tea at her flat. Lucy went to have a 'long talk' with Angela's mother on the day after McInnes told her, and heard from Angela herself on the 15th. On the day she was 'allowed to announce her engagement', Angela visited in the morning, and stayed to luncheon. There are no letters surviving from this time, but we can assume that the engagement caused a certain amount of angst for Lucy − not to mention Graham Peel.[58]

It was probably also not so welcomed by the Mackails, who saw to it that the announcement contained no mention of McInnes's parents, as his father, an engraver, had been an alcoholic.[59] The marriage took place on 5 May 1911 in a quiet ceremony at St Philip's Church, Kensington. Lucy did not attend, though she must have been invited. She stayed home instead, poignantly playing Bach cantatas to herself and watching the clock between 9:30 and 10 am while the marriage was taking place. Afterwards she went to Woolwich to hear band arrangements of folksong, possibly to drive out any lingering thoughts of McInnes. The following day her niece Marion Broadwood, one of Harry's daughters, was married to her cousin, Michael Holland, and two separate letters − one from McInnes, the other from Angela − arrived from Sidmouth.[60] Oddly enough, they had been staying at the Knowle Hotel, which Lucy had dreamt about eight years previously.[61] Their first child, Graham (named after Peel), was born on 18 February 1912.

The End of an Era

The first few months of 1911 must have been difficult for Lucy, as her brother Harry had died in February at only 54 years of age. Lucy had had a premonitory dream about this in which she had visualized a funeral procession. The funeral itself was held at Rusper on 11 February; Ada was not present, but the two sons and daughter Marion were there.[62] Lucy returned home to find flowers from the servants and from Fanny Davies. Harry had coped with the increasingly difficult job of running a firm still run on Victorian principles and which was falling behind

[58]   The words in quotations are Lucy's from her diary entry for 20 April. The entry for 9 April, when McInnes told Lucy the news, is marked out with an emphasis. Lucy went the next day to talk to Mrs Mackail, and on the 20th invited Angela to luncheon.

[59]   Flanders, *A Circle of Sisters*, p. 323. It is not clear whether Mackail disapproved of the occupation or the disposition − possibly both.

[60]   Diaries, 5−6 May 1911.

[61]   Diaries, 8 February 1903. Lucy called it a 'telepathic dream'. She often recorded such events in her diaries as evidence of her psychic abilities.

[62]   Diaries, 6 January, 9 and 11 February 1911. This is another example of a premonitory dream recorded by Lucy.

the technological advances in the industry. Given his early death, it is small wonder that neither of his sons – Stewart and Leopold – wished to join the firm, though Stewart became a sub-manager upon his father's death. Bertha had finally been elected a director in 1910.[63]

Life was changing as England moved out of the Edwardian period into the tense period just preceding the war. The death of Edward VII and accession of George V had been accompanied by political instability as the Liberals under Asquith clung to power and eventually established the pre-eminence of the House of Commons in the face of a Conservative-dominated House of Lords; Lucy, still a member of the Primrose League, kept track of both elections in 1910. The following year she had faced the premature death of her second brother and the loss of various friends, either through death or unexpected marriage. Even her own household was breaking up: three days after the triumphant concert of Gaelic song at the AGM of the Folk-Song Society in 1912, her two loyal servants, Lily and Elizabeth Bendall, left her service after 12 years. The comment in her diary at this time that she was 'too tired to go to Mrs Henry Gladstone's party to meet Princess Louise of Schleswig Holstein' is revealing: the era of genteel music-making in Edwardian salons was drawing to a close.[64]

[63]   David Wainwright, *Broadwood by Appointment* (London: Quiller Press, 1982), p. 276.

[64]   Diaries, 19 March 1912.

Chapter 7

The War Years

Relieved of the editorship of the *Journal* – at least temporarily – after the publication of the Tolmie volume, Lucy was free to pursue her interests in areas outside Gaelic song, though it remained a dominant part of her life.[1] The pursuit of English folksong of course continued, and in September 1912 she travelled to Plymouth where she stayed with Bertram and Margaret Craster, using their home, Compton Lodge, as a base from which to visit the Baring-Goulds at Lew Trenchard for the first time in 18 years.[2] She then moved on to Exeter, staying with the Wyatt-Edgells, with whom Charlotte Burne was staying.[3] Lucy collected songs from various local people, later hiring a phonograph for the purpose. Even with her gift for languages, it seems that Lucy did not learn Scots Gaelic, so she conscripted Farquhar MacRae and John MacLennan, both Gaelic speakers who had helped her in her collecting, to go through her collection in preparation for a concert given for the 1912 AGM of the Folk-Song Society in March. She kept up her network of collectors in the field, maintaining a correspondence with Janet Blunt and various others.

Female Networking

By the close of the Edwardian era, Lucy's network of friends was dominated by single, independent women. As she reached her fifties, such ties became important, for life as a single woman was not easy. Though she was comfortably ensconced in Carlisle Mansions, her income was not large, especially given the financial difficulties of the family firm. Her work for the Folk-Song Society was unpaid and she did not take on piano or voice pupils. Her niece and cohabitant, Barbara Craster, helped with indexing the *Journal* but, like her aunt Bertha, was increasingly involved in nursing, and had joined the Red Cross; she was to pass its formal exams in March 1913.[4] Family was still important, and Lucy occasionally

---

[1]   VWML, Minutes of the Folk-Song Society (hereafter Minutes), Annual Report, 1910. Lucy was still editing the Tolmie volume at this time. Her successor was Frederick Keel.

[2]   Diaries, 27 September 1912.

[3]   The violinist Lucy Wyatt-Edgell (1878–1934) was from a Devon family. Interested in folk dance, she was also a friend of Sharp. See Fox-Strangway's idiosyncratic obituary, *Journal of the English Folk Dance and Song Society*, 3/1 (1936): 79.

[4]   Diaries, 12 March 1913.

saw sisters Amy and Bertha for short visits. Fanny Davies and the Sichel sisters, Edith and Gertrude, remained staunch friends, and the friendship with fellow folksong scholar Anne Gilchrist deepened.

The era before the First World War was marked by the increased activities of the women's suffrage movement. Many of Lucy's women friends had become involved with various factions of the movement; indeed, at this time it was impossible to remain unaware of it. We have seen that one of these was Mary Neal, who had connections with the suffrage movement through her former Esperance partner, Emmeline Pethick (later Pethick-Lawrence upon her marriage in 1901), though she did not formally join it. Lucy was supportive of Neal's approach to folk dance, if only because of Sharp's bullying, and attended a gala in May, joining Neal and Clive Carey, who succeeded Hugh MacIlwaine, who had joined forces with Sharp, as her music director. The young Carey (he was in his late twenties at this time) was a classically trained singer who, like McInnes, had studied with de Reszke in Paris, and had been educated at Cambridge and the Royal College of Music. Lucy had met him in October 1911, after he had collected some Surrey folksongs with Dorothy Marshall; he was also a composer and, like Lucy, still involved in the art music scene.[5] The connection continued into 1912, when Lucy took her sister Evelyn Forsyth to the May Day celebrations at the Globe Theatre. Altogether a bigger event, this occasion featured Neal and Carey's Esperance girls, plus dances arranged by Nellie Chaplin who, with her sisters Kate and Mabel, were reviving historical courtly and country dance. The sisters were all musical and played various instruments: Nellie on harpsichord, Mabel on cello/gamba and Kate on violin/viola d'amore.[6] All this was topped off with some 'real morris-dancers from Bampton in the Bush'.[7] Somewhat later, Lucy commiserated with Neal over a poor review of her book co-authored with Kidson, *English Folk-Song and Dance*.[8]

Still interested in family matters, she spent the summer visiting various old friends and relations before leaving for healthy walks and genealogical research in Switzerland. On her return to London she was saddened to hear that Richmond Ritchie had fallen ill with toxaemia and septic pneumonia after years of overwork in the India Office, and had been admitted to a nursing home in the summer. She went to visit Annie at home two days before his death on 11 October 1912, but did not attend the funeral.[9]

---

[5]   Diaries, 16 May 1912. The earlier meeting had taken place on 6 October 1911. Notes from his collecting at Thaxted are in VWML, LEB file 5, nos 106–12.

[6]   For more on the Chaplin sisters see M. Duncan, 'Miss Nellie Chaplin's Renewal of Ancient Dances and Music', *Cremona, the Magazine of Music*, 5/61 (1911): 129; and E. Minshall, 'The Chaplin Trio', *The Musical Journal*, 23:271 (1910): 152–3.

[7]   Diaries, 1 May 1913.

[8]   The offending review appeared in the *Musical Times*, 2 November 1915, and was written by Phillips Barker, a friend of Sharp's. Lucy wrote to protest.

[9]   Diaries, 11 October 1912.

Musical Life

Vaughan Williams was gaining a reputation as one of England's leading composers, and in February Lucy, Mary Venables and Barbara Craster were invited by Herbert Birch Reynardson to hear the premiere of the *Sea Symphony*. McInnes was one of the soloists and was enjoying a successful career; he had already performed Vaughan Williams's arrangement of Purcell's 'Evening Hymn' at a Promenade concert in the Queen's Hall.[10] In 1913 Harry Plunket Greene was still active on the folksong scene, and Lucy attended his lecture on Irish folksong (mostly of the drawing room variety by Stanford, Wood, Harty and others) at the AGM of the Folk-Song Society at Steinway Hall in February. Dorothea Webb sang some of Lucy's arrangements of English folksongs, plus others collected by Sharp, Kidson and Gardiner. For Lucy, the London concert scene had rarely been so exciting, as in the same month she attended performances of Stravinsky's *The Firebird* danced by the Russian ballet.[11]

With McInnes apparently successfully launched in his career in this heady pre-war period, Lucy needed another protégé to entertain her guests at her musical parties. None could be better than the brilliant young Brazilian pianist Guiomar Novaës, who had made her London debut in 1910 and was returning to the capital in 1913. A week after her concert on 6 May, Lucy invited her to tea with her agent Lesley McIntyre with a view to arranging a programme for the next party. On 23 May 1913 a party of 49 people gathered to hear Novaës play a programme of Bach, Liszt, Chopin, Schumann's *Kinderszenen* and a piece by her teacher, Isidor Philipp. As usual, Lucy tended to keep her life compartmentalized, and there were no folksong colleagues present.[12]

The Quest Society

Though Lucy continued to be active in the Folk-Song Society at this time – indeed, they could not do without her – she continued to pursue her interest in folklore and music of other cultures, spreading her wings beyond the British Isles. The Folklore Society had fulfilled this need, but eventually the Quest Society proved to be a more satisfying forum. Already familiar with James Frazer and *The Golden Bough*, Lucy was fortified with contemporary theory and eager to explore further. Founded in 1909 by George Mead as an offshoot of the Theosophical Society, itself beset by factionalist politics, The Quest Society became a forum for Mead 'to promote investigation and comparative study of religion, philosophy and

---

[10]   Diaries, 11 October 1912.

[11]   Diaries, 24 February 1913.

[12]   Diaries, 23 May 1913. Among the guests were Eva Ashton, the Farrers, Louise Douste de Fortis, the Henschels, Benton Fletcher, Norman O'Neill, William Shakespeare and various Spring Rices.

science, on the basis of experience' and had an associated journal.[13] Mead, with his interests in early Christianity, Gnosticism, Rosicrucianism and mysticism, proved to be a kindred spirit for Lucy, who was keen to explore spiritual matters. She had always been interested in religion and, living in the shadow of Westminster Cathedral, could not really escape it. The Quest Society encouraged scholarly discussion of philosophical topics as well as music, and featured such high-profile speakers as Rabindranath Tagore.[14] In due course Lucy reviewed a book of Indian folksongs for the Quest Society journal. Mead and his wife Laura (née Cooper) became close friends and were always invited to social events at Carlisle Mansions. At Christmas 1913 they were her guests along with Mrs Bram Stoker and William Toynbee. She also befriended Jessie Weston, an authority on the Holy Grail, and was influenced by her work. The Quest Society was not without its excitement: in a meeting in December 1913 at which Lord Haldane was a speaker, a militant suffragist with a male companion got in, and a scuffle ensued. It was none other than Lucy who forced the woman down and pinned her hands behind her, before she and her companion were dragged out. Lord Haldane continued his Hegelian theme.[15]

The Grinding Organ

By the beginning of 1914 Lucy had consolidated her group of friends and her reputation as an editor and adjudicator. Still wanting to compose – or at least arrange – music, she jumped at an opportunity offered by Mary Venables to write some incidental music for *The Grinding Organ* by the eighteenth-century feminist and writer Maria Edgworth. The performance, given at Taphouse's Music Room in Oxford, was in aid of the Oxford branch of the National Union of Women's Suffrage Societies; a note added in parentheses clarified that they were the 'law-abiding' section. It is not clear exactly what Lucy composed for this, but it probably involved arrangements of contemporary traditional tunes.[16] Given the title, it is not surprising that the music involved a harmonium and a barrel organ.

---

[13]   R.A. Gilbert, 'Mead, George Robert Stow (1863–1933)', *Oxford Dictionary of National Biography* (Oxford: Oxford University Press, 2004) at: http://www.oxforddnb. com.ezproxy.library.yorku.ca/view/article/53879 (accessed February 2008).

[14]   Diaries, 19 June 1913.

[15]   Diaries, 18 December 1913.

[16]   Diaries, 22 January 1914.

Folksong Matters

Lucy continued to go to meetings of the Folk-Song Society, whose membership was buoyant after the publication of Gaelic songs.[17] She was an active committee member, making suggestions about the future publication of the *Journal*, and ways of increasing membership. In March she read a paper on sea shanties for the indisposed Anne Gilchrist, who had been working on the subject for some time. Musical examples were sung by Margaret Layton and Clive Carey.[18] She also had her own musical publications to think about: new legislation regarding mechanical reproduction had come into effect on 1 July 1912. The proliferation of piano rolls, gramophones and other mechanical means of reproducing music soon raised questions about copyright and remuneration for the author: the situation was somewhat similar to the 'royalty ballad' system instituted by Boosey, and, indeed, Boosey was at the forefront of the performing right movement.[19] Cramer wrote to Lucy somewhat tardily, asking if she would authorize them, as her publishers, to look after these fees, under an arrangement where they would take a percentage of a third, if divided between author, composer and publisher, or a half if divided between composer and publisher only. As it was a form letter, there was no mention of 'singer' or arranger.[20] They reached an arrangement shortly after, by which she would receive two-thirds (as author and composer) for recordings of the most popular songs from *English County Songs*, which were 'The Keys of Heaven', 'Twankydillo' and 'Robin-a-Thrush'; by April 1915 she had accrued royalties of the princely sum of £6 11s ½d.[21] Cramer took four years to reply to Lucy's repeated requests for information on the companies recording the songs, which were the Gramophone Co. (for 'Keys' and 'The Crocodile', and Columbia (for 'Sally Gray', 'Twankydillo' and 'Robin-a-Thrush').[22]

The Gathering Storm

Frederick Keel and Clive Carey had collected some material for No. 19 of the *Journal*, which Lucy would edit. Unfortunately Keel and his family made an ill-advised journey to Germany in July of 1914 and were promptly arrested and made political prisoners upon the outbreak of war. Keel's wife and child were allowed to stay with her parents in Bavaria, while he was held in prison in

---

[17]   Annual Report, 1911–12; 101 members had joined. See Chapter 6, fn. 45.

[18]   Diaries, 7 March 1914.

[19]   For more on the evolution of the Performing Right Society around this time, see Cyril Ehrlich, *Harmonious Alliance: A History of the Performing Right Society* (Oxford: Oxford University Press, 1989), pp. 1–21.

[20]   Publishers' letters, 2185/LEB/3, no.79, 10 October 1912.

[21]   Ibid., nos 81 and 87.

[22]   Ibid., no. 93, 22 December 1919.

Frankfurt. At the end of the year Keel's family was sent back to England, while Keel himself was interned with other civilian prisoners of war at the Ruhleben camp, a converted race-course, near Berlin. While Keel was away, Lucy started a fund which raised enough money to provide food parcels and books for him during his incarceration. Clive Carey eventually went to the Front, as did the composer George Butterworth, who had recently joined the Society; both were valuable collectors. Butterworth, also a fine composer of song, died in action in 1916, a great loss not only to folksong, but also to British music generally.[23]

Sensing the uneasiness on the Continent, Lucy had avoided Keel's fate by abandoning her plans to travel to Switzerland with Barbara Craster, though her sister Evelyn had decided to go and reproached her sister for not venturing forth; she had arrived there on 5 August.[24] Life was becoming increasingly unstable, not just in Europe, but also in Lucy's personal life. Barbara, whose life had been interwoven with that of her aunt's, had been hinting that she might not continue to live at Carlisle Mansions, and on the eve of her forty-second birthday announced that she wished to strike off on her own. She had found her calling with the Red Cross and wished to pursue a career in nursing, perhaps influenced by her aunt Bertha. Astounded and dismayed, Lucy tried to dissuade her.[25] She would lose not only a flatmate at a time of financial insecurity, but also a folksong colleague, for Barbara had dabbled in collecting and had provided indexes for the *Journal*. How would she manage? How could she afford to retain household staff? Would she have to move? The summer was unsettling as world events marched on inexorably, with Germany declaring war on Russia on 2 August. Lucy and Barbara threw their belongings into boxes and left for Ockley Station to visit the Shearmes. Two days later, after the German invasion of Belgium, England declared war on Germany.

Outbreak of War

The beginning of the war was marked by the unexpected and premature deaths of two close friends, Edith Sichel and Gavin Greig, both of which saddened Lucy greatly. Sichel, aged 52 at the time of her death, was a great friend of Emily Ritchie, who had joined her in doing philanthropic work with East End girls in the 1890s, much as Mary Neal had done with Emmeline Pethick. Later, Sichel had distinguished herself as a historian and writer, focusing on France and the life of Catherine de Medici: in so doing she presaged much later work in social and feminist history. Her philanthropic work continued, and at the end of her life

---

[23]   For Butterworth's collecting, see VWML, LEB file 5, nos 96–105; Carey's can be found in nos 106–12, the last of which was collected with Mary Neal. Carey's songs were published in the *Journal of the English Folk Dance and Song Society*, 1932.

[24]   Diaries, 29 July 1914.

[25]   Diaries, 24 June 1914.

she was teaching at Holloway Prison. She died at the home of Fuller Maitland at Carnforth, possibly due to the strain caused by overwork in London.[26] Greig, too, had been a leading spirit in his community as an influential schoolmaster, though, owing to distance, Lucy had never met him (she called him 'a corresponding friend'). However, they had shared not only that friendship via letter, but also a passion for folksong and scholarship. Knowing that his widow would be struggling financially, Lucy started a campaign to make sure that she would receive an annual pension from the Civil List treasury.[27] Other musicians she had known in the past – notably the pianist Henry Bird – had left families in need, and Lucy also campaigned to raise money for them.[28]

The war meanwhile was making its presence felt. The year 1915 opened with special intercession services in all the churches, particularly Westminster Cathedral, where Lucy became a frequent visitor, possibly for the comfort it offered in troubled times, but also for its sublime music. Conscious of the war effort, Lucy was already doing some clerical work at the Women's Work office and was also involved with helping refugee Belgians, who had fled to England to escape the German invasion which had precipitated the war. With Edouard Garceau, the sisters Jeanne and Louise Douste de Fortis and her friend Marianne Harriet 'Mitty' Mason, Lucy helped to organize a charity concert, held in the elegant Grafton Gallery, in aid of Belgian soldiers and musicians. A tea party held at the home of the Douste sisters afterwards realized £180.[29]

Juliette Folville

Lucy had meanwhile found another artist worthy of her support in the extraordinarily gifted Belgian violinist, composer and pianist, Juliette Folville. Born in Liège in 1870, Folville had received her musical training at the Conservatoire in her home city, studying violin and counterpoint, winning the *premier prix* for fugue in 1887. She was also an accomplished harpsichordist who did much to promote music of the *clavecinistes* and their contemporaries. She was appointed a professor of music at the Liège Conservatoire in 1898, 10 years

---

[26]   Rosemary Mitchell, 'Sichel, Edith Helen (1862–1914)', *Oxford Dictionary of National Biography* (Oxford: Oxford University Press, 2004) at: http://www.oxforddnb.com.ezproxy.library.yorku.ca/view/article/55974 (accessed February 2008).

[27]   Diaries, 2 February 1916. Greig's widow was given a yearly pension of £40 by the Civil List treasury.

[28]   Diaries, 22 February 1916. The Bird fund reached £2,150 yielding an annuity of £100.

[29]   Diaries, 12 February 1915. Lucy sent her two maids to help and felt too poorly to go herself.

after her London debut, where she had received complimentary reviews, one of them deeming her an 'artist *jusqu'au bout des ongles'*.[30]

Lucy quickly befriended the 'magnificent' Folville, who generously offered to play *gratis* at Lucy's flat in March.[31] Lucy insisted on paying her, and in the end Folville 'enchanted' a party of 23, including Lucy's old friend Eva Ashton, Mr and Mrs George Mead and others. Not surprisingly there was a Belgian element to the programme in the form of Franck's *Prelude, Chorale and Fugue* and works by Vincent d'Indy, but she also included some etudes by Liszt and Chopin. A little later, Folville played again at a private *recital-causerie*, where she gave a historical programme of *musique ancienne et moderne*, with a commentary in French. Lucy attended with Marian Arkwright and Angela Mackail's younger sister Clare.[32] A few days later, Lucy gave a second party where she poured tea for 26 friends, including Juliette's octogenarian mother. Playing from 5 pm to 6.30, Folville included some early music by Handel and Couperin in this concert, as well as Mozart, Chopin, Franck, Borodin and her own compositions. The inclusion of earlier repertoire here is interesting, for, like Fuller Maitland, Folville was interested in the harpsichord, and one wonders if she played the Handel and Couperin pieces on that instrument.[33] Folville, who was staying in Bournemouth, soon began playing at private parties throughout London.

Such concerts offered only temporary respite from the very real concerns of the war, now well underway. Lucy and the world at large were horrified to learn of the fate of the nurse, Edith Cavell, executed by the Germans for her heroic work in helping English and Belgian soldiers escape. Zeppelins often floated overhead. The newspapers published dire threats from Germany, promising the wholesale destruction of all England's ships and steamers. Gerald Bray, the husband of her niece Joan (the daughter of James and Eve) died at Gallipoli. Even the Broadwood piano factory was manufacturing munitions instead of pianos, and Lucy made the long journey out to Old Ford to visit the factory on New Year's Eve 1915. Many of the workers were women, who had been introduced to the shopfloor when the men had gone off to war, combining work on ammunition boxes with activities such as French polishing and key-making associated with piano manufacture.[34] Lucy had seen advertisements in the newspaper inviting 'educated women of the leisured class', such as herself, three weeks' training in munitions factory work such as shell-making in order to relieve female factory hands at the weekends. However, she did not take up this option, but instead

---

[30]   *Musical Times*, 29 (1888): 137.

[31]   Diaries, 14 March 1915.

[32]   Diaries, 24 March 1915. The recital was held at the home of a Mrs Fowler at 26 Gilbert Street.

[33]   Diaries, 28 March 1915.

[34]   David Wainwright, *Broadwood by Appointment* (London: Quiller Press, 1982), p. 284. See also Diaries, 31 December 1915. Lucy made her first visit to Old Ford with May Crofton and Ada.

registered with the Union of Women Workers and began working at the Camp Library on the site of the Broadwood firm's old Horseferry Road factory, doing the hot, heavy work of unpacking huge sacks and sorting the contents.[35] The firm was able to keep up limited piano production throughout the war, though methods of production had to be altered and rationalized.[36] Despite entreaties from various friends and relations to leave London, Lucy remained in her flat, occasionally visiting friends in the country, particularly during the summer, when she made her usual peregrinations. In April she went to stay with the Vaughan Williamses at Leith Hill and then went on to adjudicate choirs at Holmwood. The chief judge was Percy Buck, whom Lucy deemed a poor conductor. Her sense of humour intact, she poked fun at him in one of her rhymes:

> The guinea fowls of Leith Hill Place
> Are very down in luck:
> 'We cried, "Come back" for Ralph' they say,
> 'Twas thought we said "Come Buck!"'[37]

In June she decided to take a motoring trip with her friend Julia Freeman to the West Country, taking in picturesque villages in Somerset and Wiltshire, visiting her publisher on the way. Back in London, she resumed her war work and discovered that she had an enlarged caecum, which required medical treatment.[38]

The Folk-Song Society

The Folk-Song Society continued to meet during the war years, though its membership became somewhat depleted. The Annual Report for 1915 acknowledged, with some understatement, that the war 'was not conducive to collecting' and that the membership stood at 262. Sharp was collecting in America, and the Society's business was being administered by Lucy and Mrs Keel, who had recently returned from Germany. Despite wanting to escape the drag of administrative duties on her time, Lucy was almost forced to continue playing a strong administrative and editorial role, overseeing issues no. 19 (which appeared in 1915 and included some of her material) and no. 20. By 1916, however, she asked to be released from such duties, and agreed to be only a signatory of cheques.[39] Keel had evidently taken material for issue no. 19 with him to Germany, which made publication impossible, so that issue carried songs collected by Lucy,

---

[35]   Diaries, 12 October 1915.
[36]   Wainwright, *Broadwood*, p. 285.
[37]   Diaries, 22 April 1915.
[38]   Diaries, 1 November 1915.
[39]   Diaries, 4 February 1916.

Anne Gilchrist, Clive Carey and Walter Ford. No. 20 carried Lucy's article on Padstow May Day songs and ceremonies.

The membership began to dwindle as members of the old guard passed away. Laurence Gomme died in 1916, and the stalwart Ernest Clarke was ailing. Sharp returned from his Appalachian collecting mid-war at the end of 1916, full of songs collected from North Carolina. Dorothy Marshall, who had helped Clive Carey to collect in Surrey and Hampshire and had encouraged the performance of mummers' plays, dances and songs, died in 1917, as did the Reverend James B. Duncan, who had collaborated with Gavin Greig in collecting the music of the north-east of Scotland. Butterworth was dead at 30, and Clive Carey and Vaughan Williams were at the Front. The enterprising Keel, languishing in the Ruhleben camp, but far from finding time heavy on his hands, was finding a captive audience for his talks on British and foreign folk music and was studying 'comparative folksong and folklore' once his materials arrived, thus fulfilling his mission to lecture on British and foreign folk music – with illustrations – and include it in 'soldier concert programmes'. Martin Freeman, who had joined in 1915, was on active service but eventually would provide material on Irish song 'to form two large journals'.[40]

Lucy continued to maintain her contacts in the field during the war years, though she did not actively collect herself. She maintained a connection with the collector Janet Blunt, who, with her cousin Dorothy, had sent songs to Lucy before the war. Janet continued to write to Lucy during the war, and her chatty letters are valuable for their insights into what awaited the collector in the field, and how using the phonograph could make their task much easier:

One comes across <u>other</u> songs, in searching for one; and the people's interest in them is so delightful. One dear old lady of 84 has been 'tuning' for me. She was very fond of singing in her youth – over her work in the fields. Her father would say 'That's right, – wench – sing it out' – (he was a fine singer & made songs) – & the farmer would say to her & her sister Betsy 'There you be! Hollering again! & merry as usual!' ... Well, her two songs (so far) are a version of William Taylor ... It is so very difficult unless one could write shorthand to get the verses complete & consecutive as she sings – & once stopped for repetition she gets '<u>lost</u>', like so many folk-singers. This has made me long to be able to take phonograph records of songs. Can you tell me if it is a very difficult process to learn? And also if it is a very expensive machine to get to work? I have no idea how to set about it. I was reading the instructions how to <u>use</u> a phonograph to record Folk songs – in one of the <u>early</u> journals I recently got & it seems so very necessary, if one is to keep a record of dialect & varieties of time, tune & expression. For instance, it seems to me there is a 4/4 bar in the ¾ tune to 'Fair Lamkin' but not in every verse etc a phonograph wd record this exactly. One old man, William Walton, used to be a very good singer – & esp part songs – which

---

[40]   Annual Report, 1917.

he seemed fonder of than solos. He sang me one all through; quite oldish, of an early type & rather nice – but, no doubt, not 'folk' ... He was a morris dancer too – & is coming to sing me a morris tune that I did not recognise, to a very jolly 'clapdance'. ...There is an elderly man at Bloxham too, who sings 'Green Broom' & one or two other songs so well – I long to get them in a Phonograph record – for he is very much worried if one stops him – & I am not good at musical dictation <u>without</u> a piano.[41]

Despite the efforts of collectors such as Blunt, the war in general was not kind to folksong research. Inspired by his American adventures, Cecil Sharp returned (after another trip) in December 1918, determined to found a school of English Folk Song and Dance. A meeting was held in January 1919 at Wigmore Hall to discuss 'Reconstruction in Music', largely glorifying Sharp's work, and with various luminaries seated on the platform. Lucy was not included among these, and noted with some despair that there was no mention of pre-war pioneers such as herself, Baring-Gould, Kidson, Vaughan Williams or Butterworth.[42] But by this time Sharp had moved into folk dance, and it is possible that this meeting dealt more with Sharp's reconstruction of English dances rather than folksong.

Ruhleben

Ruhleben had been another story. Finding that there were a number of musicians in the camp after the initial shock and settling-in period, the prisoners began to give impromptu concerts, eventually holding regular events in the large hall that had been the race-course refreshment bar. Musical instruments were somehow obtained from Berlin, and an orchestra and choir were formed. The programmes eventually included symphonic and chamber music, solo recitals, and choral and ballad concerts.[43] The returning prisoners gave a concert at Central Hall in early February, and Keel was among them. Keel himself had done much to promote folksong while interned in the camp, singing and lecturing on folk music, and encouraging madrigal groups. Far from restricting himself to British folk music, he had noted some songs from a Breton prisoner.[44]

---

[41]   VWML, LEB 5, no. 47, letter from Janet Blunt, Adderbury Manor, Banbury, 14 April 1916.

[42]   Diaries, 23 January 1919.

[43]   E.L. Bainton, 'Music in Ruhleben Camp', *Musical Times*, 60 (1919): 72.

[44]   VWML, Minutes, Annual Report, 1916.

Publishing Ventures

Lucy was also publishing outside the *Journal*, working with Lavinia Edna Walter, whose speciality was nursery rhymes. Walter was planning two volumes, one comprising English rhymes and the other a mixture of Russian, French and Belgian verses. Lucy set to work on the 30 rhymes after negotiating with the publisher A. & C. Black. Neither volume was particularly scholarly – certainly nothing compared to the work Lucy did for the *Journal* – and must have appealed to a completely different market. Both volumes were sumptuously illustrated, in contrast to the musical arrangements, which were slender though pretty. The continental rhymes appeared only in English translation, with no reference to the original. The Belgian verses appeared to be of Walter's own collecting, from wartime munitions workers she had befriended.[45] All this was reminiscent of the work her old friend Harriet 'Mitty' Mason had done in *Traditional Nursery Rhymes and Country Songs*, which Lucy had mined for *English County Songs*. A second edition of Mason's book had appeared in 1908, and Lucy had kept up the friendship, corresponding with her after she moved to South Africa to stay with her brother and pursue her botanical interests in retirement. She exhibited some of her watercolours in London in 1916.[46]

James Campbell McInnes

Though Lucy's life was filled mainly with female friends, she was still in communication with James Campbell McInnes, who was trying to keep his career afloat in difficult times. He was a constant correspondent, keeping in touch more by letter than in person; his relationship with Graham Peel also appeared to be ongoing, which might have been symptomatic of his failing marriage, or indeed its cause. Lucy heard from McInnes immediately after the outbreak of war; by September he reported that he was doing police duty in London, 'watching a gate and a roof four hours at a stretch'.[47] A second son, Colin, had been born on 21 August, amidst a crumbling and increasingly turbulent marriage. Some years later his older son Graham wrote of witnessing his father's scenes of 'towering violence' 'He was a giant with a troubled stormy visage, a huge black moustache and a deep rumbling voice which filled me with fear and admiration'.[48]

   Though McInnes was still a strong singer, his performances were less frequent during the war, though Lucy did go to hear him sing Brahms's *Zigeunerlieder*

[45]   Letters, 2185/LEB/1, no. 107, from L. Edna Walter, 12 March 1916.

[46]   Katherine Field, 'Mason, (Marianne) Harriet (1845–1932)', *Oxford Dictionary of National Biography* (Oxford: Oxford University Press, 2004) at: http://www.oxforddnb.com.ezproxy.library.yorku.ca/view/article/48847 (accessed October 2007).

[47]   Diaries, 2 September 1914.

[48]   Graham McInnes, *The Road to Gundagai* (London: Hamish Hamilton, 1965), p. 11.

in a vocal quartet accompanied by a distraught Ilona Eibenschütz, still reeling from the catastrophic effect of the outbreak of war on her husband's business.[49] An article about him appeared in the *Musical Standard* in October 1915, and he dropped by for lunch 'and a long talk' during the following winter.[50] Lucy was still his musical mentor and sent him some books on Handel. She treated both his sons as godsons and sent them little presents from time to time, and remained in touch with both parents. But the McInnes marriage was doomed. Its failure could have been foreseen: the couple, 18 years apart in age, had married in haste – he at 39, she at just 21 – only to repent in leisure, as both adjusted to a union in which McInnes's sexuality was compromised: it is significant that their first son was named after his lover, Graham Peel. The article in the *Musical Standard* may well have been a desperate bid to keep a career afloat, difficult in wartime in any case.

The effects of a thwarted sexuality and a career adversely affected by the war combined to turn McInnes into an alcoholic. Angela gave birth to a third child in May 1917, by which time the marriage had plunged into stormy, violent battles. The daughter, Mary, never really had a chance to thrive and died in infancy; Angela herself went into denial and would not attend the funeral. In her divorce petition in November 1917, Angela blamed Mary's death on her husband, citing his 'violent habits, drunkenness and abuse' as reasons for divorce. McInnes was also accused of committing adultery with the nursemaid; there were also rumours of an assault on Angela's sister Clare.[51] The disgraced McInnes did not attend the hearing, at which a decree nisi with costs and custody of the two children were granted to Angela.[52]

McInnes was banished permanently from the family home and did not see his sons until they reached adulthood, though there was a brief encounter in Kensington while they were still children. He eventually served in the Royal Flying Corps. Lucy was aware of what was happening and had heard about Mary's death from Graham Peel.[53] Paradoxically, Mary's birth coincided with one of McInnes's most successful society concerts, at which Lucy had been present along with various distinguished guests; he had sung George Butterworth's setting of Housman's *A Shropshire Lad* as a tribute to the late composer.[54]

It seems that alcohol was truly McInnes's demon. Angela remarried in 1918 and moved to Australia in 1920 with her two sons; a third son was born shortly afterwards. Never happy in her adopted country, Angela eventually returned home, effectively ending the marriage. She began to write, becoming a successful author under her second married name, Angela Thirkell. Her novel, *O, These Men,*

[49]   Diaries, 21 October 1914. Eibenschütz performed as Mrs Derenburg.

[50]   Diaries, 20 January 1916.

[51]   See Judith Flanders, *A Circle of Sisters* (London and New York: Macmillan, 2005), p. 326.

[52]   Law Report, *The Times*, 19 November 1917, p. 2, issue 41639.

[53]   Diaries, 8 June 1917. The letter is no longer extant.

[54]   Diaries, 8 November 1916.

These Men!, published in 1935, long after the marriage was over, superficially resembles her years with McInnes in its theme of uncontrollable alcoholism: she even named the drunken character James and had the female protagonist state that '[m]arriage is no cure for alcoholism'. The characterization is shallow and the plot feeble: Thirkell was clearly no Jane Austen, though her many 'Barsetshire' novels enjoyed some popularity.[55]

McInnes sought treatment for his alcoholism, but by December 1918 was evidently considered a 'hopeless case' after being transferred from one home to another.[56] His career in England over, he moved to Toronto in 1919, where he began anew, teaching English at the university and singing at the Conservatory (then still part of the university), performing mostly in oratorio, and organizing concerts. He became known for his role as Christus in the St Matthew Passion. He managed to keep his career as a performer and teacher afloat by eschewing drink altogether. By the time his son Graham visited him in the 1930s, he seemed a bit of an anachronism – a rather sad and lonely figure, but not without presence:

> In the instant before hesitant recognition dawned in his eyes, I saw an artist's wide floppy, black hat above a heavy square, grey face with grey-black eyebrows and a smudge of white moustache. The face was sunk deep in a spotted brown silk foulard scarf and a heavy navy blue overcoat with a velvet collar. He wore spats and funny half-galoshes and he carried a heavy silver-knobbed stick. He looked like someone out of the cast of *Trelawny of the Wells.*[57]

McInnes was sharing a small shabby house near the university with some friends, and maintained a covert homosexual relationship, though Graham McInnes is not explicit about this. McInnes and his partner also shared a cottage north of Toronto, in the Muskoka lakes region. Graham wrote of this area that:

> … it was here in the northwoods that my father was most fulfilled and was most himself. He gave Canada all he had of creative talent and example. In return Canada gave him a home, a chance to make a fresh, if more muted career; the respect of hundreds of its young music lovers; and the affection of his equals. And in the end it gave him peace of mind.'[58]

---

[55]   Katherine Mullin, 'Thirkell, Angela Margaret (1890–1961)', *Oxford Dictionary of National Biography* (Oxford: Oxford University Press, 2004); online edn, May 2005 at: http://www.oxforddnb.com.ezproxy.library.yorku.ca/view/article/36466 (accessed February 2008).

[56]   Diaries, 5 December 1918. Lucy received 'a melancholy account' from Entwistle Bury of the PCS, who provided this information.

[57]   Graham McInnes, *Finding a Father* (London: Hamish Hamilton, 1967), p. 32.

[58]   McInnes, *Road to Gundagai*, p. 223.

The voice was still powerful, though not up to its former glory. Colin MacInnes recalled it thus:

> His rich treacherous voice had not lost its power to grab your intestines and tie them in knots against your will. Listening to him breached social fortresses, made castles crumble and found you alone on the darkling plain filled with a nameless dread. It was a voice that unmanned you: the rich gritty bray of the authentic bard.[59]

Home Life

By 1917 the war was taking its toll on Lucy's household. In January Carlisle Mansions felt the tremors caused by an explosion in Woolwich, where a large munitions factory was blown up, killing some 700 people.[60] March brought the news of revolution in Russia and the abdication of the czar to make way for the new government of Alexander Kerensky, and ultimately Lenin's regime. Air raids were frequent, and Lucy's household tended to cower in a neighbour's flat downstairs when they happened.[61] The damage around her in Victoria was sobering: thousands of windowpanes shattered, masonry wrecked, shops and houses with their fronts torn. There were many casualties, including children. It was difficult to run a household: never without staff, Lucy had retained two maids and a cook, but found it difficult to keep them; her cook, Louise Challenger, left in February, to be replaced by Maud Holmes, who had been employed by Lucy's sister-in-law Ada at Bone Hill for 14 years.[62] Meals were carefully planned, and by the time of Challenger's departure Lucy was keeping track of how much meat was being consumed per person per month. The hardship of the war had the beneficial effect of making neighbours more neighbourly, and she befriended a Mrs Tudor who lived opposite at no. 85, occasionally taking tea with her. Worse still, there were strange noises (strumming and howling) emanating from neighbouring flats, and several tenants banded together to complain.

Her sister Amy was leading an eccentric life in Lausanne, constantly moving but not giving people her change of address, and visiting spas to relieve her rheumatism.[63] Lucy sought refuge in the novels of George Sand, whom she had read when much younger, and noted her quotation on 'l'amitié', or friendship, from her autobiography, *Histoire de ma vie* (1855):

---

[59] Tony Gould, *Inside Outsider: The Life and Times of Colin MacInnes* (London: Chatto and Windus, Hogarth Press, 1983), p. 61. Colin officially changed the spelling of his surname to MacInnes.

[60] Diaries, 20 January 1917.

[61] Diaries, 1 October 1917. The neighbour was a Mrs Carpmael.

[62] Diaries, 6 March 1917.

[63] Diaries, 19 August 1917.

Vous verrez bientôt que quand on a réussi à devenir excellent pour quelqu'un on ne tarde pas à être meilleur pour tout le monde, et si vous cherchez l'amour idéal, vous sentirez que l'amitié idéale prépare admirablement le coeur à en recevoir le bienfait.

[You will soon see that once one gets along well with somebody, it is not long before you get along with the whole world, and if you search for ideal love, you will see that ideal friendship prepares the heart admirably for this blessing.]

Was there something in George Sand's life which appealed to Lucy, or seemed relevant to her at this time? Was she still hoping for an ideal love, personifying it in McInnes who could clearly never provide it? Was this, after all, the end of the long saga of defining her relationships, and was she resigned to finding it solely with the women who were her closest friends? Nonetheless, she continued to obsess about McInnes, hallucinating about him in her dreams, searching for an explanation for his appalling and inexplicable behaviour.[64]

Life became desperate as the war dragged on. Staple items such as cheese, meat and margarine (there was no butter) were scarce, and were exorbitantly priced even when available. Scouring the shops on foot, lugging provisions (when found) in a large bag proved to be wearing, so the gift of a pheasant, vegetables and butter from her sister Mary in Sussex was exceedingly welcome. Shortly afterwards, a ration system was imposed and meat and margarine ration cards began to be used, thus ensuring a fairer distribution of goods. The years of war and hardship were taking their toll and it is not surprising that Lucy, at the age of 60, should have felt world-weary, admitting as much in her diary. Always prone to low spirits, she found her condition worsening as she began to experience deep bouts of depression and almost irremediable sadness.[65]

The approval of votes for women passed by the House of Lords in January 1918 – clearly a landmark event – did little to improve Lucy's spirits. She sought solace instead in her work, preparing a lecture on Gaelic song for the Pioneer Club, itself devoted to women's interests and run by an all-women committee. It held regular meetings and dinners, and made its library available to members. There was also a lending fund for women wishing to train professionally. Lucy's paper, which she gave at the end of the month at 9 Park Place, St James's, SW1, was well received. Though the audience was small, discouraged by the heavy fog and fear of the air raids which still plagued the city, the Scottish portion responded enthusiastically to the tunes, which Lucy illustrated at the piano.[66]

---

[64]   Diaries, 14 January 1918. Lucy dreamt about a letter floating before her eyes, but could not make out the contents: 'For a moment it seemed to turn into J C McI's writing. Lay awake rather long afterwards'.

[65]   Diaries, 6 February 1918: 'felt *horribly* depressed and sad'.

[66]   Diaries, 31 January 1918.

Street Cries

Though Gaelic song remained a strong interest, Lucy's days of collecting in far-flung places such as Scotland were over. But virtual imprisonment in the city during the war meant that her ears were attuned to music at her doorstep. The coming of spring to the besieged city brought some rewards, as early in the morning on 1 June she heard the 'beautiful cry' of a street vendor outside her window and bought a feather broom from him.[67] She had found a collaborator in the collection of street cries in Juliet Williams, a Chelsea-based painter who had an interest in music, and was also soliciting material from others, who were sending in cries they had noted. This activity began to occupy her as she prepared material for publication in the *Journal*.

Richard Terry and Westminster Cathedral

Lucy also consolidated her friendship with Richard Terry at Westminster Cathedral, inviting him to dinner barely a fortnight after Armistice Day, to regale him with a mummers' carol.[68] Terry would become a good friend in a world which was rapidly changing, both on a personal and national level. A Catholic convert (he was received into the Church in 1896), Terry had come to the Cathedral in 1901 from Downside, where he had been music director after graduating from King's College Cambridge. Like Lucy and her circle, he had a passion for early English music and had developed an interest in folk music while working in Antigua. Disenchanted with the sentimentality of late Victorian church music, he had found inspiration at Downside in the music of Tudor composers such as Tye, Tallis and Byrd, whose music he continued to promote at the Cathedral. These shared interests, plus the peace of the newly built cathedral on her doorstep, attracted Lucy to weekly masses, though there is no evidence that she became a Roman Catholic herself. With the publication of the *Motu Proprio* by Pope Pius X in 1903, which advocated the performance of 'grave and serious music' in Roman Catholic churches, replacing the more modern sentimental fare that had dominated services up to that point, Terry found an opportunity to promote the music of the Italian Renaissance, introducing the masses of Palestrina, Lassus and other composers to the Cathedral canon. Byrd swiftly became a favourite composer. His biographer Hilda Andrews characterized him as 'a dynamo of reform'.[69]

Lucy already had some acquaintance with this music through her old tutor, William Rockstro, and Barclay Squire. Whether it was for inner peace, the love of the music, the desire for some sort of affiliation with Terry, or simply

---

[67]   Diaries, 1 June 1918.

[68]   Diaries, 23 November 1918.

[69]   Information from Hilda Andrews, *Westminster Retrospective: A Memoir of Sir Richard Terry* (London: Oxford University Press, 1948), p. 6.

because it was on her doorstep, she began to attend mass weekly following the
end of the war, going first with her favourite nephew Leo (son of Harry and
Ada) in December. In mid-December 1918 women went to the polls for the first
time (although there were a number of restrictions regarding those who were
allowed to vote), and two weeks later the victory of the coalition government was
announced. Lucy recorded in her diary that she 'did not register [her] first vote
for MP' as the candidate for her area, William Burdett-Coutts, was unopposed.[70]
Barbara Craster, well-established and successful in her naval career, had left 84
Carlisle Mansions in March and was appointed principal of the WRNS College
near Crystal Palace in October.[71] Sister-in-law Ada was threatening to take her
place, much to Lucy's horror; she was relieved when this plan was abandoned.
The year 1919 opened with a performance of her mummers' carols from Sussex
at the Cathedral, conducted by Terry himself.[72] Lucy had come full circle in this
nostalgic reference to her childhood, which perhaps provided some comfort as
she contemplated the years ahead.

[70]   Diaries, 14 December 1918.
[71]   Diaries, 3 October 1918.
[72]   Diaries, 6 January 1919. Lucy commented that these were *beautifully done*.

Chapter 8

The Last Decade

Westminster Cathedral had become an important locus for Lucy who, though not a practising Catholic, nevertheless found its choral offerings and atmosphere comforting, particularly during the war years. It was her first destination on Armistice Day (she had already gone with Leo the previous day) before visiting the Abbey for a service at noon. She returned to the Cathedral with Leo in the evening to hear 'a gorgeous ancient Te Deum'. Crowds continued to throng Buckingham Palace, and St Paul's where she noted 'a terrifying crowd'.[1] But, despite all the delirium and relief, the aftermath of war left Lucy feeling restless and disturbed, mourning the deaths of Hubert Parry in October and of friends and family during the war itself. The McInnes affair had slammed the door on her pre-war past. Once again, the family firm was going through a crisis, with financial implications for everyone. Her 'delightful and true friend', Annie Ritchie, died at Freshwater in February 1919, but Lucy was too ill to attend the funeral. Constant strikes and unrest made daily life difficult. But friendships remained: Lucy still saw much of Fanny Davies, who had resumed her concerts at her studio in Holland Park, exploring new territory with her Tschudi harpsichord and playing duets with Hélène Dolmetsch, who was still playing her viola da gamba. Fanny's birthday in March was marked by a concert in which the pianist and her friends performed a programme of Bach. Davies played the piano rather than the harpsichord, and the tenor Gervase Elwes sang arias. The performance was crowned by a performance of the 'Peasant' cantata accompanied by a quartet; Lucy provided introductory remarks. Musical life was beginning to return to normal.[2]

Leaving Carlisle Mansions

As if the general political and social upheaval after the war were not enough, Lucy was faced with the major problem of having to move. By 1920 leaving the flat was a certainty, and she began to sort out her affairs. She went to the Cathedral to hear Taverner's 'Western Wynde' mass on Easter Sunday and then got down to clearing the flat, helping the warehousemen remove Barbara's things. On 20 April

---

[1]   Diaries, 10–12 November 1918.

[2]   Diaries, 21 March 1919. Lucy had experimented with the harpsichord as long ago as 1906, at the height of her Gaelic song-collecting activity; see Diaries, 23 April 1906, where Lucy played Couperin and Rameau on the harpsichord at a Whitehall concert. She also maintained a connection with Benton Fletcher.

Frank Pryor took the lease for his wife Hilda and himself, and by 12 May Lucy had packed up all her things and was staying with her neighbour, Ethel Portal, at no. 82.

Given the family firm's precarious state, Lucy's finances were not all that secure, and this may have been a reason for having to give up the lease to Pryor, who was an old family friend and, by day, a Lloyds underwriter.[3] Carlisle Mansions had been Lucy's home for some 20 years, and her musical life was inextricably tied up with it. To leave was a major disruption for a woman of 60, especially combined with the departure of a niece whom she considered as almost a daughter. Post-war society was quite different from the Edwardian gentility associated with her old home: servants were increasingly difficult to find, and, after a few unsuccessful attempts, in 1923, when she finally moved into another mansion flat at 41 Drayton Court, Drayton Gardens, Chelsea, she eventually found a loyal retainer in May Scrivener.[4]

Society had changed, and Lucy had to change with it. The war had brought a new lease of life for her niece Barbara, who had moved up in the ranks of the Red Cross and was determined to maintain her independent life after the war, without her aunt. Her outstanding work with the Voluntary Aid Detachment (VAD) and Women's Royal Naval Service (WRNS) was recognized by the award of an MBE in 1919, and she had led the WRNS in the peace celebrations in July in Hyde Park.[5] In her search to find herself after the war, she joined the Gurdjieff cult in Fontainebleau. Meanwhile it was left to Lucy to supervise the removal of her belongings as well as her own. Various things were auctioned off, though with disappointing results; other items were donated to a local hostel.[6]

This was just the beginning, though. It would take some time to find somewhere else to live, and Lucy still had to sell much of the contents, which were put temporarily into storage. Perhaps needing to escape London in the heady aftermath of the war, she arranged to go to Henley to visit her old friend Julia Freeman, who was not only a good travelling companion, but also had the services of a chauffeur, Palmer, who took the pair on a driving tour of the West Country. But the business of the flat rolled on, with financial details reaching her as she travelled. It had to be thoroughly cleaned and renovated for the new tenant and, given its size, this would take some time. On her return, she arranged to stay elsewhere in London – she eventually went back to Mrs Gerling's boarding house in Belgravia, where she had stayed just before the war, and from where she could supervise the workmen in the flat. Priority had to be given to finding a new place to live and ensuring that no. 84 would be ready for its new tenant.

---

[3]   David Wainwright, *Broadwood by Appointment* (London: Quiller Press, 1982), p. 227.

[4]   Diaries, 21 March 1923. The wage was £1 per week, and May was to 'find her own uniform'.

[5]   Diaries, 19 July 1919.

[6]   Diaries, 21 April 1920. The auction realized only £14 6s 0d.

The Family Business

Lucy's financial future, always precarious, was dependent on the fortunes of the family firm, which found itself in difficult straits at the end of the war. In early October Lucy was informed that Bertha was no longer her trustee and that her money would be managed by Robert, Seton and/or Frank Pryor. The board met on 20 December 1918 to discuss the future of the firm. There had already been some changes, as Frank Pryor had now replaced Bertha as Lucy's trustee. Lucy attended with Bertha, who joined a number of family members, including Ada, and her sons Stewart and Leopold (known as Leo), who was a favourite of Lucy's and often stayed with her while in London, and James's son Captain Evelyn Broadwood, who was elected a director. Cuthbert Heath took over the chairmanship from W.H.P. Leslie. The possibility of a takeover (called an 'amalgamation' by Lucy in her diary) by Vickers of Dartwood, which had been a project of Leslie's, was rejected, and no shares were transferred. However, despite the relief at not being taken over, there were post-war challenges to be faced in the form of unionization and the abolition of the contract system.

Leo Broadwood began to take more of a leading role in the firm, dealing with disputes and introducing a more open management style to the company, which, not surprisingly, was mired in pre-war practices.[7] Still wary of German competition, the firm briefly began to concentrate on making grand pianos instead of the upright cottage pianos which had been the staple of their trade both before and during the war. More significantly, they began to manufacture gramophones, though this quickly subsided when electrical models began to be developed in the United States.

Though the production of pianos began to increase, the company had yet to escape its financial straits, and in 1924 it moved its showroom from the spacious quarters in Conduit Street to a smaller space in New Bond Street. As the piano trade began to improve, the company's production of both grands and uprights began to increase, though the General Strike of May 1926 hit the firm hard, exacerbated by the sudden and unexpected death of Stewart Broadwood, killed in an accident while working at home in the same month. In 1928 Leo Broadwood resigned his post as company secretary, but remained a member of the board.

By this time the company was heavily in debt, bailed out by Cuthbert Heath. The board had become merely a rubber stamp for Heath's decisions, and had ceased to take an active part in running the firm. In the end, the firm was reconstructed, with the Old Ford factory let as industrial units and the workforce transferring to the Challen company unit at Hendon, still making Broadwood pianos. Evelyn Broadwood took over as chairman.

---

[7]   Wainwright, *Broadwood*, p. 289.

Family and Friends

During the decade after the war, family affairs assumed even more importance as the sisters grew older and their world changed. Amy became ill and needed constant care. Bertha was still no easier to get along with, and Lucy reported 'feeling increasingly ill during her visit' from her home in Painswick for tea.[8] The upheaval over Home Rule in Ireland precipitated an armed raid by Sinn Fein on the home of Edith Dobbs and her daughters Mildred and Sybil in Camphire, which resulted in their eventually moving back to England in November 1922.[9] The words of Bridget Geary's clarion call to freedom, 'The Blackwater Side', must have rung in their ears.

More than ever, Lucy relied on her old friends Eva Ashton, Fanny Davies and Mary Venables, often travelling to stay with the latter in Oxford. She could combine a visit to Mary's home, Larkbeare, with one to Herbert Craster, now sub-librarian at the Bodleian, and his wife Ida. She was saddened to lose her old friend the composer Marian Arkwright, who died suddenly in her sleep in 1922 after conducting a choral concert.[10] Arkwright was secretary of the English Ladies' Orchestral Union and also a well-known local conductor, and had been the first woman to be awarded the Mus.Doc from Durham University. She and her brother Godfrey, a music historian, had shared Lucy's enthusiasm for folksong, and Godfrey had been active in promoting early English music, including Purcell. Marian's death came a year after that of Julia Freeman, with whom she had shared a motor tour of the West Country in 1920, and who died in the scourge of 'encephalitis lethargica' which swept the country over the following decade.[11]

Lucy herself had resumed her travels after the war. Eager to resume her Swiss connections, she set off in July 1920 for Glarus via Basel and celebrated her sixty-second birthday on 9 August in Glarus, visiting Hans Tschudi, a cultivated and rich bachelor in his 'lovely old Haus in der Wiese' (house in the field), taking in the French 'empire' wallpaper and well-stocked library while indulging in a literary and musical conversation. The purpose of the trip was not only to reconnect with the Tschudi branch of the family, but also to do some genealogical spadework as well as some healthy hill-walking, though this was curtailed because of a recent outbreak of foot and mouth disease. Lucy visited the local archives and also took in

---

[8]   Diaries, 7 March 1919.

[9]   See Lucy's ms extract (1921) from Edith Dobbs's letter of 18 May 1921, SHC 2185/LEB/11/14. Lucy also mentions the event in her diary: see Diaries, 28 May 1921, where she mentions that she has heard from Bertha.

[10]   Announced in *The Times*, 24 March 1922, issue 42988, col. C, p. 9. The short notice was headed simply 'Woman Musician's Death'. Lucy's own tribute appeared in the *Journal of the Folk-Song Society*, 7/26 (1922): 27.

[11]   Julia died on 26 January 1921. Encephalitis lethargica, a viral disease of the central nervous system, swept the world between 1917 and 1928, paralysing its victims. The influenza epidemic of 1918 was not linked to it.

various church services, celebrating the Assumption (15 August) in a local church with her friends the Cookes.[12] On subsequent visits she sought out other branches of the Tschudi family in Schwanden and St Gallen, usually travelling with her friends Evelyn and Rosa Cooke who met her in Basel and could be counted on to make a fuss of her on her birthday, presenting her with flowers and cake; they were also ideal climbing and picnicking companions. In 1925 she invited Fanny Davies to join her, meeting her in St Moritz. On this occasion the musician and scholar Marion Scott, another friend of Fanny's, joined them. In addition to taking Fanny for a walk on the side of a glacier, Lucy presented her with a specially composed ode, written in her usual clever doggerel, in which the first letter of each line spells out the recipient's name, which she delivered on Assumption Day:

Ode to Fanny Davies
Faithful she, to all her friends;
Artist – soul to fingers ends.
Noble things of every kind
Needs must fill her heart and mind.
Years but ripen what she sowed,
Days but add to her rich load,
Art's wide field is hers, yet she
Valiant is in husbandry.
In her field a Bach runs clear,
Exquisite! And, very near,
Schumann lives, with Clara dear.[13]

After a break of two years, in 1928 Lucy made her last visit to Glarus for her seventieth birthday, accompanied by Mildred Dobbs and Julia and Margaret Pryor, after hearing of the death of her old friend Dr Ernst Buss in May; he had shown her much hospitality on her previous visits. She took in Schwanden and Elm, staying in a comfortable hotel in Braunwald before travelling to Glarus, where she was cordially received by Hans Tschudi. By this time she was more interested in sightseeing than walking or climbing, and left on 31 August via Basel. She went directly to Oxford to stay with her old friends Mary Venables and Anne Thackeray, before travelling to the Isle of Wight to see her widowed sister Mary, whose husband had died in 1925.

Her old friend Juliette Folville was still in England, living in Bournemouth, where she and her aged mother had established themselves.

---

12   Diaries, 9–23 August 1920. She also visited the parents of Jakob Wach, a young musician she had befriended and who had been killed in the war. Hans Wach (his father) died on a glacier in September 1923.

13   Diaries, 15 August 1925.

Illustration 8.1   Lucy and friends at Greplang Castle, Switzerland. Standing,
                    left to right: Beryl Reeves, Lucy Broadwood, Anne Thackeray,
                    Mary Venables. Seated: Fanny Davies
Source: Copyright of Surrey History Centre.

Juliette was fortunate to have, in Dan Godfrey, a charismatic and gifted
conductor of the local symphony, and in May the two joined forces in a
performance of Juliette's piano concerto in the Winter Garden Hall. Lucy
pronounced it 'extremely beautiful and magnificently played by herself, and very
well by the band'.[14] Later on in the year Lucy gave one of her pre-war-style
afternoon performance parties for Juliette in London, inviting old friends such as
the Maitlands, the Henschels, Emily Ritchie, Isobel Manisty and Aida Freeman

---

[14]   Diaries, 8 May 1919.

to hear her friend play. She recorded that Henschel was 'in raptures over Juliette's playing'.[15]

Folklore as well as folksong remained an interest, and in the 1920s the discipline of folklore began to merge with the newer one of cultural anthropology. The Polish scholar Maria Antonina Czaplicka was one of the earliest cultural anthropologists and had been brought to England by her mentor, Malinowski. She had conducted fieldwork in Siberia, publishing a book on the subject in 1914, and was appointed Lecturer in Ethnology and Folklore at Oxford in 1915. Lucy met her at Lady Margaret Hall in May 1919, where she had been invited by the Denekes to give a lecture on Gaelic folksong.[16] This marked Lucy's first foray into a serious academic environment, but she did not keep up any correspondence with Czaplicka, possibly because their ages and areas of interest were so different. Fanny Davies subsequently introduced her to the scholar of Russian music Rosa Newmarch and to a Professor Kolisek, who was working on Czech and Slovakian folksong, in 1921.[17] Sadly that year also marked the death of Czaplicka, who committed suicide when she could no longer find employment. The return of men at the end of the war meant that women were forced out of the jobs they had held during their absence, and it seems that Czaplicka, unmarried and without any financial safety net, became one of the victims of this circumstance.

Lucy's unmarried sister Amy, who had been staying in Lausanne during the war, was giving cause for some concern. Before the end of the war, Evelyn had written a circular letter (sent round to all the sisters) describing her eccentric living habits and health problems – mostly rheumatism. Amy seems to have been a bit of an individualist, refusing to give her changes of address, making it difficult for family and friends to keep track of her.[18] After the war she moved back to England, though Lucy had to help her resettle at a time when she herself was hunting for a new flat. Amy was not well, perhaps owing to her idiosyncratic lifestyle and the deprivations of war, and subsequently retired to Bath, where her health remained precarious owing to an acute infection of the lungs. Finding her looking grey and unwell, Lucy took over her financial and other affairs, finding her at first indifferent to her attentions, but ultimately sentimentally grateful.[19] Amy eventually went into a nursing home to convalesce, and regained some of her health.[20]

---

[15]   Diaries, 14 December 1919.

[16]   Diaries, 16 May 1919.

[17]   Diaries, 6 June 1921. Lucy's diaries do not record anything about this tragic event; she may have been unaware of it.

[18]   Diaries, 19 August 1917.

[19]   Diaries, 26 January 1922.

[20]   Diaries, 21 January 1922.

Ballad Operas

As the sister closest to her age (she was five years older), Amy might well have discovered a real friend in her younger sister Lucy once she returned to England. The two went to see the new production of the eighteenth-century ballad opera, *The Beggar's Opera*, at the Lyric Hammersmith on 19 June 1920. Featuring a revised version of the original by Frederic Austin, this performance brought back to public attention the traditional tunes which Lucy had known for years. Before long all London was humming the music – and thinking of spin-offs.

Among these was Lucy's cousin Frank Pryor, who approached Lucy in 1922 about the possibility of contributing to a ballad opera herself.[21] Frank had been an enthusiastic thespian since his Cambridge days and had maintained a connection with the theatre through playwriting. She met him at her old flat in Carlisle Mansions, where he and his wife Hilda were now living. They were joined by John Hastings Turner, a young writer who had made his name writing wartime revues, who was to provide the libretto taken from an opera he had been working on. The composer was Gerrard Williams, a young conductor and composer of mostly light music, who was to provide the music to the production, titled (at this point) *Kate the Cabin Boy*. Pryor was to provide the 'book', or the spoken dialogue, and Lucy's role was to supply some traditional tunes to be arranged and orchestrated, *à la* Pepusch (who had harmonized *The Beggar's Opera* tunes), by Williams.[22] In the end, Lucy spent much time on the tunes, providing alternative lyrics for songs such as 'Bristol City'. While Frank prepared the book, she had numerous meetings with Williams himself, occasionally giving him lunch.

The play had financial support from producer Donald Calthrop, and was to be performed at the Kingsway Theatre. Lucy and her nephew Evelyn attended a rehearsal on 18 October and met the cast. By the end of the session Lucy could barely hide her horror at the poor quality of the libretto and the way in which her tunes had been treated. Dismayed by the general ineptness of the musical side of the production, with its sloppy orchestration and inappropriate tempos, Lucy began to think twice about her involvement. Did she really want her name attached to this? It was difficult to get through the tea party in the foyer without saying what she really thought. She went with some relief to a meeting of the Quest Society afterwards. Brooding over the next few days, she eventually wrote to Frank Pryor about her reservations, hoping that they might be able to put things right.[23] A few days later she visited him at her old flat, finding him in a 'highly agitated, anxious state'.[24]

The situation appeared to be irremediable. The play was already well underway, and clearly neither Williams nor anyone else associated with the production

---

[21]   Diaries, 26 January 1922.
[22]   Pryor presented the book on 21 March 1923.
[23]   Diaries, 21 October 1923.
[24]   Diaries, 27 October 1923.

wished to take any notice of what Lucy thought. Whatever discussions took place were to no avail. The play, now called *Kate, or Love will find out the Way*, had its premiere at the Kingsway Theatre on 25 February 1924, and was billed as 'a fantastic ballad opera in two acts'. Lucy was disgusted and horrified. Her own music had been 'chopped and turned about ruthlessly' without her consent, and the lyrics of the original scrapped opera by Hastings Turner had been 'mutilated'. Lucy had spent two years selecting music from her own collection and from her knowledge of traditional tunes, only to have them reworded and badly orchestrated. She was furious, as were Pryor and his collaborators, and all of them asked to be dissociated from the project altogether and for their names not to be mentioned in the programme. Lucy fumed in her diary that she had not been kept informed of the 'book' of Kate, even though the plot was based on two of her own folksongs, and that her musical suggestions had been resented. Writing unusually in the third person, she noted that this was 'the first time in her life that she had been treated with marked discourtesy and ungentlemanly behaviour by men of education'.[25]

The absence of reference to the playwright in the programme did not go unremarked: it was noticed with amused curiosity by the reviewer for *The Times*, who mused that the play 'such as it is, just grew up round the Old English songs and ballads … and all the jolly things which the composer and the lyric writer thought it would be fun to bring in'.[26] A review in the *Musical Times*, published after the opera closed, decried the lack of a Gilbert or Gay. Both reviews mentioned the attractiveness of the music, though the latter remarked that it was hardly current and that it owed much to Cecil Sharp, which must have vexed Lucy.[27]

The play closed less than a month after opening, on 22 March 1924, an inauspicious day which coincided with a crippling bus and tram strike. She heard from Boosey regarding her royalties, and from Frank Pryor saying that the work might reappear to a new libretto in the autumn. She went to see the penultimate performance in the afternoon, taking Aida and Martin Freeman with her, perhaps in the hope that things had improved. Unfortunately, the production was still disappointing, with 'very ragged orchestral accompaniment'. As if to add insult to injury, all was not well at the flat either, and she had to deal with a collapsed bathroom ceiling. She soon retreated to bed with her usual complaints of laryngitis, influenza and lumbago. Once the dust had settled from the close of the unfortunate *Kate*, and when she had had time to recover, she was visited by Anthony Bernard, the conductor, who appeared to want to make amends, blaming Williams for the failure of the production. But it was really too late.[28]

Despite this disastrous experience, *Kate* was not the end of Lucy's collaboration with Williams, though sadly the relationship did not improve.

---

[25]   Diaries, 25 February 1924.

[26]   *The Times*, 26 February 1924, issue 43585, p. 10.

[27]   *Musical Times*, 65/975 (1 May 1924): 453.

[28]   Diaries, 10 April 1924.

Undeterred, Williams composed another ballad opera, *Charming Chloe*, using nine of Lucy's folk tunes, presumably with her permission. This time, the book was acknowledged to be by Rodney Bennett and F.G. Wilson. The opera was broadcast on 2 October 1928 from the new BBC studios in Daventry, with Lucy's young protégé, the tenor Henry Wendon, singing one of the roles.[29] Most upsetting to Lucy was the omission of her name in the broadcasting programme, though the other contributors were acknowledged there and in the book. Lucy protested to Williams, but there is no record of any apology or amends.[30]

Reissuing *English County Songs*

Though such lack of recognition was hurtful, there was a silver lining in that such productions had heightened public awareness of the beauty of traditional tunes, and as a result there was a demand for such music. Though *English County Songs* was out of print, many of the songs were popular and sold well in single, sheet-music form. Influenced by the wide distribution of Cecil Sharp's songs in this way, particularly in schools, Lucy and Fuller Maitland overcame their initial reluctance to follow Sharp's approach and allowed a number of their tunes from *English County Songs* to be issued as single songs. The financial inducements were clear: it was unfeasible to reprint the original volumes and selected single songs would probably sell well. Lucy especially needed some financial security. A number of songs from that collection remained popular, and were even issued in tonic sol-fa form with Lucy's blessing.[31] Somewhat belatedly, by 1928 Cramer had become aware of increased piracy of the material by others who simply took the songs and issued them without permission. Citing works by Walford Davies, Warren & Phillips and others, Cramer declared:

> The unauthorised issue of so many copyright songs from works published by ourselves has increased so much ... that we have been compelled to make a rigid rule that under no circumstances can we grant permission to other publishers to use them, as the use of unauthorised versions is the cause of a serious loss not only to ourselves, but to the composers and authors whom we represent. We have been compelled to take a strong stand in this matter.[32]

---

[29]   Born in Plymouth in 1900, Wendon had made his debut as Radames in *Aida* in 1925. Lucy had met Wendon some time before and had tried to foster his career in the way she had done for others, but he never achieved the place in her life that McInnes had occupied. He did, however, go on to have a successful career unmarred by personal tragedy.

[30]   Diaries, 2 October 1928.

[31]   SHC Publishers, 2185/LEB/3, no. 104, 19 June 1925. 'It will be absolutely necessary to have tonic sol-fa. I will, of course, get this done'.

[32]   Ibid., no. 125, 16 April 1928.

The songs were not always pirated, however. They drew the attention of the composer Alec Rowley, well known in the educational field, who arranged them for piano duet despite Lucy's initial reservations, and, in turn, a Dr Sweeting asked for the rights to the choral arrangements of some of the tunes, including 'A Shepherd's Requiem'. A Mr Thompson asked to use some of the tunes for a Holiday Association songbook. But piracy of such popular material was rife: many did not ask for permission, and Lucy began to regret Fuller Maitland's earlier generosity in releasing the tunes without adequate consideration of compensation for her or himself, and drafted a note to Cramer accordingly:

> At one time [Fuller Maitland] was inclined – years ago – to give away our 'English County Songs' much more readily that I was! But he may perhaps now see that, owing to the masses of school song-books, community song-books etc we cannot possibly give away our original privileges, right & left. Perhaps you, who have been in touch with him lately about this matter, will kindly tell me what his reply to you was. He is a busy old friend & I don't want to put him to the trouble of writing to me on the subject if you can tell me the gist of his business-reply to you. In any case you will recollect that I do not ever approve of parting with our privileges. The reason is obvious: if we allow one person or publisher to use our best (or 2d best) songs we must allow all other applicants to do so.[33]

Cramer replied a few days later, agreeing that it was inadvisable 'to give leave for publications' (that is, reprints of their work by other publishers), to which Lucy replied with her own, plus Fuller Maitland's, view that they felt entitled to royalties on arrangements of their material by other composers: 'Mr Maitland & I both feel strongly that should we give our permission in the case of composers wishing to make & publish instrumental or vocal arrangements of our songs we ought to have a share in royalties on those publications'.[34] Lucy was also concerned about other accompaniments being supplied – 'given the words, anyone familiar with the now well-known tune can indefinitely vamp accompaniments to the songs, which have already been too much pirated' – citing a performance of 'Twankydillo' at a recent PCS concert, where the singer had used a substandard accompaniment and apparently had been unaware of Lucy's arrangement.[35]

Meanwhile there were dealings with Boosey & Co. over individually printed songs from *English Traditional Songs and Carols*. By 1926 Boosey & Co. was reducing its stocks of Lucy's single sheet songs, and agreed to pay a sixth of the cover cost as royalty. They were also negotiating rights in the United States, to

---

[33]   Ibid., no. 132, draft letter, 6 April 1929.

[34]   Ibid., no. 134C, 11 April 1929.

[35]   Ibid., no. 134D.

which Lucy agreed, though the law there protected only the accompaniment and not the tune, which was fair game.[36]

The Folk-Song Society

The Folk-Song Society held its first post-war AGM in Steinway Hall, Lower Seymour Street on Friday 23 May at 8 pm. Lucy was voted chair in the absence, through illness, of Sir Ernest Clarke. Cecil Sharp lectured on his folksong collecting in the Appalachians, with illustrations by Maud Karpeles and Owen Colyer. Gathering strength after the debilitating war years, the Society began to plan the next journals. Sharp had contributed material for no. 20, in which Lucy had published an article on Padstow May Day songs, and Keel was preparing no. 21 with material collected before the war. After the success of the Tolmie volume, the Society turned to Irish song and the work of Martin Freeman, whose Gaelic songs collected from Ballyvourney, County Cork, would be divided among three volumes. As Freeman had been away during the war, once again Lucy had been involved in the editing, working with Robin Flower, although Freeman later was scathing about Flower's abilities as a musician.[37]

The first post-war volume to be published included Juliet Williams's collection of street cries, with additional contributions by Lucy Broadwood and Annie Gilchrist. Williams was a synaesthesic artist, a painter of landscapes, flowers, gardens and music subjects, whose art was inspired by music; she noted down tunes she heard outside her studio in the area of west Chelsea bordered by Oakley Street and Upper Cheyne Row. This stretch lies close to the Thames in what is still a pleasant backwater which at the time must have been filled with artists' studios. To these tunes Lucy added cries she had noted from her own area of Westminster, offering descriptions of some of the criers and her experiences in collecting their cries. Most of the tunes were noted in the original pitch, or as close to it as possible; Lucy noted that 'the best street-criers pitch their voices in the same key, year in, year out'.[38] The cries usually involved the sale of household items such as feather brooms, fire logs, flowers, lavender, strawberries ('storbies') and even goldfish. As usual, Lucy was not interested in merely saving the cries, but also in tracing their origins; she noted the similarity of one cry to a theme used by Gibbons for viol, suggesting that he may have used contemporary street cries as inspiration for their compositions. In her note on lavender cries at the end of the article, Gilchrist suggested that they might be traced back to rosemary cries, such as those noted by Deering [Dering] in his 'Madrigal on Street Cries' ['The City Cries'].

While the tunes were not difficult to note down, getting the words proved difficult. To the middle-class ears of Williams and Broadwood, the words of the

---

[36]   Ibid., no.153, 17 June 1926.
[37]   SHC, 2185/LEB/1, no. 551, 21 May 1929.
[38]   'London Street Cries', *Journal of the Folk-Song Society*, 22 (1919): 55.

working-class sellers were often incomprehensible, though this had the advantage of forcing encounters with them. Even so, the words often remained a mystery, making one wonder how many goods the hawkers actually sold. After several encounters with a particular broom-seller (who sang consistently in a rich A flat), Lucy gave up, remarking that she supposed 'he uses a rhythmical and consistent chant into which he fits whatever words come into his head at the time, lopping them and running them into each other in the process'.[39] She assumed that the man was a gypsy owing to his appearance and distinctive, expressive voice. She did not take his name, assuming that he would not have given it, and ventured the theory that he might have had superstitious reasons for not sharing the words of the cry, as it might have diminished his own luck or power. Even the disaffected Barbara Craster contributed some of the street cries she had heard while working with the Voluntary Aid Detachment in Boulogne – her last bit of work for her aunt.

The Final Years of the Folk-Song Society

The successful publication of the Tolmie collection prompted the Society to continue its efforts in the publication of Gaelic song, particularly as their publication tended to increase the membership, at least temporarily. Tolmie herself died in 1926. After the publication of the Freeman volumes, Celtic song remained a preoccupation and volumes 28 to 30 were devoted to Manx song collected by John Clague, one of the Society's earliest members. Published in 1924–6, these volumes were prepared with the help of Gilchrist and Freeman, and were the last issues of the *Journal* edited by Lucy.

During the 1920s the Folk-Song Society lost a number of crucial members, notably Cecil Sharp in 1924 and Frank Kidson in 1926. The two men represented polar opposites in their approach to folksong. Kidson was more allied with Lucy in his more academic, somewhat antiquarian approach. Sharp, though, had galvanized the Society into action, and had been accepted with some reservations; he remained a member even when he founded the English Folk Dance Society in 1911. Though publicly courteous, Lucy had never taken to Sharp, finding him too pushy and not 'a gentleman'. It is notable that even after Sharp's death, the Society remained strong and pursued interests outside his domain. Kidson maintained his researches in both music and dance, but made few contributions to the *Journal* itself. His influence was felt, though, in Lucy's academic approach, and his death marked the end of an era.

On the death of Tennyson, it was proposed at the AGM of 12 December 1928 that Lucy Broadwood should 'be elected' to that position. Lucy was not at the meeting and did not even send regrets, but she noted in her diary that it was taking place. A formal letter arrived on 15 December from Lydia John, on behalf of the Folk-Song Society, asking Lucy to accept the presidency, which she did the next day.

---

[39] Ibid., p. 58.

Final Days

Basking in this honour, Lucy spent Christmas at Adwell with the Birch Reynardsons in the company of the famous ballerina Anna Pavlova, who danced some Russian dances in Russian peasant costume. Ever the royalist, Lucy kept constant track of the King's health during this period – perhaps a reflection of her preoccupation with her own health. The new year began with the usual worries over her sisters' health – both Mary and Edith were ill, and Amy was flat-hunting in London. The usual rigours of winter ensued, replete with frozen pipes and no hot water. She wrote to congratulate Arthur Somervell on his knighthood, noted in the New Year Honours list. The year proceeded fairly quietly, punctuated by visits to friends and family and the writing of reviews. In March she attended the premiere of Vaughan Williams's opera *Sir John in Love* and found it interesting but 'ineffectively modern' in its angularity and occasional grotesqueness. She heard her song, 'A Shepherds' Requiem' performed in Sweeting's arrangement at Dorking in April. Frank Pryor was still writing plays, and his *Autocrat* was performed in May to bad reviews, noted by Lucy perhaps with a touch of *schadenfreude*. She spent her seventy-first birthday with Mary Venables and Anne Thackeray at Larkbeare and then left to see her old friend Eva Ashton, making a day trip to Pevensey on the coast.

She had taken up an invitation from the Rivazes to attend a festival at Dropmore, near Canterbury, and spent her first day there talking with them on their veranda and writing letters. She then attended a performance of Marlowe's *Dr Faustus* and walked back home. The last letters she received were from Percy Grainger, who had married and was hoping to see her on her return to London, and Graham Peel. She would not see Grainger and his wife though, for on 22 August 1929 she died suddenly at the home of her hosts.

News of her death was received with a mixture of dismay and surprise. Though not naturally robust, she had not been seriously ill, and most summers had been taken up with travel and some form of exercise. She had finally achieved some domestic stability in her new flat and with her maid, May Scrivener, with whom she seemed to have had an affectionate relationship. She was at last president of the Folk-Song Society, an appointment that was richly deserved but which had come far too late. Perhaps it was this honour, bestowed so late in her life, which created a sense that her life's work was complete. She had outlived her most serious rival, Cecil Sharp, to be sure, but the battle had been long one, and she had already perceived that it was his legacy, and not hers, that would survive. The choice of Vaughan Williams as her successor as president signalled a vote for change, and for new directions in folksong research.

Epilogue

Lucy's death effectively closed the Folk-Song Society. In its Annual Report, the Society which she had helped to found, and to which she had given years of dedicated service, described her loss as 'irreparable', and its obituary celebrated her pioneering work in folksong research. The editor unfortunately overlooked the fact that it also got the date of her death wrong, giving it as 27 August instead of the 22nd.[1]

Today, the obituaries seem curiously stilted and impersonal, perhaps in the character of that genre at that time and possibly because they were all written by men. One can only imagine what a scholar of the calibre of Anne Geddes Gilchrist would have written. The unpublished memoir written by Lucy's old friend, the violinist Mary Venables, is the only account to cast any light on Lucy's personality as well as her achievement.[2]

In the journal which she had done so much to shape, the task of writing her obituary was given to Walter Ford, a long-time member of the Society and a singer in the tradition of Plunket Greene, as well as a contemporary of Sharp at Cambridge. He traced the usual landmarks and reduced her achievement outside the folksong world to her 'small but pleasant voice' and the 'quiet charm and refined taste' of her singing in amateur circles.[3] Writing in the *Musical Times*, Frank Howes, a much younger contemporary who admired but barely knew the older woman, wrote of her own compositions and of the 'felicitous piano accompaniments' to the folksongs she had collected. Neglecting all mention of her sole-authored *English Traditional Songs and Carols*, he acknowledged the seminal importance of *English County Songs*, which was unfortunately mistyped as *English Country Songs*. He praised her 'immense amount of varied antiquarian learning' and her knowledge of printed ballads and broadsheets, summarizing that 'she thus combined in herself the two parallel streams of English traditional music – the written and the oral'. By the end, the reader is left with the impression of Lucy Broadwood as a respected but somewhat dry scholar, who, as a 'lynx-eyed' editor, was a stickler for erudition and order.[4]

---

[1]   'Annual Report of the Committee for the Year 1928', *Journal of the Folk-Song Society*, 8/33 (December 1929): xi.

[2]   SHC, LEB 2297/3/2, no.6, Memoir by Venables, February 1930.

[3]   *Journal of the Folk-Song Society*, 8/33 (December 1929): 168–9.

[4]   F[rank] H[owes], 'Obituary', *Musical Times*, 70 (1929): 943.

Illustration 9.1   Mary Venables, July 1925
Source: Copyright of Surrey History Centre.

A more personal impression was given by Fuller Maitland in his obituary for the *Monthly Musical Record*, who in addition to recording Lucy's accomplishments in folksong, gives a disproportionate amount of space to a reminiscence of a long-ago occasion in the 1870s when they had improvised on the tune, 'The Noble Lord', on two pianos. Naturally there is mention of their collaboration on *English County Songs* and of her sensitivity to creating modally appropriate accompaniments; but the success of her own compositions and arrangements is overlooked, and the important publication of *English Traditional Songs and Carols* is omitted altogether. He praises her 'scientific research' for the *Journal*, but surprisingly gives her no credit for her many years as editor, merely lumping her together with Kidson and Gilchrist as annotators. As Fuller Maitland was a fellow member of the People's Concert Society, it is surprising that he omits all mention of her performances in that context, and of her contribution to the editing of works by Purcell and J.S. Bach; this was, after all, an obituary in a mainstream musical journal. The final paragraph paints her as a typical gentlewoman of the upper classes, who was possessed of not just musical accomplishment but who 'drew very cleverly', and whose conversation was 'full of both wit and humour' and who used her influence to help younger musicians (none of whom is mentioned) attain 'a recognized place in the musical world'.[5] From this portrait, she seems not far removed from the placid, anodyne perfection of Coventry Patmore's 'Angel in the House': Mary Venables made the same points, but painted a far more dynamic picture, describing a brilliant conversationalist and companion – a woman who 'excelled in all writing games and in making comical drawings and delightful sketches and rhymes'. She also ascribed to her Swiss ancestry 'many of her sterling qualities including a certain sturdiness of outlook that had its counterpart in her actions and appearance'. Venables gives us some idea of Lucy's true personality, in contrast to the patronizing, bloodless accounts of her male contemporaries.[6]

Vaughan Williams

It is striking that Vaughan Williams, the Society's new president, did not write the obituary for the *Journal*, but instead contributed one to the *Journal of the English Folk Dance Society*, and even then not until the third issue of 1930.[7] Conceding that the activities of the English Folk Dance Society were 'as nothing' unless they were based on 'scientific knowledge', he characterized the dance group as being

---

[5]   J.A. Fuller Maitland, 'Lucy Broadwood: 1858–1929', *Monthly Musical Record*, 59 (1929): 296–7.

[6]   Mary Venables, 'Lucy Etheldred Broadwood', unpublished manuscript, February 1930, Surrey History Centre (SHC), Woking, UK, Accession no. 2297/6.

[7]   R. Vaughan Williams, 'Miss Lucy Broadwood', *Journal of the English Folk Dance Society*, 2nd series, no. 3 (1930): 61.

all about action rather than theory, the implicit criticism being that Broadwood had been more of a cerebral collector.

The obituary was a faint echo of a somewhat double-edged 'appreciation' that Vaughan Williams had written for the *Journal of the Folk-Song Society* in 1927, when Lucy finally relinquished her position as editor.[8] Here, he praises her scholarly work as evidenced in *English County Songs*, and links her with Kidson and Baring-Gould as pioneers in the movement. He points to her work on no. 5 of the *Journal* ('Surrey and Sussex Songs') and no. 10 ('Songs from Ireland') as being exemplary. But it is the final paragraph that damns as much as it praises: the picture is of an austere, reclusive scholar pondering over her precious songs 'in the quiet of her study', wilfully withholding them from the public gaze. She was credited with some reparation for this in the publication of *English Traditional Songs and Carols*, but Vaughan Williams ironically gets the title wrong, omitting 'English' – somewhat of a Freudian slip. What Vaughan Williams and others failed to acknowledge or appreciate was the huge scholarly effort that went into editing and annotating the *Journal*, particularly when it moved into the more obscure areas of Scottish, Manx and Irish song. The coyness of the penultimate sentence: 'Rumour has it that there is also a collection of beautiful Gaelic airs known at present only to a privileged few' and the concluding question: 'is it too much to hope that … she will find time to issue these also to the world?' must have been hurtful in the extreme. True, her own standards of perfection, and possibly the sheer effort of producing the Tolmie volume, delayed the publication of the Gaelic songs until after her death, but we have seen that the final decade of her life was far from idle.

Vaughan Williams had clearly never forgiven Lucy for siding with Fuller Maitland and others against Sharp back in 1906 and had supported him in his campaign 'to give folksong back to the people' as his life's work. Sharp had separated 'folk' from 'composed' music, whether the latter was of the popular or art variety. Sharp theorized folksong as a communal and racial product, 'the expression, in musical idiom, of aims and ideals that are primarily national in character'.[9] Folksong was a 'completely different species' from 'national' song, a confusing use of nomenclature, by which he meant popular traditional songs from printed sources. Lucy, on the other hand, simply wanted to trace the origins of the songs she had collected: her emphasis was more on quality whereas Sharp was intent on 'rescuing' and disseminating as many songs as possible. Both approaches were valid. Like Sharp, Vaughan Williams took a nationalist view of folksong, restricting himself to England, while Lucy's view was more diverse.

Vaughan Williams later supported Sharp in the formation of the English Folk Dance Society, but remained in the Folk-Song Society. The reasons for his attitude

---

8   R. Vaughan Williams, 'Lucy Broadwood: An Appreciation', *Journal of the Folk-Song Society*, 8/31 (September 1927): 44–5.

9   Cecil Sharp, 'Introduction', in *English Folk Song: Some Conclusions* (Taunton: Barnicott and Pearce, 1907).

probably lay in his profession as composer, where everything was in the doing – performing, composing and conducting – and where there was little time for scholarly effort. While Lucy, too, was active in her earlier days as a performer and composer, she had had much to learn on her own, which might have led to her developing a more scholarly temperament.

To be sure, Vaughan Williams was also a skilled folksong collector. Galvanized by Sharp, he began collecting in 1904, when the Folk-Song Society was just emerging from its doldrums, visiting various parts of England in addition to the home counties. In all, he collected 810 songs, 234 of them in his first year. Some of them were from Lucy's own sources, notably Henry Burstow. Primarily interested in their musical content, he absorbed much of this idiom into his own composition, much as Bartók had done. In the words of James Day, 'What he gained from it was a tonal freedom and a melodic idiom that fertilized his own creative imagination; what he made of it was the creation of his own genius'.[10] It was also in 1904 that, with his cousin's wife Margaret Massingberd, he began plans to establish the Leith Hill Festival, a musical competition which would involve local villages and which Lucy supported, particularly in its early days. The first competition was held in 1905, and Vaughan Williams conducted at every Festival until he retired in 1953 at the age of 80. Through all this time, Lucy was an ally: in his early days she had been a mentor, and, as his career progressed, she was always supportive though not uncritical. True, the relationship must have been affected by Vaughan Williams's avid support of Sharp, whom Lucy grew to detest, venting her feelings in a letter to Bertha towards the end of her life:

> Mr Cecil Sharp unfortunately took up old songs & old dance-collecting as a profession, &, not being a gentleman, he puffed and boomed and shoved and ousted, and used the Press to advertise himself; so that, although we pioneers were the people from whom he originally learnt all he knew of the subjects, he came to believe himself to be King of the whole movement, & was by the general ignorant public taken at his own valuation.[11]

Vaughan Williams did not write about Lucy again until 1948, in an article for the *Journal of the English Folk Dance and Song Society* celebrating the fiftieth anniversary of the Folk-Song Society.[12] The Folk-Song Society and The English Folk Dance Society had amalgamated in 1931, when Douglas Kennedy, Sharp's successor as director of the English Folk Dance Society, had proposed that the Folk-Song Society should share the resources of the building erected in memory of Sharp (Cecil Sharp House). A conference was held to discuss the formation of a joint society and, despite some objections, the English Folk Dance and Song

---

[10]   James Day, *Vaughan Williams* (Oxford: Oxford University Press, 1998), p. 27.

[11]   SHC, LEB 2297/3/2, no. 3, Letter from Lucy to Bertha, 22 July 1924.

[12]   R. Vaughan Williams, 'Lucy Broadwood, 1858–1929', *Journal of the English Folk Dance and Song Society*, 5 (1948): 136–8.

Society was formed, and Cecil Sharp House was designated as home to both folksong and folk dance.[13] Unlike the obituaries, in his portrait of Lucy mentioned above, Vaughan Williams acknowledges her background which combined rural knowledge with urban sophistication, and made some complimentary remarks about her musicianship as a singer, pianist and composer. She, and not Sharp, was credited with the revival of the Folk-Song Society, whose early meetings he described as 'of a dilettante and "tea-party" order'. The comparison with Sharp, whom Vaughan Williams felt Broadwood had 'misunderstood', comes later, in a return to the criticism for keeping the songs to herself: 'To her, folk songs were largely a matter for the study[;] treasure to be pondered over in solitude and only occasionally to be displayed to the chosen few'. She had been reluctant to 'bring them into the glaring light of the concert room and theatre, or to make them a cog in the educational wheel'. She had had little sympathy for Sharp's campaign of dissemination, and had thought him in 'too much of a hurry', which Vaughan Williams conceded was probably true. He allowed that Lucy's and Sharp's ideals 'could never coalesce', and regretted that the English Folk Dance Society 'could not command her wide knowledge and understanding'.[14]

Vaughan Williams's inability to understand Lucy's scholarly habits prevented him from acknowledging her breadth of knowledge, editorial abilities, generosity and her vital contribution to Gaelic song, to which he felt little connection. He was also unable to see that her apparent lack of interest in folk dance – though she in fact had made some forays into this area – had everything to do with Sharp's approach to it.

If Vaughan Williams was cautiously generous in print, though with reservations, he was not so in private. A decade later, Lucy's niece Joan Bray wrote to him asking if he would write a centenary article about the work of her late aunt. In it she echoed Lucy's view that Sharp, 'following in my aunt's footsteps, & using her methods of folk song researching etc, stole much of the limelight that should have been rightly hers'.[15] Clearly, this letter struck an unpleasant chord. An irritated Vaughan Williams replied tersely that 'Miss Broadwood was mistaken in keeping the folk songs as a study for the few, and also misunderstood Cecil Sharp's attitude towards our duty to disseminate Folk Song as broadly as possible'. The remainder of the letter was more rancorous, even sarcastic, as Vaughan Williams noted that Sharp had never been part of the charmed circle headed by Fuller Maitland, who of course was closely associated with Broadwood: 'he had no musical degree, probably was not much good at counterpoint, had had a quarrel with one of the Vice Presidents of the Folk Song Society, and all together did not belong to the right musical set! Therefore he must be ignored, or his work denigrated'.[16] Clearly,

[13]   See Frederick Keel, 'The Folk Song Society', *Journal of the English Folk Dance and Song Society*, 5/3 (1948): 125.

[14]   Vaughan Williams, 'Lucy Broadwood: An Appreciation', pp. 44–5

[15]   SHC, LEB 2297/7/1–7, no. 8, 14 July 1958.

[16]   SHC, LEB 2297/8/2, 19 July 1958. Vaughan Williams died on 26 August 1958.

Joan Bray's letter had reopened old wounds, and he would not support any undue celebration of Lucy's work: a brief acknowledgement by Frank Howes in *The Times*, where he was music critic, would surely be more than sufficient.

In fact, it was Lucy's own work that was ignored. The 1958 volume of the *Journal of the English Folk Dance and Song Society*, the successor to the journal which she founded and edited, contains no mention of her name or her work, whereas the 1959 volume is dedicated entirely to Sharp. Howes's only tribute appeared in the more specialized *Musical Times*, where he wrote only of the sixtieth anniversary of the founding of the Folk-Song Society.[17] Broadwood is mentioned only in passing. The harshness of Vaughan Williams's letter is surprising, especially given the time that had elapsed since the deaths of the two collectors. While Vaughan Williams must have been aware of her antipathy towards Sharp, one wonders whether Lucy herself – or her niece, who must have been hurt and even distressed by this response – had been aware of his partisan attitude. The comments are unfair and disingenuous, and his rejection of Lucy's contribution seems unduly harsh and a complete negation of what she probably regarded as a mutually respectful friendship.

Broadwood and Sharp

It was probably not Sharp's Cambridge degree in mathematics (not music) and perceived deficiencies in counterpoint that made him an outsider – even Vaughan Williams had read history before gaining his MusBac at Cambridge – but the forcefulness of his personality and his intolerance of views other than his own, which grated against the more refined sensibilities of stalwarts such as Fuller Maitland, who generally adhered to an unwritten gentlemanly code of avoiding unnecessary conflict. Fuller Maitland was also a critic, a breed not beloved of composers. Certainly Sharp's track record in relation to his adversaries, especially if they were women, was not good, as in the case of Mary Neal. Like Sharp, the youthful Percy Grainger also challenged the Folk-Song Society and indeed Sharp himself, but he did not alienate so many people in the process.

Moreover, Vaughan Williams must have realized that self-promotion was anathema to most women of Lucy's generation and background. This was hardly surprising, given her upbringing: only one sister, Bertha, had a public persona, but in the female-dominated profession of nursing. Lucy found her domineering and difficult, preferring to spend time with her other less forceful sisters, especially Amy. Bertha seemed to return this lack of affection, arguing (unsuccessfully) against dedicating a memorial to her sister in St Mary Magdalene's Church in Rusper. On the whole, the sisters lamented her death, blaming it on her 'overwork' for the Folk-Song Society. The omission of any mention of the major works she

---

[17] Frank Howes, 'A Folk-Song Jubilee', *Musical Times*, 99 (1958): 251–2.

published and edited on her own is an unfortunate but revealing lacuna in all the memoirs and obituaries about her.

For Mary Venables, she was reserved, and 'an aristocrat in every sense of the word' – whose sense of humour and sturdy outlook won her an 'enormous circle of friends'. She was 'a rock, dependable, and immoveable in friendship'. Like Venables herself, she had loved the independence that remaining single had given her. Disliking dispute, she held strong convictions 'without asserting them', in order to avoid unnecessary controversy. Her precision and love of order, amply reflected in her editing, were offset by her 'brilliant talk, lively wit and gift of story telling'.[18] The other side of Lucy manifested itself in frequent bouts of depression (though Venables does not mention these as such) and a retreat into mysticism. This latter aspect remained with her all her life, from the early forays to a London synagogue, her attraction to the liturgical music of the early English composers heard at Westminster Cathedral, to her fascination with folklore and the issues raised in the Quest Society. This academic breadth and general curiosity linked her to her fellow pioneers Baring-Gould and, to a certain extent, Kidson, but not necessarily to Sharp or even Vaughan Williams.

Broadwood and her Contemporaries

While comparison with Sharp is inevitable, it is perhaps more useful to link Broadwood to others, particularly women such as Alice Gomme, Charlotte Burne and Maria Czaplicka. Though she did not become involved politically with social reform or the women's movement, she had to function in a male-dominated world where women were not expected to research or publish scholarly work. None of the previous generation of collectors had been women, and her model had clearly been her uncle. A university education had been denied her, but her relentless self-education and role within the Folk-Song Society more than compensated for that lack. Like Gomme, Burne and Czaplicka, she had dared to enter the field, at first tentatively and then with more certainty when she realized how satisfying the activity could be. Her collecting in Scotland and Ireland has to be seen as her culminating work, and it is significant that she formed personal relationships with both Kate Maclean and Bridget Geary. Unlike the pioneering Czaplicka she would never find a home in a university, which would have been a congenial environment for her, but even then the younger woman was unable to maintain her career after the war, despite her significant accomplishments. As Czaplicka opened up the new field of cultural anthropology, building on the work of her mentor, Malinowski, so Lucy used the work of earlier collectors and her contemporaries to establish new standards in the field which would eventually become ethnomusicology. Unlike Czaplicka, who sadly became a victim of the society in which she lived, Lucy used her often precarious financial independence to ride out the difficult years of the war

---

18   Venables, 'Lucy Etheldred Broadwood'.

and its aftermath. Her family, always close, gave her solid foundations on which to build and a sense of social belonging which many other women lacked. From this she was able to build long-lasting friendships with both men and women, which sustained her throughout her life.

Broadwood's biography affords important insights into the life of women in this period. Resolutely single, 'having adhered to spinsterhood in spite of many pressing opportunities of quitting it' (in the words of Venables),[19] she relied on an income from the family firm which, as we have seen, was struggling against foreign competition and began to go seriously downhill after her father's death. Any money from the firm had to be shared among the unmarried sisters, and only Bertha seemed to have some limited influence in the running of the company. Nonetheless Lucy seemed to enjoy a reasonably comfortable lifestyle and only later suffered some financial hardship. As a woman in a male-dominated society, she was perhaps advantaged by belonging to a family with many daughters, and whose sons were hardly forceful. This might also have been the cause of much frustration as they stood by, watching the steady and inevitable decline of the family firm in which they had a stake but no voice.

Unlike Sharp, who had been unsuccessful in the 'art music' world, Lucy straddled both worlds easily. Her background had prepared her for this: the family firm provided pianos for the concert hall, but the family seat lay in the countryside, among the folk who tenanted the cottages on their estate. Always good landlords with a social conscience, the Broadwoods looked after their servants and appreciated their music. Both Lucy's father and his half-brother John had made a point of noticing – and notating – what they heard. Lucy was as comfortable in the concert hall as she was in the field; her own musical training as singer and pianist equipped her for both as well. All these aspects made her vastly different from Sharp.

This biography is but a first step in assessing the legacy of this courageous and capable woman. As she grew older, she collected less but began to see where new directions might lie: the street cries lay at her doorstep, and she mentored the younger collector Juliet Williams in her work. It is entirely possible that editing the *Journal* provided an escape (or a distraction) from her own collecting and the necessity of publishing the results. Her relationship with her publishers was never entirely happy, and the results were certainly not financially very rewarding. Sharp was never free of the exigencies of earning a living to support a wife and family: he moved from school-mastering to publishing folksong, as editing did not pay. Lucy, on the other hand, did not face the same pressures. The income, though slender, would always be there, and in any case women of her class and generation were not expected to earn a living, though we have seen that the war began to change matters. Editing was a safe, scholarly activity and suitable for a women of her class and education. As she grew older, active fieldwork of the kind she had conducted in the south-east and in Scotland probably became less attractive.

---

[19]   Ibid.

Editing was a pleasant and viable alternative. But was Vaughan Williams partly right? Did her relentless pursuit of authenticity prevent her from enjoying the real fruits of collecting? Did her social class militate against her collecting comfortably from those outside her class? Was this a woman who collected because of her background, or in spite of it?

Along with Frances Tolmie and Anne Gilchrist, Lucy joined a phalanx of determined (mostly single) women who sought to exercise their wits in a field where they could compete equally with their male counterparts. They all brought a professionalism to a quintessentially amateur field. Music also afforded, for Lucy, at least, an area where she could be both performer and scholar. Her reserved personality, unlike that of Kate Lee and Mary Neal, did not lead her into social reform, though she counted Neal among her friends and remained close to Harriet Mason, who had made a career of working with the poor. She always insisted on viewing folksong collection as a detached activity, and did not usually befriend her informants, though something akin to friendship developed between her and Kate Maclean, Bridget Geary and Frances Tolmie. Her friendships with women such as Fanny Davies, Juliette Folville and Mary Venables afforded her an ongoing participation in the art music world and opportunities to nurture younger talent. The case of McInnes brought a tragically flawed genius to her doorstep and into her heart; Novaës was the rising star and Folville the mature, brilliant refugee artist. It is impossible to separate Lucy Broadwood from all the worlds she inhabited: to paraphrase her favourite poet, Tennyson, she had been 'part of all that she had met'. Her diaries, field notes and network of correspondents allow us a glimpse not only into her own rich life, but also into a society which had benefited from – but could only barely begin to acknowledge – her dedication and spirit.

Appendix

English Traditional Songs and Carols, collected and edited with Annotations and Pianoforte Accompaniments by Lucy E. Broadwood (London: Boosey & Co., 1908).

The following lists the titles of the songs with their provenance, editorial tempo indication, time signature; first line; number of verses; mode; name of singer and date. Square brackets indicate editorial additions regarding mode, and notes on the singers and songs taken from the introduction and appendix.

1. Van Diemen's Land, or The Gallant Poachers. Sussex. Allegro e ben marcato; 4/4
   'Come, all you gallant poachers, that ramble free from care'; 8 verses.
   [Dorian]. Sung by Mr H. Burstow, 1893. ['This ballad is very much like the broadside formerly printed by H. Such, Union St., Borough, with the same title'.]

2. The Bold Pedlar and Robin Hood. Sussex. Allegro; 4/4
   'There chanced to be a pedlar bold'; 15 verses.
   [Dorian influence]. Sung by Mr H. Burstow, 1893. [Words can be found on Catnach and Such broadsides.]

3. Through Moorfields. Sussex. Lento; 4/4
   'Through Moorfields, and to Bedlam I went'; 8 verses.
   [Dorian]. Sung by Mr H. Burstow, 1893. ['The tune here given was noted by Mr Buttifant, late organist of Horsham Parish Church, in 1893, and is faithfully accurate to the version then sung by Mr Burstow, as heard by the editor. The variants printed show the alterations made by the same singer, and recorded by phonograph in 1907, after an interval of fourteen years'.]

4. Bristol Town. Sussex. Allegro; 2/4
   'In Bristol Town, as I have heard tell'; 11 verses.
   [Dorian]. Sung by Mr H. Burstow, 1893. [Noted first in 1893; sung into phonograph in 1907 with variants.]

5. I must live all alone. Sussex. Andante moderato; 3/4
   'As I was a-walking one morning by chance'; 4 verses.
   [Aeolian]. Sung by Mr H. Burstow, 1893. ['Verse 4 has been partially rewritten, while preserving the general idea of the original 5th'.]

6. Rosetta and her gay Ploughboy. Sussex. Allegro; 4/4
    'You constant lovers give attention while a tale to you I tell'; 8 verses.
    [Mixolydian influence]. Sung by Mr H. Burstow, 1893. [Words almost
    identical to Such broadside.]

7. The Ages of Man. Sussex. Moderato; 3/4
    'In prime of years, when I was young'; 11 verses.
    [Mixolydian]. Sung by Mr H. Burstow, 1893. [Tune noted by 'Mr Buttifant,
    late organist of Horsham Parish Church'.]

8. The Duke of Marlborough. Sussex. Con solennità, ma non troppo lento; 3/4
    'You generals all, and champions bold, that take delight in the field';
    5 verses.
    [Mixolydian]. Sung by Mr H. Burstow, 1893. ['The singer's version of
    words followed the broadside (till lately still printed by Such), here given
    … The ballad is a great favourite amongst country people; the airs sung to
    it are usually very fine, and most often modal'.]

9. The Wealthy Farmer's Son. Sussex. Allegro; 4/4
    'Come all you pretty fair maids, and listen to my song'; 8 verses.
    [Ionian]. Sung by Mr H. Burstow, 1893. [Words printed by Such. Tune
    noted by Mr Buttifant.]

10. The Merchant's Daughter, or The Constant Farmer's Son. Sussex. Moderato;
    3/4
    'It's of a merchant's daughter in London town did dwell'; 9 verses.
    [Ionian]. Sung by Mr H. Burstow, 1893. [Words follow Such and other
    printers; links with Boccaccio's *Decameron*.]

11. Henry Martin, or Salt Seas. Sussex. Allegro con spirito; 3/4
    'There were three brothers in merry Scotland'; 7 verses.
    [Ionian]. Sung by Mr H. Burstow, 1893. [Words probably from Catnach
    broadside.]

12. Georgie, or Banstead Downs. Sussex. Moderato; 4/4
    'As I rode over Banstead Downs'; 7 verses.
    [Ionian]. Sung by Mr H. Burstow, 1893. [Based on the execution of
    George Stoole in 1610; 'Such, until lately, printed a broadside "The Life
    of Georgey"'.]

13. Boney's Lamentation, or Abdication. Sussex. Pomposo e ben marcato; 4/4
    'Attend, you sons of high renown, to these few lines which I pen down:';
    3 verses.
    [Aeolian]. Sung by Mr H. Burstow, 1893. ['In this ballad, the singer, whilst
    preserving the correct sequence of events, corrupted the names of persons
    and places very puzzlingly ... The misplacement of several sentences has
    been adjustable by help of the triple rhymes. The Lamentation ends with
    Napoleon's abdication, and, as the battle of Waterloo is not mentioned, we
    may infer that the ballad was composed in the year 1814'.]

14. Belfast Mountains. Sussex. Andante espressivo; 4/4
    'All on these/the Belfast mountains I heard a maid complain'; 5 verses.
    [Ionian]. Sung by Mr H. Burstow, 1893. [Words follow ballad sheet printed
    by Shelmerdine, Manchester, and Catnach.]

15. The Young Servant Man, or The Two Affectionate Lovers. Sussex. Allegro
    con spirito; 3/4
    'It's of a damsel both fair and handsome'; 7 verses.
    [Ionian]. Sung by Mr Walter Searle, 1901. ['The time is usually irregular,
    and not often so well defined as in the version here given'.]

16. Death and the Lady. Sussex. Andante non troppo lento; 4/4
    Death: 'Fair Lady, throw those costly robes aside'; 23 verses.
    [Ionian]. Sung by Mr H. Burstow, 1893. ['Mr Burstow's version is a
    wonderful proof of a country singer's memory. Lately (1908), at the age of
    83, he sang it all through without a slip, and with every word precisely as
    here given. Some of his lines seem an improvement on the printed broadside
    versions. He however despises the tune, as being "almost all on one note."']

17. The Three Butchers, or Gibson, Wilson and Johnson. Sussex. Allegro con
    spirito; 4/4. 'A story I will tell to you, it is of butchers three'; 10 verses.
    [Ionian]. Sung by Mr H. Burstow, 1893. ['This is a version of an old ballad
    found in various forms on ... broadsides of the 17th century ... The editor
    has not, so far, met with the Sussex tune elsewhere'.]

18. The Unquiet Grave, or How Cold the Winds do blow. Surrey; version 1
    Andante espressivo; 4/4. '"How cold the winds do blow, dear love!"';
    7 verses.
    [Ionian]. Sung by Mr James Bromham, 1896.

19. The Unquiet Grave, or How Cold the Winds do blow. Surrey; version 2
    Andante espressivo; 4/4. '"How cold the winds do blow, dear love!"';
    7 verses.
    [Ionian]. Sung by Mrs Rugman, 1896.

20. The Unquiet Grave, or Cold Blows the Wind. N. Devonshire; version 3 Andante espressivo; 3/4. '"Cold blows the wind o'er my true love"'; 8 verses.
[Ionian]. Sung by Mrs Jeffreys, 1893. [Mrs Jeffreys's great age and ill-health made it impossible to note more than the tune and the two beautiful concluding verses here printed. The other verses were so much the same as in the Shropshire version ..., that the latter as been re-printed here, up to the point where Mrs Jeffreys's materially differed ... In dealing with this, one of our most popular and most poetical traditional ballads, Child shows how ancient and universal is the idea that immoderate grief prevents the dead from resting'.]

21. Oh, the Trees are getting high. Surrey. Lento e espressivo; 2/4
'"Oh! The trees are getting high and the leaves are growing green;"'; 5 verses.
[Aeolian]. Sung by Mr Ede, 1896. ['The version given here was sung first to the editor by Mr Ede whilst he was trimming hedges, and the fierce snap of his shears at the words "So there was an end of his growing" came with startling dramatic effect. A few words of Mr Ede's version have been transposed or slightly altered where rhyme or metre absolutely necessitated it, and one stanza has been omitted'. Original in *JFSS*, 1, p. 214]

22. Our Ship she lies in Harbour. Surrey. Moderato; 4/4
'"Our ship she lies in harbour, just ready to set sail"'; 9 verses.
[Ionian]. Sung by Mr Sparks, 1896. [Also exists in a broadside printed by Such. 'The tune is sometimes used in Sussex to the words of the Sussex Mummers' Carol'.]

23. The Irish Girl, or The New Irish Girl. Surrey. Allegro moderato; 4/4
'Abroad as I was walking, down by the river side'; 6 verses.
[Mixolydian]. Sung by Mr James Bromham, 1896. ['The Surrey singer's words have here been given. His is the only printed or traditional version known to the editor in which sense seems to be made of verse 3, by describing the suffering and broken-hearted "love" as a woman'.]

24. The Little Lowland Maid. Surrey. Allegro con spirito; 6/8
'It's of a pretty sailor lad who ploughed the stormy sea'; 8 verses.
[Ionian]. Sung by Mr Baker, 1896. [Broadside version printed by Ryle, successor to Catnach. 'The singer's words "courtmaid," "valliant," and "manastree" being obviously "comrade", "villain," and "monster," have been altered in the version here given'.]

25. The Rich Nobleman and his Daughter. Surrey. Allegro; 3/4
    'It's of a rich nobleman lately, we hear;' 7 verses.
    [Ionian]. Sung by Mr Grantham, 1892.

26. The Poor Murdered Woman. Surrey. Allegro Moderato; 3/4
    'It was Hankey the squire, as I have heard say'; 8 verses.
    [Dorian]. Sung by Mr Foster, 1897. ['This fine Dorian tune was noted in
    1897 by the Rev. Charles J. Shebbeare at Milford, Surrey, from the singing
    of a young labourer, with whom it was a favourite song. Mr Foster wrote
    out the doggerel words, and had heard that they described a real event …
    This song is only one of many proofs that "ballets" are made by local,
    untaught bards, and that they are transmitted, and survive, long after the
    events which they record have ceased to be a reality to the singer'.]

27. The Valiant Lady, or the Brisk Young Lively Lad. Surrey. Allegro risoluto;
    2/4
    'It's of a brisk young lively lad/Came out of Gloucestershire'; 8 verses.
    [Ionian]. Sung by Mr Baker, 1896.

28. King Pharaoh [Gypsy Christmas Carol]. Sussex and Surrey. Andante; 4/4
    'King Pharim/Pharaoh sat a-musing'; 9 verses (two versions)
    [Ionian]. Sung by Gypsies of the name of Goby, 1893.

29. The Moon shines bright. [Christmas Carol]. Sussex and Surrey. Andante;
    4/4
    'Oh, the moon shines bright, and the stars give a light;'; 6 verses.
    [Ionian]. Sung by Gypsies of the name of Goby, well known in Sussex and
    Surrey, n.d.

30. The Hampshire Mummers' Christmas Carol. Andante; 4/4
    'There is six good days all in the week, all for a labouring man'; 8 verses.
    [Ionian]. Sung by Mummers of Kingsclere, 1897. [Noted by Godfrey
    Arkwright.]

31. The Sussex Mummers' Christmas Carol. Andante; 4/4
    'When righteous Joseph wedded was unto a virtuous maid'; 7 verses.
    [Ionian]. Sung by Mummers from the neighbourhood of Horsham about
    1878–1881.

32. Bedfordshire May Day Carol. Allegretto; 4/4
    'I've been rambling all the night'; 8 verses.
    [Ionian]. Sung near Hinwick. n.d. [contributed by Sir Ernest Clarke.]

33. The Lost Lady found. Lincolnshire. Allegro; 3/4
   ''Twas down in a valley a fair maid did dwell'; 9 verses.
   [Dorian]. Sung by Mrs Hill, 1893. [Mrs Hill, an old family nurse, and a native of Stamford, learned her delightful song when a child, from an old cook who danced as she sang it, beating time on the stone kitchen-floor with her iron pattens ... Mrs Hill followed the ballad-sheet version printed by Such, which is here given.' Cf 'The Lament of the Duchess of Gloucester' and 'Green Bushes'.]

34. Died of Love, or A brisk young Lad he courted me. North Lincolnshire. Andante espressivo; 3/4.
   'A brisk young lad came courting me'; 3 verses.
   [Dorian]. Sung by Mr Joseph Taylor, of Saxby-All-Saints, 1906. [The singer remembered only two verses of words. Of these the first verse, though beautiful, is too painfully tragic for general use. It has therefore been omitted here, and two stanzas from a variant of a similar ballad, noted by Mr H.E.D. Hammond in Dorsetshire have ... been used for verses 1 and 2'.]

35. King Henry, my Son. Cumberland. Moderato; 4/4
   'Oh, where have you been wand'ring, King Henry, my son?'; 3 verses.
   [Aeolian]. Air, with a longer version of the ballad, sung by Miss Margaret Scott [Thorburn], some years before 1868. ['Miss M.B. Lattimer, living in Carlisle, noted this fine air, which she learned in childhood, some time before 1868, from Margaret Scott (now Mrs Thorburn), a young servant in her home. The singer came from Wigton, in Cumberland, and had learnt the ballad from her father, who died when she was nine years old. Miss Lattimer recollected only a part of the words, and completed the ballad from another version, giving the three verses used in the harmonised arrangement.' Cf 'Lord Randal', 'Lord Donald', and 'The Croodlin' Doo'.]

36. Travel the Country round. Sussex. Allegro; 6/8
   'I am a jovial ranger, I fear no kind of danger'; 8 verses.
   [Ionian]. Sung by Mr H. Burstow, 1893.

37. Oh, Yarmouth is a pretty Town. Sussex. Andante; 3/4
   'Oh, Yarmouth is a pretty town, and shines where it stands'; 4 verses.
   [Ionian]. Sung by Mr H. Burstow, 1893. ['The accompanist may bring out the quotations from "The British Grenadiers," "Rule Britannia," and "The Girl I left behind me" judiciously'.]

38. Some rival has stolen my true love away. Surrey. Allegro moderato; 3/4
   'Some rival has stolen my true love away'; 3 verses.
   [Ionian]. Sung by Mr Lough, Dunsfold, 1898.

Select Bibliography

Books and Articles

Andrews, Hilda, *Westminster Retrospective: A Memoir of Sir Richard Terry* (London: Oxford University Press, 1948).
Austen, Jane, *Pride and Prejudice* (Cambridge: Cambridge University Press, 2006).
Bainton, Edgar. L., 'Music in Ruhleben Camp', *Musical Times*, 60 (1919): 72–3.
Baker, Anne Pimlott, 'Alfred James Hipkins (1826–1903)', *Oxford Dictionary of National Biography* (Oxford: Oxford University Press, 2004), at: http://www.oxforddnb.com./view/article/33890.
Baring-Gould, Sabine, *Old Country Life* (London: Methuen, 1892).
——, ed., *English Minstrelsie: A National Monument of English Song*, vols 1–8 (Edinburgh: Jack & Jack, 1895–8).
—— and H. Fleetwood Sheppard, eds, *Songs and Ballads of the West: A Collection Made from the Mouths of the People*, 2nd edn, vols 1–4 (London: Methuen, Patey & Willis, 1895). First published London: Patey & Willis, 1889–92.
Bashford, Christina and Leanne Langley, eds, *Music and British Culture, 1785–1914: Essays in Honour of Cyril Ehrlich* (Oxford: Oxford University Press, 2000).
Bassin, Ethel, *The Old Songs of Skye: Frances Tolmie and Her Circle* (London: Routledge & Kegan Paul, 1977).
Bearman, C.J., 'The Lucy Broadwood Collection: An Interim Report', *Folk Music Journal*, 7/3 (1997): 357–65.
——, 'Kate Lee and the Foundation of the Folk-Song Society', *Folk Music Journal*, 7/5 (1999): 627–43.
——, 'The English Folk Music Movement 1898–1914', PhD dissertation, University of Hull, 2001.
——, 'Percy Grainger, the Phonograph and the Folk Song Society', *Music and Letters*, 84/3 (2003): 434–55.
Bird, John, *Percy Grainger* (Oxford and New York: Oxford University Press, 1999).
Blacking, John, *'A Common-sense View of All Music': Reflections on Percy Grainger's Contribution to Ethnomusicology and Music Education* (Cambridge: Cambridge University Press, 1987).
Blatchford, Robert, *Merrie England* (London: Clarion Press, 1894).
Boosey, William, *Fifty Years of Music* (London: Ernest Benn, 1931).

Boyes, Georgina, 'Alice Bertha Gomme, 1852 [*sic*]–1938: A Reassessment of the Work of a Folklorist', *Folklore*, 101 (1990): 198–209.

——, *The Imagined Village* (Manchester: Manchester University Press, 1993).

——, 'Alice Gomme' in C. Blacker and H.E. Davidson, eds, *Women and Tradition: A Neglected Group of Folklorists* (Durham, NC: Academic Press, 2001), pp. 65–86.

Briggs, Asa, *The Age of Improvement* (London: Longmans, Green & Co., 1960).

Broadwood, John and G. Dusart, eds, *Old English Songs, as Now Sung by the Peasantry of the Weald of Surrey and Sussex* (London: Betts & Co., 1843).

Broadwood, Lucy, 'On the Collecting of English Folk Song', *Proceedings of the Royal Musical Association*, 31 (1904–05): 89–109.

——, 'Songs from County Waterford', *Journal of the Folk-Song Society*, 3/10 (1907): 3–38.

——, ed., *English Traditional Songs and Carols* (London: Boosey & Co., 1908).

——, 'Ten Gaelic Folk Songs', *Journal of the English Folk Dance and Song Society*, 1/1 (1932): 42–51.

——, 'Eleven Gaelic Folk Songs', *Journal of the English Folk Dance and Song Society*, 1/2 (1933): 89–96.

—— and J.A. Fuller Maitland, eds, *English County Songs* (London: Leadenhall Press, 1893).

——, Frank Howes, A.G. Gilchrist, A. Martin Freeman, eds, 'Twenty Gaelic Songs', *Journal of the Folk-Song Society*, 8/35 (1931): 280–303.

Burstow, Henry, *Reminiscences of Horsham, being the Recollections of Henry Burstow*, ed. William Albery (Folcraft, PA: Folcraft Library Editions, 1975). First published 1911.

Caine, Barbara, *Destined to Be Wives: The Sisters of Beatrice Webb* (Oxford: Oxford University Press, 1986).

Campbell, Katherine, 'Lucy Broadwood and John Potts: A Collecting Episode in the Scottish Borders', *Folk Music Journal*, 9/2 (2007): 219–25.

Campbell, Margaret, *Dolmetsch, the Man and his Work* (London: Hamish Hamilton, 1975).

Cannadine, David, *Class in Britain* (London and New Haven, CT: Yale University Press, 1998).

Chappell, William, ed., *Popular Music of the Olden Time: A Collection of Ancient Songs, Ballads and Dance Tunes, Illustrative of the National Music of England*, 2 vols (London: Chappell, Simkin, Marshall & Co., 1838).

Collinson, Francis, *The Traditional and National Music of Scotland* (London: Routledge & Kegan Paul, 1966).

Cook, Chris, *Britain in the Nineteenth Century, 1815–1914* (London and New York: Longman, 1999).

Cox, Gordon, *A History of Musical Education in England, 1872–1928* (Aldershot: Scolar, 1993).

——, *Sir Arthur Somervell on Music Education: His Writings, Speeches and Letters* (Woodbridge: Boydell Press, 2003).

Curney, Vanessa, 'Beer, Rachel (1858–1927)', *Oxford Dictionary of National Biography* (Oxford: Oxford University Press, 2004), at: http://www.oxforddnb. com./view/article/48270.

Dakers, Caroline, *The Holland Park Circle: Artists and Victorian Society* (London and New Haven, CT: Yale University Press, 1999).

Dale, William, *Tschudi the Harpsichord Maker* (London: Constable, 1913).

Day, James, *Vaughan Williams* (Oxford and New York: Oxford University Press, 1998).

Dean-Smith, Margaret, 'The Preservation of English Folk Song in the Journal of the English Folk Song Society', *Journal of the English Folk Dance and Song Society*, 6/3 (1951): 69–76.

——, *A Guide to English Folk Song Collection 1822–1952* (Liverpool and London: Liverpool University Press with the EFDSS, 1954).

——, 'The Work of Anne Geddes Gilchrist, 1863–1954', *Proceedings of the Royal Musical Association*, 84 (1958): 43–53.

——, 'Letters to Lucy Broadwood: A Selection from the Broadwood Papers at Cecil Sharp House', *Journal of the English Folk Dance and Song Society*, 9 (1964): 233–68.

de Val, Dorothy, 'The Transformed Village: Lucy Broadwood and Folksong', in C. Bashford and L. Langley, eds, *Music and British Culture, 1785–1914: Essays in Honour of Cyril Ehrlich* (Oxford: Oxford University Press, 2000), pp. 341–66.

——, '"Legitimate, Phenomenal and Eccentric": Pianists and Pianism in Late 19th-century London', in J. Dibble and B. Zon, eds, *Music in Nineteenth-century Britain* (Aldershot: Ashgate, 2002), pp. 182–95.

——, '"A Messenger for Schumann and Brahms"? Re-evaluating Fanny Davies' in T. Ellsworth and S. Wollenberg, eds, *The Piano in Nineteenth-Century British Culture* (Aldershot: Ashgate, 2007), pp. 217–38.

Dibble, Jeremy, *C. Hubert H. Parry: His Life and Music* (Oxford: Oxford University Press, 1992).

——, 'Maitland, John Alexander Fuller (1856–1936)', *Oxford Dictionary of National Biography* (Oxford: Oxford University Press, 2004), at: http://www. oxforddnb.com./view/article/34838.

Dixon, James Henry, ed., *Ancient Poems, Ballads and Songs of the Peasantry of England* (London: The Percy Society, 1846).

Dolmetsch, Mabel, *Personal Recollections of Arnold Dolmetsch* (London: Routledge & Kegan Paul, 1958).

Dorson, R.M., *The British Folklorists: A History* (London: Routledge & Kegan Paul, 1968).

Dreyfus, Kay, ed., *The Farthest North of Humanness*: *Letters of Percy Grainger, 1901–1914* (South Melbourne: Macmillan, 1985).

Duncan, M., 'Miss Nellie Chaplin's Renewal of Ancient Dances and Music', *Cremona, the Magazine of Music*, 5/61 (1911): 129.

Dunglison, Robley and Dunglison, Richard James, *A Dictionary of Medical Science* (London: J. & A. Churchill, 1876). Originally published 1833.

Ehrlich, Cyril, *The Piano: A History* (Oxford: Clarendon Press, 1990).

——, *Harmonious Alliance: A History of the Performing Right Society* (Oxford: Oxford University Press, 1989).

Engel, Carl, *An Introduction to the Study of National Music* (London: Longmans, Green, Reader & Dyer, 1866).

Field, Katherine, 'Mason, (Marianne) Harriet (1845–1932)', *Oxford Dictionary of National Biography* (London: Oxford University Press, 2004), at: www.oxforddnb.com/articles/48/48847-article.html.

Flanders, Judith, *A Circle of Sisters* (London and New York: Macmillan, 2005).

Ford, Walter, 'Lucy Etheldred Broadwood', *Journal of the Folk-Song Society*, 8/3 (1929): 168–9.

Francmanis, John, 'The Musical Sherlock Holmes: Frank Kidson and the English Folk Music Revival, c. 1890–1926', PhD dissertation, Leeds Metropolitan University, 1997.

——, '"The "Folk-Song" Competition: An Aspect of the Search for an English National Music', *Rural History*, 11/2 (2000): 181–205.

——, 'The Roving Artist: Frank Kidson, Pioneer Song Collector', *Folk Music Journal*, 8/1 (2001): 41–66.

——, 'National Music to National Redeemer: The Consolidation of a "Folk Song" Construct in Edwardian England', *Popular Music*, 21/1 (2002): 1–25.

Frazer, James, *The Golden Bough: A Study of Magic and Religion* (London: Macmillan, 1890).

Frogley, Alain, ed., *Vaughan Williams Studies* (Cambridge: Cambridge University Press, 1996).

Fuller Maitland, J.A., *A Door-keeper of Music* (London: John Murray, 1929).

——, 'Lucy Broadwood: 1858–1929', *Monthly Musical Record*, 59 (1929): 296–7.

Gammon, Vic, 'Folk Song Collecting in Sussex and Surrey, 1843–1914', *History Workshop Journal*, 10 (1980): 61–89.

——, '"Not Appreciated in Worthing?" Class Expression and Popular Song Texts in Mid-Nineteenth-Century Britain', *Popular Culture*, 4 (1984): 5–24.

——, *Desire, Drink and Death in English Folk and Vernacular Song 1600–1900* (Aldershot: Ashgate, 2008).

Gérin, Winifred, *Anne Thackeray Ritchie: A Biography* (New York: Oxford University Press, 1981).

Gilbert, R.A., 'Mead, George Robert Stow (1863–1933)', *Oxford Dictionary of National Biography* (Oxford: Oxford University Press, 2004), at: http://www.oxforddnb.com./view/article/53879.

Gillett, Paula, *Musical Women in England, 1870–1914* (London: Macmillan, 2000).

Gillies, Malcolm G.W. and David Pear, eds, *Grainger on Grainger* (Rochester: University of Rochester Press, 2002).

Godman, Stanley, 'John Broadwood: New Light on the Folk-Song Pioneer', *Monthly Musical Record* (1957): 105–8.

——, 'John Broadwood, the Earliest English Folksong Collector', *West Sussex Gazette*, 30 January 1964.

Gomme, Robert, 'Gomme, Alice Bertha, Lady Gomme (1853–1938)', *Oxford Dictionary of National Biography* (Oxford: Oxford University Press, 2004), at: http://www.oxforddnb.com. /view/article/38616.

——, 'Gomme, Sir (George) Laurence (1853–1916)', *Oxford Dictionary of National Biography* (Oxford: Oxford University Press, 2004), at: http://www. oxforddnb.com./view/article/38353.

Gould, Tony, *Inside Outsider: The Life and Times of Colin MacInnes* (London: Chatto & Windus, Hogarth Press, 1983).

Graebe, Martin, 'Sabine Baring-Gould and his Old Singing Men', in Ian Russell and David Atkinson, eds, *Folk Song: Tradition, Revival, and Re-Creation* (Aberdeen: Elphinstone Institute, University of Aberdeen, 2004), pp. 175–85.

Grainger, Percy, 'Collecting with the Phonograph', *Journal of the Folk-Song Society*, 3/12 (1908–09): 147–62.

——, 'The Impress of Personality in Traditional Singing', *Journal of the Folk-Song Society*, 3/12 (1908–09): 163–6.

——, L. Broadwood *et al.*, 'Songs Collected by Percy Grainger', *Journal of the Folk-Song Society*, 3/12 (1908–09): 170–242.

——, 'The Impress of Personality in Unwritten Music', *Musical Quarterly*, 1/3 (1915): 416–35.

——, 'Arnold Dolmetsch: Musical Confucius', *Musical Quarterly*, 19/2 (1933): 187–98.

Grand, Sarah, *Ideala: A Study from Life* (Charleston, SC: Bibliobazaar, 2006). First published 1888.

Gregory, E. David, *Victorian Songhunters: The Recovery and Editing of English Vernacular Ballads and Folk Lyrics, 1820–1883* (Lanham, MD: Scarecrow Press, 2006),

——, 'Before the Folk-Song Society: Lucy Broadwood and English Folk Song, 1884–97', *Folk Music Journal*, 9/3 (2008): 372–414.

——, *The Late Victorian Folksong Revival: The Persistence of English Melody, 1878–1903* (Lanham, MD: Scarecrow Press, 2010).

Gutmann, Edward, *The Watering Places and Mineral Springs of Germany, Austria, and Switzerland* (London: Sampson, Low, Marston, Searle & Rivington, 1880).

Harding, Rosamund, *The Piano-Forte, its History Traced to the Great Exhibition of 1851* (London: Gresham Press, 1979).

Harker, Dave, *Fakesong: The Manufacture of British 'Folksong' 1700 to the Present Day* (Milton Keynes: Open University Press, 1985).

Harris, Jose, *Private Lives, Public Spirit: Britain 1870–1914* (Oxford: Oxford University Press, 1993).

Henschel, George, *Musings and Memories of a Musician* (London: Macmillan, 1918).

Hipkins, A.J., *Musical Instruments: Historic, Rare and Unique* (Edinburgh: Adam and Charles Black, 1888).

——, *A Description and History of the Pianoforte* (London: Novello, 1896).

Hipkins, Edith, *How Chopin Played – From Contemporary Impressions Collected from the Diaries and Notebooks of A.J. Hipkins F.S.A.* (London: Dent, 1937).

Hobsbawm, Eric, *Industry and Empire* (Harmondsworth: Penguin, 1983).

Hoppen, K. Theodore, *The Mid-Victorian Generation, 1846–1886* (Oxford: Clarendon Press, 1998).

Howes, Frank, 'A Folk-Song Jubilee', *Musical Times*, 99 (1958): 251–2.

——, *The English Musical Renaissance* (London: Secker & Warburg, 1966).

——, *Folk Music of Britain – And Beyond* (London: Methuen, 1969).

Huffman, Joan B., 'Balfour, Lady Frances (1858–1931)', *Oxford Dictionary of National Biography* (Oxford: Oxford University Press, 2004), at: http://www. oxforddnb.com/view/article/30554.

Hughes, Meirion and Robert Stradling, *The English Musical Renaissance, 1840–1940: Constructing a National Music* (Manchester: Manchester University Press, 2001).

Jekyll, Walter, *Jamaican Song and Story: Annancy Stories, Digging Songs, Ring Tunes, and Dancing Tunes* (London: David Nutt, 1907).

Joyce, Patrick W., ed., *Ancient Irish Music* (Dublin: McGlashan & Gill, 1873).

Judge, Roy, 'Mary Neal and the Esperance Morris', *Folk Music Journal*, 5/5 (1989): 545–91.

Karpeles, Maud, *Cecil Sharp: His Life and Work* (London: Routledge & Kegan Paul, 1967).

——, *An Introduction to English Folk Song* (Oxford: Oxford University Press, 1973).

Kaul, Chandrika, 'Ritchie, Sir Richmond Thackeray Willoughby (1854–1912)', *Oxford Dictionary of National Biography* (Oxford: Oxford University Press, 2004), at: http://www.oxforddnb.com./view/article/35764.

Keel, Frederick, 'The Folk Song Society', *Journal of the English Folk Dance and Song Society*, 5/3 (1948): 111–27.

Kennedy-Fraser, Marjory, *Songs of the Hebrides*, 3 vols (London: Boosey & Co., 1909–21).

Kidson, Frank, *Traditional Tunes: A Collection of Ballads and Airs* (Oxford: Chas. Taphouse & Sons, 1891; facsimile edition Wakefield, 1970).

——, *A Garland of English Folk-Songs* (London: Ascherberg, Hopwood & Crew, [1926]).

—— and Alfred Moffatt, eds, *The Minstrelsy of England: A Collection of 200 English Songs with their Melodies, Popular from the 16th Century to the Middle of the 18th Century* (London: Bailey & Ferguson, 1901).

—— and Mary Neal, *English Folk-Song and Dance* (Cambridge: Cambridge University Press, 1915).

Lehmann, Liza, *The Life of Liza Lehmann, by Herself* (London: T. Fisher Unwin, 1919).

Lloyd, A.L., *Folksong in England* (London: Lawrence & Wishart, 1967).

Mason, M.H., ed., *Nursery Rhymes and Country Songs: Both Tunes and Words from Tradition* (London: Metzler, 1878).

McInnes, Graham, *The Road to Gundagai* (London: Hamish Hamilton, 1965).

——, *Humping my Bluey* (London: Hamish Hamilton, 1966).

——, *Finding a Father* (London: Hamish Hamilton, 1967).

——, *Goodbye Melbourne Town* (London: Hamish Hamilton, 1968).

Minshall, E., 'The Chaplin Trio', *The Musical Journal*, 23/271 (1910): 152–3.

Mitchell, Rosemary, 'Sichel, Edith Helen (1862–1914)', *Oxford Dictionary of National Biography* (Oxford: Oxford University Press, 2004), at: http://www.oxforddnb.com./view/article/55974.

Onderdonk, Julian, 'Vaughan Williams and the Modes', *Folk Music Journal*, 7/5 (1999): 609–26.

Palmer, Roy, ed., *Folk Songs Collected by Ralph Vaughan Williams* (London: J.M. Dent & Sons, 1983).

——, 'Kidson's Collecting', *Folk Music Journal*, 5/2 (1986): 150–75.

Parry, Sir Hubert, 'Inaugural Address to the General Meeting of the Folk-Song Society, 2nd February 1899', *Journal of the Folk-Song Society*, 1/1 (1899): 2.

Pickering, Michael, *Village Song and Culture: A Study Based on the Blunt Collection of Song from Adderbury North Oxfordshire* (London: Croom Helm, 1982).

——, 'Recent Folk Music Scholarship in England: A Critique', *Folk Music Journal*, 6 (1990): 37–64.

Plunket Greene, Harry, *Interpretation in Song* (London: Macmillan, 1912).

Porter, James, 'Muddying the Crystal Spring: From Idealism and Realism to Marxism in the Study of English and American Folk Song', in Bruno Nettl and Philip V. Bohlman, eds, *Comparative Musicology and Anthropology of Music* (Chicago: University of Chicago Press, 1991), pp. 113–30.

Reynardson, Herbert Birch [and Lucy Broadwood], eds, *Sussex Songs* (London: Lucas & Weber, 1889 [actually 1890]).

Rubinstein, David, *Before the Suffragettes: Women's Emancipation in the 1890s* (Brighton: Harvester Press, 1986).

Russell, Dave, *Popular Music in England, 1840–1914: A Social History* (Manchester: Manchester University Press, 1987).

Sharp, Cecil, *English Folk Song: Some Conclusions* (Taunton: Barnicott & Pearce, 1907).

—— and Broadwood, Lucy, 'Some Characteristics of English Folk-Music', *Folklore*, 19/2 (1908): 132–52.

Shearme, John, *Lively Recollections* (London: John Lane Bodley Head, 1917).

Sheppard, Francis, *London, 1808–1870: The Infernal Wen* (London: Secker and Warburg, 1971).

Squire, William Barclay, 'A History of the Music Room of the British Museum, 1753–1953', *Proceedings of the Royal Musical Association*, 79 (1952): 65–79.

Strickland, Margot, *Angela Thirkell: Portrait of a Lady Novelist* (London: Duckworth, 1977).

Sumner, Heywood, ed., *The Besom Maker and Other Country Folk Songs* (London: Longmans, Green & Co., 1888).

Thirkell, Angela, *Three Houses* (Oxford: Oxford University Press, 1932).

——, *O, These Men, These Men!* (Wakefield, RI, and London: Moyer Bell, 1996). First published 1935.

Thomson, R.S., 'The Development of the Broadside Ballad Trade and its Influence Upon the Transmission of English Folk Songs', PhD dissertation, University of Cambridge, 1975.

Tolmie, Frances, Broadwood, L.E., Gilchrist, A.G. and Henderson, G., eds, 'Songs of Occupation from the Western Isles of Scotland', *Journal of the Folk-Song Society*, 4/16 (1911).

Vaughan Williams, Ralph, 'Lucy Broadwood: An Appreciation', *Journal of the Folk-Song Society*, 8/1 (1927): 44–5.

——, 'Miss Lucy Broadwood', *Journal of the English Folk Dance Society*, 3 (1930): 61.

——, 'Lucy Broadwood, 1858–1929', *Journal of the English Folk Dance and Song Society*, 5/3 (December, 1948): 136–8.

——, *National Music and Other Essays* (Oxford: Clarendon Press, 1996).

Venables, Mary, 'Lucy Etheldred Broadwood', unpublished manuscript, February, 1930, Surrey History Centre, Woking, UK, Accession no. 2297/6.

Vicinus, Martha, ed., *Suffer and Be Still: Women in the Victorian Age* (Bloomington: Indiana University Press, 1972).

——, *A Widening Sphere: Changing Roles of Victorian Women* (Bloomington: Indiana University Press, 1977).

Wainwright, David, *Broadwood by Appointment* (London: Quiller Press, 1982).

Walford, Edward, *Walford's County Families of the United Kingdom, or Royal Manual of the Titled and Untitled Aristocracy of England, Wales, Scotland and Ireland* (London: Chatto & Windus, 1860–1920).

Walter, Lavinia Edna, *English Nursery Rhymes*, ed. E. Walter, harmonised by L.E. Broadwood (London: A. & C. Black, 1916).

——, *Some Nursery Rhymes of Belgium, France and Russia ... the Belgian Airs Harmonised by L.E. Broadwood* (London: A. & C. Black, 1917).

——, *Christmas Carols*, ed. L.E. Walter, harmonized by L.E. Broadwood (London: A. & C. Black, 1922).

Williams, Iolo, *English Folk-Song and Dance* (London: Longmans, Green & Co., 1935).

Williams, Juliet, Broadwood, Lucy E. and Gilchrist, Anne G., 'London Street Cries', *Journal of the Folk-Song Society*, 6/22 (1919): 55–70.

Wolz, Lyn A., 'Resources in the Vaughan Williams Memorial Library: The Anne Geddes Gilchrist Collection', *Folk Music Journal*, 8/5 (2005): 619–40.

Yates, Michael, 'Percy Grainger and the Impact of the Phonograph', *Folk Music Journal*, 4/3 (1982): 265–75.

Original Compositions and Arrangements by Lucy Broadwood
(in date order; individual sheet music editions taken from *English County* *Songs* not included)

'Jess Macpharlane', old Scotch air arranged by L.E. Broadwood (London: Boosey & Co., 1890).

'In Loyalty', arr. Lucy Broadwood. seventeenth-century song, words by F. Semple (London: S. Lucas, Weber & Co., 1892).

'Nae Mair We'll meet', words by J. Sim (London: Weekes & Co., 1892).

'Tammy' (London: Weekes & Co., 1892).

'Annie's Tryst'. Song and words by Aytoun (London: Weekes & Co., 1893).

'When Trees did Bud' (London and New York: Boosey & Co., 1893).

'The Woodlark', words by R. Burns, and 'What Does Little Birdie say?', words by Lord Tennyson (London: J.B. Cramer & Co., 1894).

Old World Songs, edited and arranged by L.E. Broadwood and J.A. Fuller Maitland (Chappell & Co., [1895]).

'Young Colin', adapted and arranged from William Shield's air (London: Boosey & Co., 1896).

'The Jolly Comber', arr. L. Broadwood (London and New York: Boosey & Co., 1897).

'Travel the Country Round', Old Song arr. L. Broadwood (London and New York: Boosey & Co., 1897). [Later published in *English Traditional Songs and Carols*, 1908.]

'Oh, Yarmouth is a Pretty Town', old song arr. L. Broadwood (London and New York: Boosey & Co., 1897).

'As I Went Forth', traditional Sussex air arranged with new words (London: Boosey & Co., 1900).

'Some Rival has Stolen my True Love Away', Traditional Surrey Song, arranged by L.E. Broadwood (London and New York: Boosey & Co., 1900).

Songs from Alice in Wonderland and Through the Looking Glass, for voice and piano (London: A. & C. Black, 1921).

Index